T0381511

McCary Fluted Point Survey of Virginia

Point 1 to 1055

Wm Jack Hranicky RPA

authorHOUSE

AuthorHouse™
1663 Liberty Drive
Bloomington, IN 47403
www.authorhouse.com
Phone: 833-262-8899

© 2008 Wm Jack Hranicky RPA. All rights reserved.

No part of this book may be reproduced, stored in a retrieval system, or
transmitted by any means without the written permission of the author.

Published by AuthorHouse 08/28/2021

ISBN: 978-1-4343-7030-3 (sc)

Print information available on the last page.

Any people depicted in stock imagery provided by Getty Images are models,
and such images are being used for illustrative purposes only.
Certain stock imagery © Getty Images.

This book is printed on acid-free paper.

Because of the dynamic nature of the Internet, any web addresses or links contained in
this book may have changed since publication and may no longer be valid. The views
expressed in this work are solely those of the author and do not necessarily reflect the views
of the publisher, and the publisher hereby disclaims any responsibility for them.

McCary Fluted Point Survey of Virginia

Wm Jack Hranicky RPA
Survey Director

McCary Survey Point Number 1000 (Face Rubbings)

Points 1 to 1055
Special Publication Number 1

McCary Fluted Point Survey
www.archeology.org
Post Office Box 11256
Alexandria, Virginia 22312
USA

Dedicated to: Ben C. McCary

BEN C. MCCARY AND SURVEY POINT NUMBER 1000

McCary Survey Point Number 1000 was named the McCary point by the author and Michael Johnson. This photograph appears on the March 2004 issue of the Archeological Society of Virginia's Quarterly Bulletin. All Survey points have been published in the Quarterly Bulletin – for over 50 years. Photograph shows Ben McCary receiving the 1990 Society for American Archaeology's Crabtree Award.

The Society for American Archaeology (SAA) has published *Readings in Late Pleistocene North America and Early Paleoindians: Selections from American Antiquity* which was compiled by Bruce B. Huckell and J. David Kilby in 2004. Along with other classic papers, it includes Ben McCary's 1951 *A Workshop Site of Early Man in Dinwiddie County, Virginia*. This publication opened the door for Paleoindian studies in the East.

Table of Contents

Preface

Prehistoric artifacts are object d' antiques which contain its history of human makage and usage. Aside from the artifact, not everyone places values on history. Old artifacts are just that – old artifacts. Yet to others, old artifacts represent an ancient time and place which can only be visible via the artifacts. The artifact's previous owner is somehow touchable through the artifacts. The artifact simply represents a time which may or may not be of interest to human beings living today. Those who maintain a fascination with prehistory usually find its products worthy of study and preserving them for the future.

One aspect of prehistory is the people who made Clovis points. These artifacts are some of the finest stone objects that were ever made by early humans. As such, appreciation of them becomes a desire to collect them. For some people, just one is sufficient; for others, the more I have the better. Since no two Clovis points are exactly alike, collecting them becomes an obsession to own the past. Regardless of motives, 95% of Virginia's known Clovis points are in private collections. While many Clovis points are undocumented, the McCary Survey has recorded over 1000 paleopoints.

Does recording a paleopoint add to our knowledge; the answer is yes, but one paleopoint contributes very little data. Information about the point, in most cases, simply duplicates what we already know about paleopoints. And, one lone point does not make a history. When we start analyzing a 1000 or more, the prehistoric book opens in response to numerous questions about the collective nature of prehistoric artifacts. The when's and where's become time's of the past – eventually histories.

Recording paleopoints is one stem at a time, by one contributor at a time. These contributions become the basis for archaeological investigations, which become additions to our knowledge base. While people differ in the value of these histories, the long term effect is an appreciation for those who contributed artifact data. For artifacts, we (owners and trustees) are temporary custodians; the temporary custodians will be replaced by new custodians, many of whom will be forgotten. While the artifact has lost contact with its ancient owner, it does contribute to the history of mankind.

Probably the most difficult factor to deal with in recording paleopoints is the direct reference by professional archaeologists that you cannot distinguish (recognize) non-Native paleopoints from modern fakes. True, some cases are difficult, but most are not. My thoughts are, if the archaeologist cannot make and use a Clovis point, then that individual should be barred from Paleoindian archaeology. If you really want to know if a point is a fake, go to collectors, not professional archaeologists. Of course, there are numerous exceptions; let's say only nationally known archaeologists in Paleoindian studies.

Wm Jack Hranicky RPA

Part One – General Survey Information

McCary Fluted Point Survey

Ben C. McCary started the Survey in 1947, and he collected point data for over 40 years.[1] When he retired with the Survey, he turned the Survey over to Michael F. Johnson. With the assistance of Joyce Pearsall, they ran the Survey for 10+ years. With his work being too involved at the Cactus Hill site, he turned the Survey over to Wm Jack Hranicky, who is the current director. The Survey is an independent organization dedicated to recording paleopoints found in the Commonwealth of Virginia. It relies on professional and amateur archaeologists, artifact collectors, and the interested general public for obtaining paleopoints for recording.

The Survey is a collection of point metrics, personal observations, rubbings, drawings, and digital images; Survey records vary with these elements. The Survey contains 1000+ points and is presented in the following pages. Hranicky (2005) offers guidelines for setting up and running a survey. This publication is available on **www.archeology.org**.

Survey Point Number 1003
(Water Test)

This publication contains:
- **Survey history**
- **Survey references**
- **Illustrations of**
     Survey points 1 to 1000
- **Table containing basic**
     Survey point data.
- **Points 1001 to 1055**
- **Williamson Paleosite Points**
- **Appendices**

References:

Hranicky, Wm Jack (2005) *A Model for a Paleoindian Fluted Point Survey*. AuthorHouse, Bloomington, Indiana.

Hranicky, Wm Jack Hranicky (2008) *Recording Clovis Points – Techniques, Examples, and Methods*. To be published.

Hranicky, Wm Jack and Ben C. McCary (1995) *Clovis Technology in Virginia*. Special Publication Number 31, Archeological Society of Virginia.

---

[1] Initially, McCary called Clovis points Folsom points. For years, archaeologists referred to all Paleoindian points as Clovis. Today, the safe term is paleopoints.

SEPTEMBER 1947
VOLUME-2 NUMBER-1

QUARTERLY BULLETIN

123

FOLSOM SURVEY

First Publication Release of McCary Survey Paleopoints

4

McCary Survey History

The McCary Fluted Point Survey of Virginia was started by Ben C. McCary. In 1941, he invited collectors to Richmond Virginia to discuss their finds and collections (Figure 1). The idea behind this show-and-tell meeting became the Survey. These points and subsequently-reported points were published in 1947. Starting with hand rubbling of paleopoints to digital imaging, the Survey now has a database of 1000+ points. The first release of Survey points was published by the Archeological Society of Virginia (ASV). See References for Survey publications. However, these publications give little insight into McCary's recording practices and lack Big-Picture interpretations of Survey data as they apply to the archaeology of prehistory. This publication uses the Survey as a basis for reporting paleopoints.

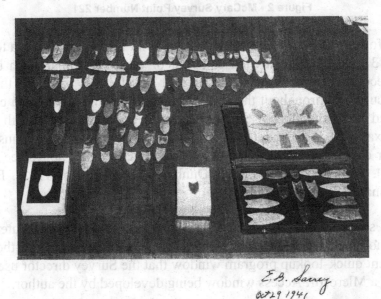

Figure 1 - Photograph of Clovis points taken at an early meeting of the Archeological Society of Virginia (ASV). It is signed by E. B. Sacrey (October 29, 1941), who was the first ASV Secretary. This Folsom/Clovis interest would eventually become the McCary Fluted Point Survey of Virginia.

Additionally this publication is essentially a continuation of Hranicky and McCary's (1995) *Clovis Technology in Virginia* that was published as ASV Special Publication Number 31. They presented early efforts to organize Paleoindina data collected by the Survey into meaningful and useful information for the archaeological community and the interested general public. As suggested then, and now in this publication, collecting and interpreting Paleoindian data is an artform that one learns with study, practice, hands-on analysis, and making public presentations. Without overly arguing the generalized philosophy of recording paleopoints, it comes down to the romance of handling and studying objects from antiquity, as in Figure 2. However, after the point infatuation wears off, work is begun to record what the point has to tell you.

Figure 2 - McCary Survey Point Number 221

The following form is used by the McCary Fluted Point Survey of Virginia to record fluted points (Figure 3). Readers are invited to use it or create a similar form based on their research and recording needs. Data collection for this form is based on the forthcoming tables with discussions throughout the text. Forms create standards in data collection; data can be recorded as hard/softcopy. See Appendix A for a Georgia, North Carolina, and Pennsylvania examples. Fogelman (2006) provides paleopoint data for Pennsylvania which can be used for comparison to the McCary Survey data. For Missouri, see Anderson and O'Brian (1998). For Florida, see Carter, Dunbar, and Anderson (1998). For all eastern states, see Brennan (1982).

There has been several paper Survey Record Forms, including one computer form. As the Survey grew, more data fields were added to ensure better descriptions of the point. Figure 4 shows a current quick-lookup program window that the Survey director uses in the field.[2] Figure 5 shows a Microsoft Access window being developed by the author.

---

[2] This program was written by the author's early days in the computer sciences as a C programmer; thus, it is maintained.

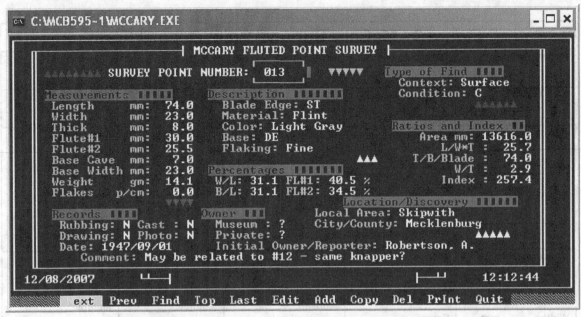

Figure 4 - Survey Quick Lookup Program Showing MC 7

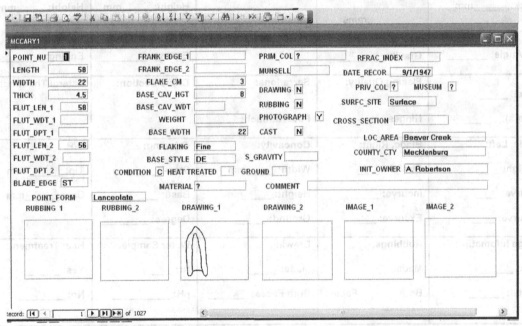

Figure 5 – Microsoft Access Survey Data Display Window (MC 1)

Figure 3 - McCary Survey® Point Record Form

Record Date:	Recorder:	Location:	Finder:	Owner:
Find Type:	Discovery Date:	County:	River Basin:	Artifact Number:

Site Information: Yes: _____ No: _____ VA Number: 44 _____ _____	Condition: Complete: _____ Broken: _____ Damaged: _____ Rechip: _____	Manufacture: Biface: _____ Flake: _____ Uniface: _____ Tool: _____	Basic Shape: Lanceolate: _____ Triangular: _____ Pentagonal: ____ Other: _____	Flakes/cm Face #1 _____ Face #2 _____ Average: _____
Measurements: Length: _____ mm Width: _____mm Thick: _____mm C to C: _____ mm Tip Angle: _____ °	Material: Grain: Source: Weight: _____ grams Specific Gravity:_____	Color: Munsell: Recording Temp: _____ °	Face #1 Flute: Single: _____ Multiple: ____ Width: _____ mm Height: _____mm Type: _____ Ending: _____	Face #2 Flute: Single: _____ Multiple: ____ Width: _____ mm Height: _____mm Type: _____ Ending: _____
Bevel: _____ Face(s): _____	Flaking Quality: Hinges:	Serrations: Fine Retouch:	Cross Section:	Lateral Thinning:
Blade, Left: Straight:____ Incurve: ____ Excurve: ____	Blade, Right: Straight:____ Incurve: ____ Excurve: ____	Concavity: Width: _____mm Height: _____mm Ground: _____	Grinding: Stem:_____ Base: _____ Degree: _____	D/P Tip: _____ mm Base: _____mm
Image Infomation: Film: _____ Digital: _____	Rubbings: Made: _____ Both Faces: _____	Drawings: Made: _____ Both Faces: _____	Water Sample: Nr: _____ pH: _____	Heat Treatment: Yes: _____ No: _____

General Observations: Patination: _____ Field _____ or Laboratory _____ Recording	Map Attached: Yes _____, No _____ Discovery witness: Yes _____, No _____

Owner's address:

City, State, Zip

Phone: Email:

Miscellaneous Notes:

Ver: 7 – 2007

8

For the historically-oriented community, 1000+ fluted Virginia points are presented. This is the largest single population containing this many projectile points in print today. It offers comparisons and morphological studies for the Middle Atlantic area and other national Paleoindian concentrations. Virginia paleopoint data are available from the Survey in electronic formats.

> The McCary Fluted Point Survey of Virginia is an independent, not-for-profit organization that is not associated or affiliated with any state-federal agency, college or university, archaeological organization, or any commercial enterprise. The survey operates as a public domain organization that is comprised of volunteers who serve for the advancement of Paleoindian studies. It is found at: www.archeology.org on the Internet.

The McCary Survey fits into scientific archaeological research; it can be used for all archaeological investigations and prehistoric interpretations (Figure 6). What are needed here, and for archaeology in general, are data warehouse accesses.[3] [4] By this nature, archaeological research should be forced to find new ways of examining data, as Kantardzic (2003) suggests:

Thus, there is currently a paradigm shift from classical modeling and analyses based on first principles to developing models and the corresponding analyses directly from data.

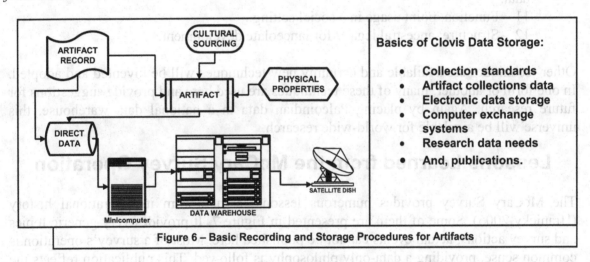

Basics of Clovis Data Storage:

- **Collection standards**
- **Artifact collections data**
- **Electronic data storage**
- **Computer exchange systems**
- **Research data needs**
- **And, publications.**

Figure 6 – Basic Recording and Storage Procedures for Artifacts

Again, the survey's processes of collecting data from scientific observations and analyzing them, such as, comparing these collected data to other reported Clovis benchmarks, provide a service that is not generally available to the professional community. This operation has always involved typical measures of central tendency, including mean, medium, mode, variance, and deviation. These factors tend to fall short of modern functional/structural analyses – they are simply *ole-tyme ways* of manipulating data. What remains from them are new ways to interpret data – such as a forecasting method, an artificial intelligence method, a modeling method for PCs, and numerous research techniques.

---

[3] Third Party Access – researchers using data only and do not have access to the original paleopoints.

[4] David Anderson, University of Tennessee, has provided a website *The Paleoindian Database of the Americas* (http://pidba.tennessee.edu/) that comes closest to being a national data warehouse.

Collecting survey data is (and always will be) one of the *fun* processes in archaeology. It allows hands-on examination and generally presents something new – the basic romance of archaeology. Clovis points and other types are more-or-less the same; they each tell a different story from the past. From this type of recording operation, the McCary Survey has built a database from which more information about Paleoindian technology can be deduced. The following analytical topics are possible:

1 – Classification: creates groups of data in predetermined classes.
2 – Regression: maps data into real-time predictive variables.
3 – Clustering: identifies finite sets of data for descriptive methods.
4 – Summarizing: provides generalities for datasets.
5 – Change: measures movement (differences) in variables, attributes, or types.
6 – Deviation: measures change in variables, attributes, or types.
7 – Modeling: creates local (or broad-range) circumstances for data analysis.
8 – Boundaries: provides restrictive ranges (distribution) for data accumulation and analysis.
9 – Prediction: provides strategies for identifying unknown data.
10 – Networking: uses artificial intelligence to recognize patterns (behavior) in data.
11 – Function: point usage in a social setting.
12 – Structure: ancestral legacy for lanceolate development.

Other techniques are available and certainly new techniques will be invented and adopted. In one form or another, many of these techniques are used here and provide suggestions for future research. Again by placing Paleoindian data in a national data warehouse, this universe will be available for world-wide research.

Lessons Learned from the McCary Survey Operation

The McCary Survey provides numerous lessons learned from its operational history (Hranicky 2005). Some of them are presented in Figure 7. It provides very generic topics and survey actions; actual events cannot be published here. Most of a survey's operation is common sense, providing a data-only philosophy is followed. This publication reflects the organizational learning from the McCary Survey's operation; perhaps a written document for lessons learned should be maintained by any survey. The McCary Survey taught the author that a survey is on a tight rope stretched from the collector/relic world to the sanity of the professional archaeological community. Lessons learn do not come easily and are ongoing.

Figure 7 – Lessons Learned from the McCary Survey	
Lesson	**Learned Activity**
Get archaeological support	A survey needs (must have) support and participation from the professional archaeological and museum communities

Figure 7 – Lessons Learned from the McCary Survey	
Lesson	**Learned Activity**
State society support	A survey needs state, county, and cities archaeological societies
Set goals for the survey	A survey must have goals and objectives to survive. It must have a purpose that supports the archaeological community
Capture point data	A survey must have published standards and procedures for capturing point data
Expert analysis	A survey must have experts for analyzing and recording points
Produce publications	A survey is not a self-serving organization; therefore, it must publish frequently the points that have been recorded
Provide benefits	A survey must provide benefits to archaeological research and provide data to the public knowledge about paleopoints
Provide education	A survey must approach the general public to educate them about archaeology, paleohistory, and the need for information about prehistory
Provide preservation information	A survey must approach the general public to educate them about archaeology and the need for preservation of prehistoric antiquities
Acceptance policy	A survey must have a written policy regarding its criteria for accepting (or rejecting) a point into the survey
Avoid cost	In order for a survey to remain independent, it should not be funded by public dollars
Setting point values	A survey must avoid any type of monetary assessment of paleopoints
Survey access	A survey must provide public access to its records and database
Looting observation	A survey must report knowledge of site looting, but take no role in stopping it
Meeting ethical requirements	A survey must publish policies that meet or exceed those set by the Society for American Archaeology
Responding to Native Americans	A survey should keep Native Americans in its coverage area informed of the survey's activities and goals
Maintaining public policies	A survey's rule: no private archaeology and all data is part of the public realm

Figure 7 – Lessons Learned from the McCary Survey	
Lesson	**Learned Activity**
Fake point submissions	A survey will always be faced with this problem, but with reasonably skill and experience with fluted point, this not a major concern.
Nonstate submissions	A survey will always be faced with this problem
Point classification	A survey personnel should never force a point into a Paleoindian type; it either has the attributes, or it does not
Review responses by survey committee	All survey review committee reports must be in writing, sometimes reviewers change their minds. If a reviewer does not submit his/her reviews, remove them.
Hiding sites	A survey must recognize that some point finders will not disclose site locations; the survey is an object-oriented focus. Points from sites are destroying the site and the survey should (or perhaps not) attempt to convert the looting behavior.
Curation value	A survey must accept that curation among collectors varies widely and is often attached to monetary values
Point values	A survey must recognize that points are personal property and have monetary values; the survey should never set (appraise) point dollar values.
Accurate recordkeeping	A survey depends on its records; thus, accurate data are of primary importance. These data will be questioned by scholars studying the database and records. Standard will ensure data validity.
Public trust	A survey must have public trust, especially within the collector community. This is more important than collector trust, but both are needed.
Public policy	A survey is part of a public policy which promotes conservation and protection of antiquity.
Public domain	A survey must contribute its data to the public domain
Missing or incomplete information	For most point recordings, there is missing information about the point's history and artifact associations
Everyone's an expert	Since there is a high interest in

Figure 7 – Lessons Learned from the McCary Survey	
Lesson	**Learned Activity**
	Paleoindian technology, there is a wide range of qualified people write and/or simply talk about it. Opinions vary from ridiculous to scholarly portrayals of yesteryear's history
Collector deaths	A survey that finds out a collector has died should talk to the family about scientifically recording the collection, regardless if it has Clovis points.
State/federal agency support	A survey needs state/federal archaeology support, but should never submit to their controls
Legal requirements	A survey must never violate and state/federal laws regarding antiquities. As a recommendation, the survey should have legal council
Copyright of survey data	Never
Point reproductions	A survey should encourage case to be made of paleopoints; they are a valuable education resource.
Never count on anything	Promises are often well intentioned, but do not rely on them; a point in hand beats a point out somewhere
Second (or more) opinion on a point	A survey should never rely on one opinion about a specific paleopoint
Privacy laws	A survey must follow the law, and operate as a public institution
Encourage point donations	A survey must encourage donation of private collections to public domain facilities.
Never trust legacy of societies	A survey must work with archaeological societies, but officers and board members change so old cooperative arrangement may change.
Publication caution	Some societies and journals copyright their materials; thus, a survey may have problems using the data under these circumstances.
Personalities	A survey cannot avoid or corporate with all human personalities
Authorities	There are no such things – only people claiming to be an authority – A survey should be careful who is quoted in their reports and publications. The basic criteria are: RPA after their name; however, numerous collectors are very knowledgeable people, so well-known is

Figure 7 – Lessons Learned from the McCary Survey	
Lesson	**Learned Activity**
	probably satisfactory..
Solutrean connection	A survey must avoid it; there is no proof of any direct technological relationship between Solutrean and Clovis technologies.
Clovis skeptics	A survey must accept the Clovis is not provable to all people
Point authentication	A survey must recognize the by entering a point into a survey, it is being authenticated, which is part of the verification and validation process.
View only	A survey must accept that collectors will only allow their collection to be viewed and points cannot be recorded
Photograph only	A survey must accept that collectors will only allow their collections to be photographed and will not provide point data
Nonfluted Clovis points	A survey needs a policy whether to record (always), but to number them.
Morphological variations	Basically, a survey needs to record all paleopoints regardless of their typology.
Keep records of known fake points	Fake points are sometimes re-submitted for inclusion in the survey; records eliminate this problem
Keeping records on collectors	Argumentative and privacy concern, but records of who collects assist in tracking artifacts
Establishing point typologies within a state	A survey must recognize that point typology is not an exact science; thus, use type nomenclature carefully
Director acceptance	The survey director must be accepted and trusted in the collector community
Collectors' broken points	Most collectors only display complete points. A Survey should always ask to examine broken point and any collected "debitage."
Survey data usage	A survey must recognize that some members of the professional community will never use survey data in their research.
Sale of paleopoints	A survey must respect private property and understand the paleopoints will be bought and sold; record when available
Clovis-like, Restone-like	If a survey is using established types, never use "like."

The aforementioned lessons were generated by the author's 10-year operation on the McCary Survey and from the Survey's former directors. Since most of the Survey's points were presented by collectors, dealing with the magnitude of personalities and authenticity of artifacts is an experience that can only be partly told in this publication. The personal need to share this experience with others drives this publication's content. In many ways, recording points is pure archaeology, and in some cases, a frustrating experience with prehistoric material destruction.

Learning from a Survey

The McCary Survey has over 70 years of data – what can we learn from these data? By computerizing the data, literally hundreds of questions can be asked and answered, all of which produce insights that simply are not viewable one point at a time. Ben McCary and Hranicky (1995) compiled Survey data which was published by the Archeological Society of Virginia (ASV) and offers a starting place for Clovis population data. As mentioned, a primary advantage to the overall survey operation is its lessons-learned records. While paper trails (letters, files, emails, etc.) are recommended, survey personnel learn over years of recording points who the players are, and what are the values of their contributions. This operation will vary among surveys and the collectors, amateurs, and professionals that they deal with.

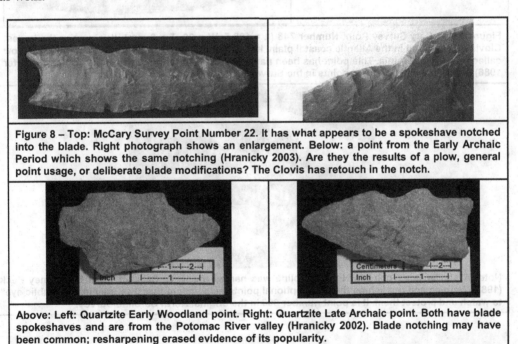

Figure 8 – Top: McCary Survey Point Number 22. It has what appears to be a spokeshave notched into the blade. Right photograph shows an enlargement. Below: a point from the Early Archaic Period which shows the same notching (Hranicky 2003). Are they the results of a plow, general point usage, or deliberate blade modifications? The Clovis has retouch in the notch.

Above: Left: Quartzite Early Woodland point. Right: Quartzite Late Archaic point. Both have blade spokeshaves and are from the Potomac River valley (Hranicky 2002). Blade notching may have been common; resharpening erased evidence of its popularity.

A learning example comes from Survey points Number 22, and Number 219 (illustrated in the Survey list) which have spokeshaves. The spokeshave was used throughout prehistory, and these points in the Survey provide two of the oldest records of this technology (Figure 8). To the best of our knowledge, paleopoint blade notching has not been reported in Virginia's literature or elsewhere. Does the spokeshave in a blade have an Old World legacy? Some archaeologists, namely Dennis Stanford and Bruce Bradly, argue that the Solutreans made numerous cross-Atlantic migrations to eastern North America.

The spokeshave was used to debark and shape small wooden, bone, and antler shafts. Two other forms (quartzite) have the notch close to the hafting area. Suggestion: later Archaic Period Indians started using quartzite because it has a higher tensile strength. See quartzite regenerative characteristics below.

No matter what the approach to the study of prehistoric stone tools (Figure 9), quoting Floyd Painter, who was the editor/publisher of the Chesopiean Archaeological Journal offers – *there is always something new to discover in Clovis archaeology.*

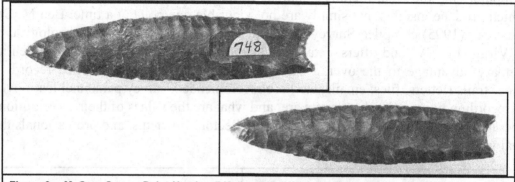

Figure 9 – McCary Survey Point Number 748 (L = 138.5, W = 30, T = 8 mm). It is among the largest Clovis points found in the Atlantic coastal plain. It was found during the 19th century at Salt Lick (now called Roanoke), Virginia. This point has been named the Loy Carter point (by Floyd Painter in Carter 1986) and is one of the longest points in the Survey. It is now in the McCary Collection.

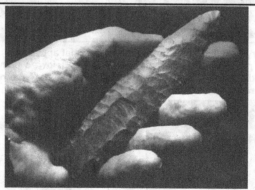

Note: A similar large point in North Carolina was named the R. E. Callicutt point by Rodney Peck (1985). Naming and publishing these exceptional points help ensure that they stay in the "public eye" to watch and protect them. It is point number 300 in the original North Carolina Survey.

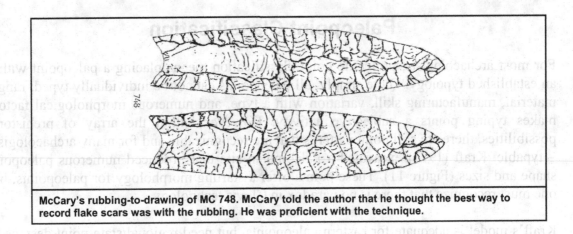

McCary's rubbing-to-drawing of MC 748. McCary told the author that he thought the best way to record flake scars was with the rubbing. He was proficient with the technique.

Survey Certificate

The McCary Survey has available a certificate for each paleopoint. It is available upon request; all paleopoints recorded after MC 1000 automatically receive a certificate (Figure 10).

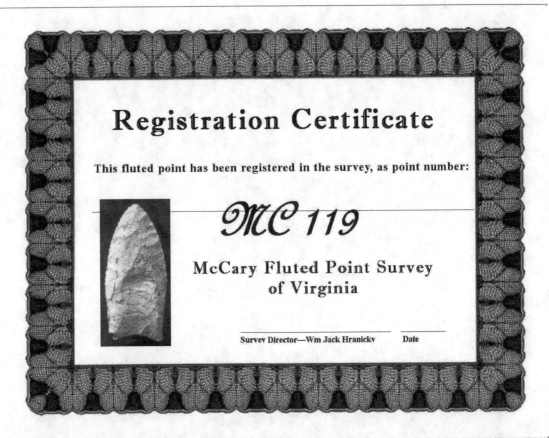

Registration Certificate

This fluted point has been registered in the survey, as point number:

MC 119

McCary Fluted Point Survey
of Virginia

Survey Director—Wm Jack Hranicky   Date

Figure 10 - Each paleopoint recorded after number 1000 in the Survey is issued a Registration Certificate.
A certificate for earlier numbers is available upon request.

Paleopoint Classification

For most archaeologists, projectile point classification means placing a paleopoint within an established typology. Quite simply, all paleopoints cannot be individually typed; range, material, manufacturing skill, variation with a type, and numerous morphological factors makes typing points a subjective activity. However within the array of prehistoric possibilities, there are still point patterns that are recognizable and for many archaeologists – typable. Kraft (1973) excavated a Paleoindian site that produced numerous paleopoint shape and sizes (Figure 11). These points offer a starting morphology for paleopoints, but one must recognize that there is no paradox in Clovis technology.

Kraft's model is adequate for eastern paleopoints, but need regional/state point designs in order to provide a state-wide framework for is tool class. His type numbers have not been adopted, but are used to reflect the original publication. While typology has its place in archaeology, note the morphological variations in the figure; then turn to the section containing the 1000 Virginia points and view their morphology. The Survey report containing points from 1000 to 1055 is also included in this publication.

Figure 11 – Morphological Shapes found at the Plenge Site in New Jersey (Kraft 1973)

Type 1 Tapered, mildly excurvate or parallel sided, fluted point	 Deep Base · Shallow Base · Abrupt Base
Type 2 Recurved, waisted and eared fluted point	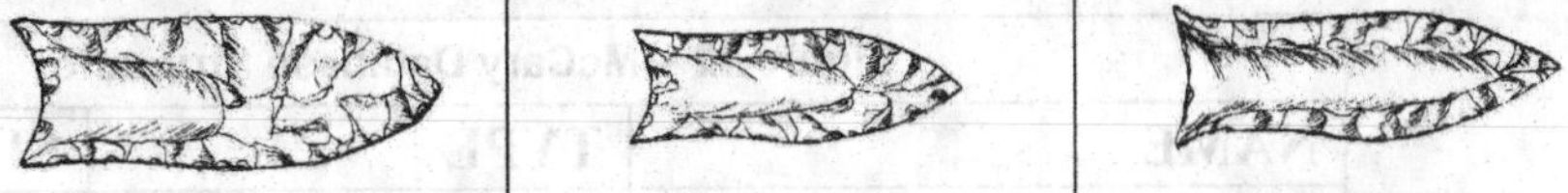 Long Point · Medium Point · Eared Point
Type 3 "Stubby" fluted point	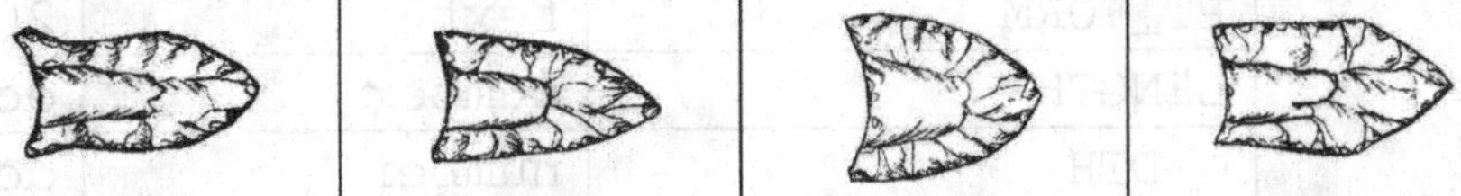 Waisted · Straight · Rounded · Pentagonal
Type 4 Convex sided fluted point	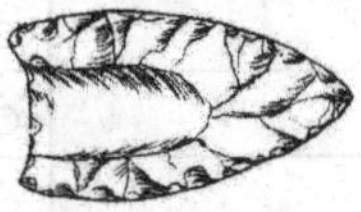 Excurvate
Type 5 Contracted stem fluted point	 Mild Taper · Pumpkin Seed · Pentagonal
Type 6 Triangular straight-sided point	 Triangle
Type 7 Reworked fluted point (knife/scraper, drill)	Knife · Scraper · Not shown. Drill
Type 10 Unfluted lanceolate point	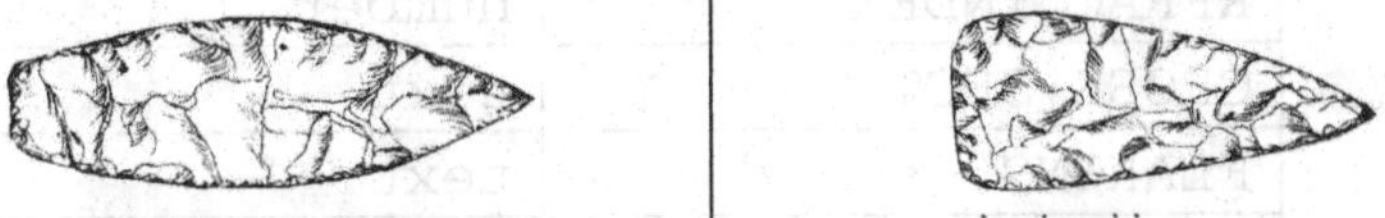 Contracting Stem · Broad Base
Type 11 Unfluted trianguloid point	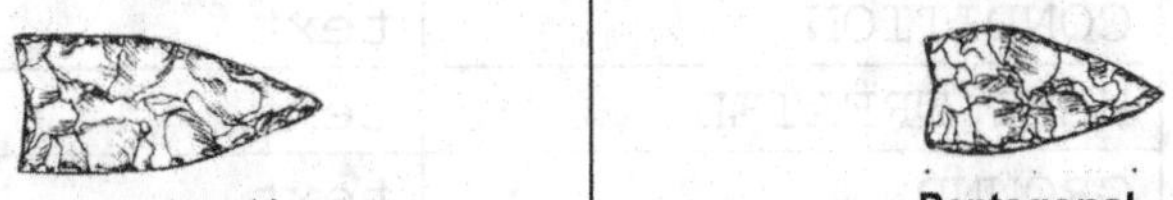 Excurvate Sides · Pentagonal
Type 12 Blade point* * Added this paper.	 Parallel Sides

Survey Database Structure

The following table (Data Dictionary) provides the McCary Survey database structure (Figure 12). The entire Survey file is available on CD; see website for availability: **www.archeology.org**

Figure 12 – McCary Database Structure		
NAME	**TYPE**	**SIZE**
POINT_NUM	number	5
PT_FORM	text	20
LENGTH	number	double
WIDTH	number	double
THICK	number	double
FLUTE_LEN_1	number	double
FLUTE_WD_1	number	double
FLUTE_DP_1	number	double
FLUTE_LEN_2	number	double
FLUTE_WD_2	number	double
FLUTE_DP_2	number	double
BLADE_EDGE	text	2
FRANK_EDGE_1	number	double
FRANK_EDGE_2	number	double
FLAKE_CM	number	double
BASE_CAV_HGT	number	double
BASE_CAV_WPT	number	double
WEIGHT	number	double
BASE_WDTH	number	double
S_GRAVITY	number	double
RFRAC_INDEX	number	Long
CROSS_SECT	text	4
FLAKING	text	4
BASE_STYLE	text	2
CONDITION	text	1
HEAT TREATED	text	1
GROUND	text	12
MATERIAL	text	20
PRIM_COLOR	text	14
MUNSELL	text	15
DRAWING	text	1
RUBBING	text	1

Figure 12 – McCary Database Structure		
PHOTOGRAPH	text	1
CAST	text	1
MUSEUM	text	1
DATE_RECOR	date/time	
PRIV_COLL	text	1
SURFAC_SITE	text	7
LOC_AREA	text	19
COUNTY	text	18
INIT_OWNER	text	20
COMMENT	text	48
NEW_COMMENT	text	65
RUBBING_1	graphic	ole object
RUBBING_2	graphic	ole object
DRAWING_1	graphic	ole object
DRAWING_2	graphic	ole object
PHOTO_IMAGE_1	graphic	ole object
PHOTO_IMAGE_2	graphic	ole object
VIDEO	Graphic	ole object

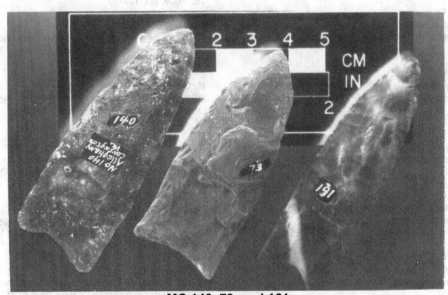

MC 140, 73, and 161
See Special Publication Number 2 – Points 1001 to 1050
McCary Fluted Point Survey of Virginia

McCary Survey
References

McCary, Ben C.
(1947) A Survey and Study of Folsom-Like Points Found in Virginia, Nos. 1-131. Quarterly Bulletin, Archeological Society of Virginia, Vol. 2, No. 1.

McCary, Ben C.
(1947) Report of Additional Virginia-Folsom Points, Nos. 132-136. Quarterly Bulletin, Archeological Society of Virginia, Vol. 2, No. 2.

McCary, Ben C.
(1948) Report of Additional Virginia-Folsom Points, Nos. 137-141. Quarterly Bulletin, Archeological Society of Virginia, Vol. 2, No. 3.

McCary, Ben C.
(1949) Survey of Virginia-Folsom Points, Nos. 142-161. Quarterly Bulletin, Archeological Society of Virginia, Vol. 4, No. 1.

McCary, Ben C., J. C. Smith, and C. E. Gilliam
(1949) A Folsom Workshop Site on the Williamson Farm, Dinwiddie County, Virginia, The Williamson Site, Nos. 162-172. Quarterly Bulletin, Archeological Society of Virginia, Vol. 4, No. 2.

McCary, Ben C.
(1952) Survey of Virginia-Folsom Points, Nos. 173-219. Quarterly Bulletin, Archeological Society of Virginia, Vol. 6, No. 4.

McCary, Ben C.
(1953) Survey of Virginia Fluted Points, Nos. 220-225. Quarterly Bulletin, Archeological Society of Virginia, Vol. 7, No. 3.

McCary, Ben C.
(1954) Survey of Virginia Fluted Points, Nos. 226-231. Quarterly Bulletin, Archeological Society of Virginia, Vol. 8, No. 3.

McCary, Ben C.
(1956) Survey of Virginia Fluted Points, Nos. 232-263. Quarterly Bulletin, Archeological Society of Virginia, Vol. 10, No. 3.

McCary, Ben C.
(1956) A Fluted Point from Rockbridge County (No. 264). Quarterly Bulletin, Archeological Society of Virginia, Vol. 10, No. 4.

McCary, Ben C.
(1958) Survey of Virginia Fluted Points, Nos. 265-281. Quarterly Bulletin, Archeological Society of Virginia, Vol. 13, No. 1.

McCary, Ben C.
(1961) Survey of Virginia Fluted Points, Nos. 282-293. Quarterly Bulletin, Archeological Society of Virginia, Vol. 15, No. 3, pp. 27-31.

McCary, Ben C.
(1963) Survey of Virginia Fluted Points, Nos. 294-314. Quarterly Bulletin, Archeological Society of Virginia, Vol. 18, No. 2, pp. 25-29.

McCary, Ben C.
(1965) Survey of Virginia Fluted Points, Nos. 315-347. Quarterly Bulletin, Archeological Society of Virginia, Vol. 20, No. 2, pp. 53-60.

McCary, Ben C.
(1968) Survey of Virginia Fluted Points, Nos. 348-384. Quarterly Bulletin, Archeological Society of Virginia, Vol. 23, No. 1, pp. 2-10.

McCary, Ben C.
(1972) Survey of Virginia Fluted Points, Nos. 385-420. Quarterly Bulletin, Archeological Society of Virginia, Vol. 26, No. 4, pp. 190-202.

For McCary Points 380-384:
Potter, Steven R.
(1968) A Report on Some Stone Paleo-Indian Projectile Points from Virginia and Nearby States. Quarterly Bulletin, Archaeological Society of Virginia, Vol. 23, No. 1, pp. 11-19.

McCary, Ben C.
(1974) Survey of Virginia Fluted Points, Nos. 421-468. Quarterly Bulletin, Archeological Society of Virginia, Vol. 28, No. 3, pp. 137-151.

McCary, Ben C.
(1976) Survey of Virginia Fluted Points, Nos. 469-507. Quarterly Bulletin, Archeological Society of Virginia, Vol. 30, No. 4, pp. 169-186.

McCary, Ben C.
(1979) Survey of Virginia Fluted Points, Nos. 508-536. Quarterly Bulletin, Archeological Society of Virginia, Vol. 33, No. 3, pp. 98-108.

McCary, Ben C.
(1980) Survey of Virginia Fluted Points, Nos. 537-603. Quarterly Bulletin, Archeological Society of Virginia, Vol. 34, No. 3, pp. 161-184.

McCary, Ben C.
(1981) Survey of Virginia Fluted Points, Nos. 604-640. Quarterly Bulletin, Archeological Society of Virginia, Vol. 35, No. 4, pp. 186-199.

McCary, Ben C.
(1982) Survey of Virginia Fluted Points, Nos. 641-679. Quarterly Bulletin, Archeological Society of Virginia, Vol. 37, No. 3, pp. 105-118.

McCary, Ben C.
(1984) Survey of Virginia Fluted Points, Nos. 680-706. Quarterly Bulletin, Archeological Society of Virginia, Vol. 39, No. 1, pp. 55-64.

McCary, Ben C.
(1985) Survey of Virginia Fluted Points, Nos. 707-732. Quarterly Bulletin, Archeological Society of Virginia, Vol. 40, No. 1, pp. 1-11.

McCary, Ben C.
(1986) Survey of Virginia Fluted Points, Nos. 733-770. Quarterly Bulletin, Archeological Society of Virginia, Vol. 41, No. 1, pp. 1-14.

McCary, Ben C.
(1987) Survey of Virginia Fluted Points, Nos. 771-800. Quarterly Bulletin, Archeological Society of Virginia, Vol. 42, No. 3, pp. 121-132.

McCary, Ben C.
(1988) Survey of Virginia Fluted Points, Nos. 801-824. Quarterly Bulletin, Archeological Society of Virginia, Vol. 43, No. 3, pp. 97-107.

McCary, Ben C.
(1990) Survey of Virginia Fluted Points, Nos. 825-845. Quarterly Bulletin, Archeological Society of Virginia, Vol. 45, No. 1, pp. 28-37.

Johnson, Michael F. and Joyce Pearsall
(1991) The Dr. Ben C. McCary Virginia Fluted Point Survey, Nos. 846-867. Quarterly Bulletin, Archeological Society of Virginia, Vol. 46, No. 2, pp. 55-68.

Johnson, Michael F. and Joyce Pearsall
(1991) The Dr. Ben C. McCary Virginia Fluted Point Survey, Nos. 868-890. Quarterly Bulletin, Archeological Society of Virginia, Vol. 46, No. 3, pp. 145-162.

Johnson, Michael F. and Joyce Pearsall
(1993) The Dr. Ben C. McCary Virginia Fluted Point Survey, Nos. 891-920. Quarterly Bulletin, Archeological Society of Virginia, Vol. 48, No. 2, pp. 45-63.

Johnson, Michael F. and Joyce Pearsall
(1995) The Dr. Ben C. McCary Virginia Fluted Point Survey, Nos. 921-941. Quarterly Bulletin, Archeological Society of Virginia, Vol. 50, No. 1, pp. 17-31.

Johnson, Michael F. and Joyce Pearsall
(1996) The Dr. Ben C. McCary Virginia Fluted Point Survey, Nos. 942-951. Quarterly Bulletin, Archeological Society of Virginia, Vol. 51, No. 4, pp. 178-185.

Johnson, Michael F. and Joyce Pearsall
(1998) The Dr. Ben C. McCary Virginia Fluted Point Survey, Nos. 952-974. Quarterly Bulletin, Archeological Society of Virginia, Vol. 53, No. 1, pp. 2-17.

Johnson, Michael F. and Joyce Pearsall
(1999) The Dr. Ben C. McCary Virginia Fluted Point Survey, Nos. 975-999. Quarterly Bulletin, Archeological Society of Virginia, Vol. 54, No. 1, pp. 36-53.

Hranicky, Wm Jack
(2004) McCary Fluted Point Survey: Points 1000 to 1008 – A Continuing Study of Virginia Paleoindian Technology. ASV Quarterly Bulletin, Vol. 59, No. 1, pp. 25-52

Hranicky, Wm Jack
(2005) McCary Fluted Point Survey - Points 1009 to 1014: A Continuing Study of Virginia Paleoindian Technology. ASV Quarterly Bulletin, Vol. 60, No. 1, pp. 15-31.

Hranicky, Wm Jack
(2006) McCary Fluted Point Survey: Points 1015 to 1035 – A Continuing Study of Virginia Paleoindian Technology. ASV Quarterly Bulletin, Vol. 61, No. 3, pp. 119-136.

Hranicky, Wm Jack
(2008) McCary Survey Fluted Points: 1036 to 1055. Special Publication No. 2, McCary Fluted Point Survey.

Part Two – McCary Survey Paleopoints

McCary Survey Points

The McCary Survey has 50+ years of recording paleopoints and, over time, numerous recording methods were used. Consequently in presenting a thousand points, the following illustrations will vary from hand-drawn to digital images. The author has presented as accurate point portrayal as possible from the Survey's point history and its points; however, due to different recording methodologies, actual point data may vary.

MC 1 **?** 58-22-5 mm Mecklenburg Co.	**MC 2** **Quartz** 63-46-7 mm Mecklenburg Co.	**MC 3** **Quartz** 53-22-5 mm Mecklenburg Co.	**MC 4** **Quartz** 35-22-9 mm Mecklenburg Co.	**MC 5** **Quartz** 52-27-6 mm Mecklenburg Co.	**MC 6** **Quartz** 33-19-x mm Mecklenburg Co.
MC 7 **Flint** 57-22-x mm Mecklenburg Co.	**MC 8** **Flint** 47-23-5 mm Mecklenburg Co.	**MC 9** **Chalcedony** 63-29-x mm Mecklenburg Co.	**MC 10** **Flint** 64-24-5 mm Mecklenburg Co.	**MC 11** **Quartz** 46-24-x mm Mecklenburg Co.	**MC 12** **Shale** 51-24-x mm Mecklenburg Co.
MC 13 **Flint** 73-24-x mm Mecklenburg Co.	**MC 14** **Flint** 65-27-x mm Mecklenburg Co.	**MC 15** **Flint** 35-17-x mm Mecklenburg Co.	**MC 16** **Flint** 43-21-4 mm Mecklenburg Co.	**MC 17** **Flint** 57-24-x mm Mecklenburg Co.	**MC 18** **Flint** 58-24-5 mm Mecklenburg Co.

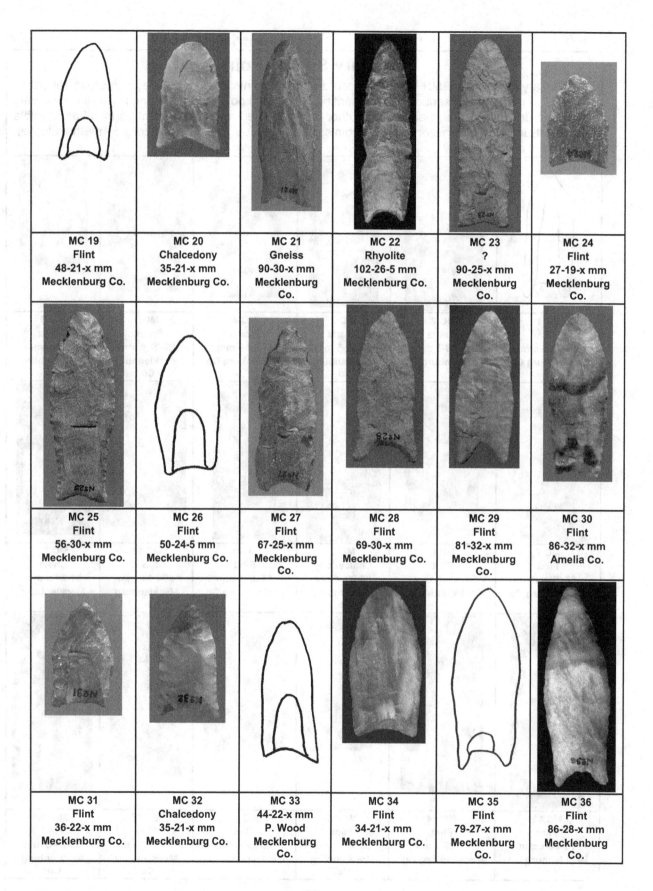

MC 19 Flint 48-21-x mm Mecklenburg Co.	**MC 20** Chalcedony 35-21-x mm Mecklenburg Co.	**MC 21** Gneiss 90-30-x mm Mecklenburg Co.	**MC 22** Rhyolite 102-26-5 mm Mecklenburg Co.	**MC 23** ? 90-25-x mm Mecklenburg Co.	**MC 24** Flint 27-19-x mm Mecklenburg Co.
MC 25 Flint 56-30-x mm Mecklenburg Co.	**MC 26** Flint 50-24-5 mm Mecklenburg Co.	**MC 27** Flint 67-25-x mm Mecklenburg Co.	**MC 28** Flint 69-30-x mm Mecklenburg Co.	**MC 29** Flint 81-32-x mm Mecklenburg Co.	**MC 30** Flint 86-32-x mm Amelia Co.
MC 31 Flint 36-22-x mm Mecklenburg Co.	**MC 32** Chalcedony 35-21-x mm Mecklenburg Co.	**MC 33** 44-22-x mm P. Wood Mecklenburg Co.	**MC 34** Flint 34-21-x mm Mecklenburg Co.	**MC 35** Flint 79-27-x mm Mecklenburg Co.	**MC 36** Flint 86-28-x mm Mecklenburg Co.

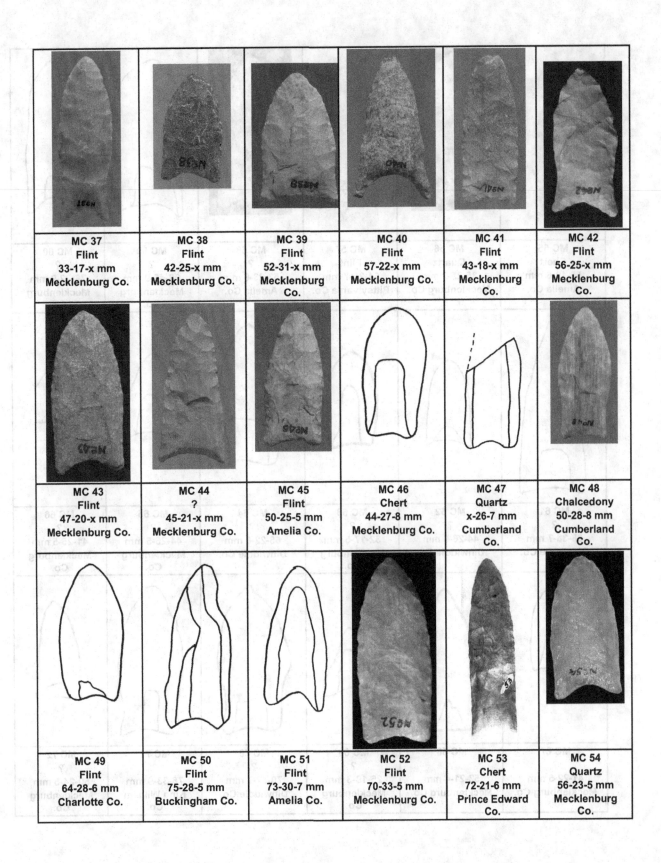

MC 37 Flint 33-17-x mm Mecklenburg Co.	**MC 38** Flint 42-25-x mm Mecklenburg Co.	**MC 39** Flint 52-31-x mm Mecklenburg Co.	**MC 40** Flint 57-22-x mm Mecklenburg Co.	**MC 41** Flint 43-18-x mm Mecklenburg Co.	**MC 42** Flint 56-25-x mm Mecklenburg Co.
MC 43 Flint 47-20-x mm Mecklenburg Co.	**MC 44** ? 45-21-x mm Mecklenburg Co.	**MC 45** Flint 50-25-5 mm Amelia Co.	**MC 46** Chert 44-27-8 mm Mecklenburg Co.	**MC 47** Quartz x-26-7 mm Cumberland Co.	**MC 48** Chalcedony 50-28-8 mm Cumberland Co.
MC 49 Flint 64-28-6 mm Charlotte Co.	**MC 50** Flint 75-28-5 mm Buckingham Co.	**MC 51** Flint 73-30-7 mm Amelia Co.	**MC 52** Flint 70-33-5 mm Mecklenburg Co.	**MC 53** Chert 72-21-6 mm Prince Edward Co.	**MC 54** Quartz 56-23-5 mm Mecklenburg Co.

MC 55 Chert 55-19-6 mm Amelia Co.	MC 56 Quartz 35-25-7 mm Mecklenburg Co.	MC 57 Flint 64-25-7 mm Pittsylvania Co.	MC 58 ? 53-23-6 mm Amelia Co.	MC 59 ? 98-45-9 mm Mecklenburg Co.	MC 60 ? 76-32-9 mm Mecklenburg Co.
MC 61 ? 88-38-7 mm Dinwiddie Co.	MC 62 ? 44-26-6 mm Dinwiddie Co.	MC 63 ? 32-17-5 mm Mecklenburg Co.	MC 64 ? 65-22-6 mm Dinwiddie Co.	MC 65 ? 44-25-5 mm Mecklenburg Co.	MC 66 ? 41-25-5 mm Mecklenburg Co.
MC 67 ? 41-22-5 mm Mecklenburg Co.	MC 68 ? 53-21-4 mm Mecklenburg Co.	MC 69 ? 25-19-3 mm Mecklenburg Co.	MC 70 ? 70-32-7 mm Dinwiddie Co.	MC 71 ? 76-33-9 mm King William Co.	MC 72 ? 50-24-5 mm Mecklenburg Co.

MC 73	MC 74	MC 75	MC 76	MC 77	MC 78
Flint	Flint	Flint	Jasper	Flint	Flint
63-25-6 mm	45-20-4 mm	66-26-5 mm	29-16-4 mm	x-20-4 mm	70-28-5 mm
Nansemond Co.	Nansemond Co.	Nansemond Co.	Shenandoah Co.	Albermarle Co.	Caroline Co.

MC 79	MC 80	MC 81	MC 82	MC 83	MC 84
Flint	Chalcedony	Quartzite	Flint	?	?
58-26-6 mm	57-26-6 mm	43-27-9 mm	59-21-5 mm	50-25-5 mm	50-27-6 mm
Scott Co.	Scott Co.	Albermarle Co.	James City Co.	Bedford Co.	Bedford Co.

MC 85	MC 86	MC 87	MC 88	MC 89	MC 90
?	?	?	Flint	Flint	?
26-21-x mm	44-22-x mm	65-30-6 mm	70-25-x mm	50-22-x mm	55-24-x mm
Bedford Co.	Bedford Co.	Bedford Co.	Bedford Co.	Mecklenburg Co.	Amelia Co.

31

MC 91 Quartz x-28-x mm ???	**MC 92** Flint 40-21-x mm Rockingham Co.	**MC 93** Quartz 50-20-x mm Mecklenburg Co.	**MC 94** ? 60-27-6 mm Mecklenburg Co.	**MC 95** ? 74-28-x mm Mecklenburg Co.	**MC 96** ? 88-27-9 mm Mecklenburg Co.
MC 97 ? 115-25-9 mm Campbell Co.	**MC 98** ? 137-52-7 mm Mecklenburg Co.	**MC 99** ? 79-30-9 mm Mecklenburg Co.	**MC 100** Flint 50-25-6 mm Mecklenburg Co.	**MC 101** Flint 63-19-6 mm Mecklenburg Co.	**MC 102** ? 44-24-6 mm Mecklenburg Co.
MC 103 Chalcedony 70-25-6 mm Page Co.	**MC 104** Quartz 55-24-7 mm Page Co.	**MC 105** Chalcedony 92-31-x mm Page Co.	**MC 106** Flint 92-29-6 mm Prince Edward Co.	**MC 107** Slate 104-31-6 mm Bedford Co.	**MC 108** Flint 47-30-6 mm Prince George Co.

MC 109 Flint 53-22-5 mm Prince George Co.	**MC 110** Jasper 62-33-7 mm Bedford Co.	**MC 111** Quartzite 93-50-7 mm Hanover Co.	**MC 112** Flint 82-28-6 mm Brunswick Co.	**MC 113** Flint 44-25-3 mm Henrico Co.	**MC 114** Congomerate 44-22-5 mm Caroline Co.
MC 115 Chalcedony 64-31-7 mm Caroline Co.	**MC 116** Jasper 97-31-6 mm Bedford Co.	**MC 117** Chert x-25-6 mm Bedford Co.	**MC 118** ? 98-32-9 mm Nelson Co.	**MC 119** ? 68-25-7 mm Prince George Co.	**MC 120** Flint 38-25-5 mm Spotsylvania Co.
MC 121 Flint 98-33-6 mm Dinwiddie Co.	**MC 122** Flint 82-30-6 mm Mecklenburg Co.	**MC 123** Chert 50-29-6 mm King and Queen Co.	**MC 124**Quartz 30-17-4 mm Caroline Co.	**MC 125** ? 83-31-7 mm Amelia Co.	**MC 126** ? 70-25-6 mm Mecklenburg Co.

MC 127 ? 40-22-5 mm Mecklenburg Co.	MC 128 Quartz 42-25-5 mm Mecklenburg Co.	MC 129 Flint 45-25-5 mm Mecklenburg Co.	MC 130 Flint 85-32-6 mm Dinwiddie Co.	MC 131 Flint 60-20-6 mm Mecklenburg Co.	MC 132 Chert 59-22-8 mm Bedford Co.
MC 133 Flint 45-30-4 mm Campbell Co.	MC 134 Flint 50-27-5 mm Campbell Co.	MC 135 Quartz 40-15-5 mm Mecklenburg Co.	MC 136 Quartz 49-25-8 mm Mecklenburg Co.	MC 137 Flint 61-24-5 mm Bedford Co.	MC 138 Flint 109-31-6 mm Bedford Co.
MC 139 Flint 47-23-8 mm Amherst Co.	MC 140 ? 69-25-8 mm Alleghany Co.	MC 141 Jasper 72-26-x mm Nelson Co.	MC 142 ? 36-20-4 mm Surry Co.	MC 143 ? 53-21-5 mm Charlotte Co.	MC 144 Flint 58-27-7 mm Campbell Co.

MC 145 Chert 55-27-6 mm Bedford Co.	MC 146 ? 60-27-8 mm Dinwiddie Co.	MC 147 ? 47-23-5 mm Dinwiddie Co.	MC 148 ? 56-21-5 mm Dinwiddie Co.	MC 149 Jasper 90-32-7 mm Pittsylvania Co.	MC 150 Quartz 59-29-7 mm Mecklenburg Co.
MC 151 ? 75-31-7 mm Dinwiddie Co.	MC 152 Flint 50-38-6 mm Sussex Co.	MC 153 Chalcedony 48-25-6 mm Pittsylvania Co.	MC 154 Quartz 53-28-5 mm Mecklenburg Co.	MC 155 ? 73-29-9 mm Dinwiddie Co.	MC 156 Chert 77-28-7 mm Rockingham Co.
MC 157 Flint 60-25-6 mm Rockingham Co.	MC 158 Quartzite 72-26-7 mm Prince George	MC 159 Chert 94-27-4 mm Mecklenburg Co.	MC 160 Flint 58-32-x mm Mecklenburg Co.	MC 161 Chalcedony 90-21-4 mm Shenandoah Co.	MC 162 Chalcedony 32-18-4 mm Dinwiddie Co.

35

MC 163 Chalcedony 40-21-6 mm Dinwiddie Co.	MC 164 Quart 31-20-4 mm Dinwiddie Co.	MC 165 Chalcedony 46-20-6 mm Dinwiddie Co.	MC 166 Chalcedony 45-24-6 mm Dinwiddie Co.	MC 167 Chalcedony 40-33-6 mm Dinwiddie Co.	MC 168 Chalcedony x-20-5 mm Dinwiddie Co.
MC 169 Chalcedony x-25-5 mm Dinwiddie Co.	MC 170 Jasper 44-23-6 mm Dinwiddie Co.	MC 171 Chert 28-12-6 mm Dinwiddie Co.	MC 172 Quartz 29-19-4 mm Dinwiddie Co.	MC 173 Chert x-27-5 mm Dinwiddie Co.	MC 174 Chert 40-21-4 mm Dinwiddie Co.
MC 175 Chert 55-32-6 mm Dinwiddie Co.	MC 176 Chert 37-18-5 mm Dinwiddie Co.	MC 177 Chert 48-20-4 mm Hanover Co.	MC 178 Chert 47-26-4 mm Chesterfield Co.	MC 179 Chert 66-25-6 mm Dinwiddie Co.	MC 180 Chert 51-24-6 mm Chesterfield Co.

MC 181 Flint 73-33-6 mm Mathews Co.	MC 182 Chert 69-25-5 mm Buchanan Co.	MC 183 Chert 56-28-7 mm Mecklenburg Co.	MC 184 Flint 60-28-6 mm Smyth Co.	MC 185 Chert 41-16-8 mm Dinwiddie Co.	MC 186 Chert 50-22-5 mm Dinwiddie Co.
MC 187 Chert 38-27-7 mm Dinwiddie Co.	MC 188 Quartzite 45-23-6 mm Dinwiddie Co.	MC 189 Quartz 26-12-6 mm Dinwiddie Co.	MC 190 Chert 63-26-8 mm Dinwiddie Co.	MC 191 Quartz x-29-6 mm Dinwiddie Co.	MC 192 Quartzite 65-28-8 mm Dinwiddie Co.
MC 193 Chert 56-31-8 mm Dinwiddie Co.	MC 194 Chert x-29-9 mm Dinwiddie Co.	MC 195 Quartzite 57-23-6 mm Dinwiddie Co.	MC 196 Quartz 50-29-8 mm Dinwiddie Co.	MC 197 Chert x-25-4 mm Dinwiddie Co.	MC 198 Chert 55-22-4 mm Dinwiddie Co.
MC 199 Quartzite 71-31-8 mm Dinwiddie Co.	MC 200 Chert 42-22-5 mm Dinwiddie Co.	MC 201 Quartz 34-20-6 mm Dinwiddie Co.	MC 202 Quartz 30-19-6 mm Dinwiddie Co.	MC 203 Chert 36-24-6 mm Dinwiddie Co.	MC 204 Chert x-24-5 mm Dinwiddie Co.

MC 205 Chert x-21-5 mm Dinwiddie Co.	**MC 206** Quartz x-24-4 mm Dinwiddie Co.	**MC 207** Chert 42-27-5 mm Dinwiddie Co.	**MC 208** Chert x-20-5 mm Dinwiddie Co.	**MC 209** Quartzite x-25-5 mm Dinwiddie Co.	**MC 210** Flint 61-24-7 mm Smyth Co.
MC 211 Chert 47-29-6 mm Dinwiddie Co.	**MC 212** Chert x-25-5 mm Dinwiddie Co.	**MC 213** Quartz 54-27-5 mm Smyth Co.	**MC 214** Chert 72-31-7 mm Dinwiddie Co.	**MC 215** Quartz 40-26-10 mm Dinwiddie Co.	**MC 216** Chert 72-31-7 mm Dinwiddie Co.
MC 217 Chert 35-24-5 mm Dinwiddie Co.	**MC 218** Flint 52-21-x mm Mecklenburg Co.	**MC 219** Chert 38-19-5 mm Greensville Co.	**MC 220** Jasper 140-32-10 mm Halifax Co.	**MC 221** Chert 70-31-7 Mecklenburg Co.	**MC 222** Chert 56-35-6 mm Mecklenburg Co.

MC 223 Quartz x-22-5 mm Brunswick Co.	MC 224 Chert 93-40-7 mm Mecklenburg Co.	MC 225 Chert 46-23-6 mm Mecklenburg Co.	MC 226 Chert 71-26-5 mm Mecklenburg Co.	MC 227 Chert 79-29-5 mm Mecklenburg Co.	MC 228 Chert 69-25-4 mm Lunenburg Co.
MC 229 Chert 65-34-10 mm Mecklenburg Co.	MC 230 Chert 47-24-5 mm Mecklenburg Co.	MC 231 Chert 52-24-5 Dinwiddie Co.	MC 232 Chert 72-35-7 mm Dinwiddie Co.	MC 233 Chert 53-30-10 mm Dinwiddie Co.	MC 234 Chalcedony 70-27-7 mm Dinwiddie Co.
MC 235 Chert 66-23-7 mm Dinwiddie Co.	MC 236 Chert 57-25-6 mm Dinwiddie Co.	MC 237 Chert 53-22-5 mm Dinwiddie Co.	MC 238 Chert 46-20-5 mm Dinwiddie Co.	MC 239 Chert x-24-5 mm Dinwiddie Co.	MC 240 Chert x-28-6 mm Dinwiddie Co.

MC 241 Chert x-27-5 mm Dinwiddie Co.	**MC 242** Chert 46-22-5 mm Dinwiddie Co.	**MC 243** Chert 35-20-5 mm Dinwiddie Co.	**MC 244** Chert x-21-4 mm Dinwiddie Co.	**MC 245** Chert 38-22-5 mm Dinwiddie Co.	**MC 246** Chert 43-19-6 mm Dinwiddie Co.
MC 247 Jasper 56-22-4 mm Nansemond Co.	**MC 248** Quartzite 50-29-5 mm Nansemond Co.	**MC 249** Chert 53-26-5 mm ???	**MC 250** Chert 77-26-5 mm York Co.	**MC 251** Chert 36-23-5 mm Dinwiddie Co.	**MC 252** Chert 37-22-5 mm Dinwiddie Co.
MC 253 Quartzite 51-24-9 mm Nansemond Co.	**MC 254** Chert 52-23-5 mm Nansemond Co.	**MC 255** Quartz x-27-5 mm Dinwiddie Co.	**MC 256** Jasper 26-17-5 mm Dinwiddie Co.	**MC 257** Quartz x-27-7 mm Dinwiddie Co.	**MC 258** Quartz x-16-5 mm Dinwiddie Co.

MC 259 Quartz 39-22-5 mm Dinwiddie Co.	MC 260 Chert 82-23-8 mm Bath Co.	MC 261 Rhyolite 58-20-6 mm Mecklenburg Co.	MC 262 Chert 63-23-6 mm Mecklenburg Co.	MC 263 Chert 40-22-4 mm Mecklenburg Co.	MC 264 Chert 49-26-7 mm Rockbridge Co.
MC 265 Quartzite 45-20-10 mm Nansemond Co.	MC 266 Jasper 36-20-4 mm Nansemond Co.	MC 267 Chert 61-26-7 mm Northampton Co.	MC 268 P. Wood 42-21-4 mm Mecklenburg Co.	MC 269 Quartz 69-25-7 mm Dinwiddie Co.	MC 270 Quartz x-27-7 mm Princess Anne Co.
MC 271 Chert 38-23-7 mm Southampton Co.	MC 272 Chert 54-24-5 mm Princess Anne Co.	MC 273 Quartzite 74-26-7 mm Southampton Co.	MC 274 Chert 71-25-6 mm Isle of Wight Co.	MC 275 Quartzite 46-20-6 mm Greensville Co.	MC 276 Chert 50-26-7 mm Dinwiddie Co.

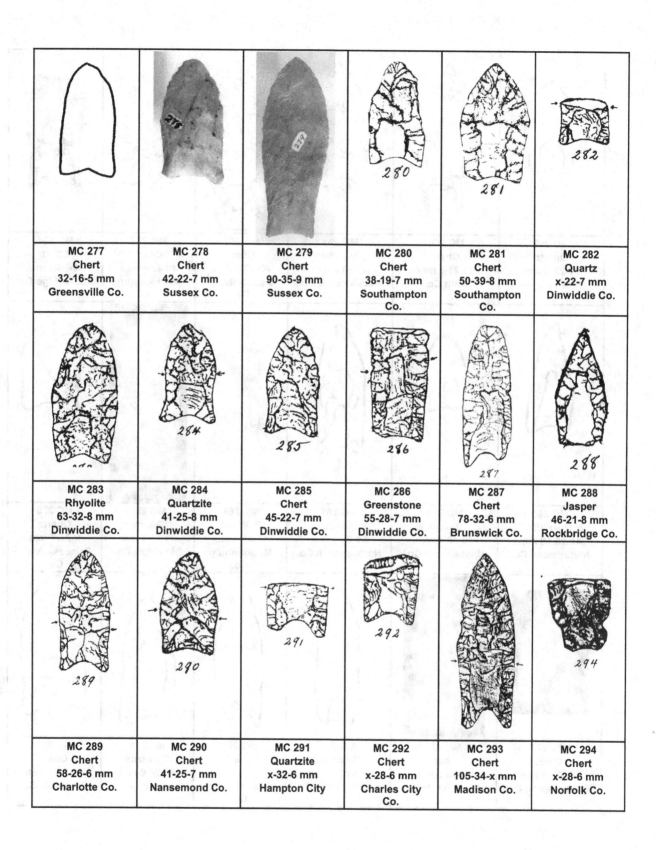

MC 277 Chert 32-16-5 mm Greensville Co.	**MC 278** Chert 42-22-7 mm Sussex Co.	**MC 279** Chert 90-35-9 mm Sussex Co.	**MC 280** Chert 38-19-7 mm Southampton Co.	**MC 281** Chert 50-39-8 mm Southampton Co.	**MC 282** Quartz x-22-7 mm Dinwiddie Co.
MC 283 Rhyolite 63-32-8 mm Dinwiddie Co.	**MC 284** Quartzite 41-25-8 mm Dinwiddie Co.	**MC 285** Chert 45-22-7 mm Dinwiddie Co.	**MC 286** Greenstone 55-28-7 mm Dinwiddie Co.	**MC 287** Chert 78-32-6 mm Brunswick Co.	**MC 288** Jasper 46-21-8 mm Rockbridge Co.
MC 289 Chert 58-26-6 mm Charlotte Co.	**MC 290** Chert 41-25-7 mm Nansemond Co.	**MC 291** Quartzite x-32-6 mm Hampton City	**MC 292** Chert x-28-6 mm Charles City Co.	**MC 293** Chert 105-34-x mm Madison Co.	**MC 294** Chert x-28-6 mm Norfolk Co.

295	296	297	298	Duplicate See MC142	300
MC 295 Chert x-26-7 mm Norfolk Co.	**MC 296** Greenstone 63-23-7 mm Mecklenburg Co.	**MC 297** Jasper 50-28-8 mm Isle of Wight Co.	**MC 298** Rhyolie 45-25-7 mm Nansemond Co.	MC 299	**MC 300** Chert 53-28-7 mm Smyth Co.
301	302	733	304		306
MC 301 Chert 70-30-7 mm Dinwiddie Co.	**MC 302** Jasper x-27-7 mm Surry Co.	**MC 303** Quartz x-26-7 mm Southampton Co.	**MC 304** Chert 62-29-9 mm Mecklenburg Co.	**MC 305** Quartz 34-20-5 mm Brunswick Co.	**MC 306** Quartz x-27-8 mm Nansemond Co.
307	308			311	
MC 307 Chert x-26-6 mm Dinwiddie Co.	**MC 308** Quartzite 42-34-9 mm Nansemond Co.	**MC 309** Chert 50-24-7 mm Greensville Co.	**MC 310** Rhyolite 71-29-7 mm James City Co.	**MC 311** Jasper x-30-5 mm Halifax Co.	**MC 312** Chert 56-28-6 mm Mecklenburg Co.

MC 313 Jasper 76-25-7 mm Richmond City	MC 314 Chert 32-24-6 mm Prince George Co.	MC 315 Quartz 41-22-6 mm Albermarle Co.	MC 316 Chert 57-28-6 mm Grayson Co.	MC 317 Chert 60-23-6 mm Grayson Co.	MC 318 Chert 54-32-6 mm ???
MC 319 Jasper 79-33-6 mm ???	MC 320 Quartzite 50-26-7 mm Pittsylvania Co.	MC 321 Chert 75-28-7 mm Pittsylvania Co.	MC 322 Chert 46-28-6 mm Pearsburg City	MC 323 Greenstone 54-20-6 mm Princess Anne Co.	MC 324 Flint 81-30-6 mm Southampton Co.
MC 325 Greemstone X-21-6 mm Dinwiddie Co.	MC 326 Chert x-27-7 mm Southampton Co.	MC 327 Chert x-30-6 mm Sussex Co.	MC 328 Schist 48-25-6 mm Sussex Co.	MC 329 Chert 26-18-4 mm Dinwiddie Co.	MC 330 Chalcedony 69-31-7 mm Brunswick Co.

44

MC 331 Quartz 52-36-8 mm Nelson Co.	MC 332 Quartzite 66-26-9 mm Southampton Co.	MC 333 Chert 62-22-7 mm Mecklenburg Co.	MC 334 Chalcedony 39-25-6 mm Surry Co.	MC 335 Chert 56-21-6 mm Dinwiddie Co.	MC 336 Quartzite 33-20-6 mm ???
MC 337 Chert 75-33-7 mm Powhatan Co.	MC 338 Chert 56-28-x mm Sussex Co.	MC 339 ? 38-18-5 mm Tazewell Co.	MC 340 Quartzite 44-24-7 mm King George Co.	MC 341 Jasper 56-22-7 mm Chesterfield Co.	MC 342 Quartz x-20-6 mm Chesterfield Co.
MC 343 P. Wood X- 21-6 mm Chesterfield Co.	MC 344 Chert 38-21-5 mm Chesterfield Co,	MC 345 Quartz 37-19-7 mm Chesterfield Co.	MC 346 Chert 33-20-6 mm Chesterfield Co.	MC 347 Chert 53-32-3 mm Shenandoah Co.	MC 348 Chert 35-15-4 mm Dinwiddie Co.

45

MC 349 Chert 37-15-5 mm Dinwiddie Co.	**MC 350** Chert 32-15-4 mm Dinwiddie Co.	**MC 351** Chert 32-21-5 mm Dinwiddie Co.	**MC 352** Chert x-18-5 mm Dinwiddie Co.	**MC 353** Chert 61-29-7 mm Dinwiddie Co.	**MC 354** Quartzite 50-30-8 mm Sussex Co.
MC 355 Quartzite 43-25-6 mm Sussex Co.	**MC 356** Jasper x-25-5 mm Sussex Co.	**MC 357** Chert x-32-7 mm Bedford Co.	**MC 358** Chalcedony 74-28-x mm ???	**MC 359** Chert 64-27-7 mm Tazewell Co.	**MC 360** Chert 75-30-7 mm Tazewell Co.
MC 361 Chert 30-15-x mm Scott Co.	**MC 362** Slate 47-25-6 mm Nansemond Co.	**MC 363** Quartzite 79-34-8 mm Isle of Wight Co.	**MC 364** Chalcedony 36-21-6 mm Princess Anne Co.	**MC 365** Chert 62-31-8 mm Hanover Co.	**MC 366** Chert 47-23-6 mm Amherst Co.
MC 367 Chert x-25-6 mm Virginia Beach	**MC 368** Quartzite 32-19-6 mm Dinwiddie Co.	**MC 369** Quartzite 51-25-7 mm Norfolk Co.	**MC 370** Chert 30-17-5 mm Dinwiddie Co.	**MC 371** Jasper x-22-6 mm Henrico Co.	**MC 372** Chert 56-24-7 mm Brunswick Co.

MC 373 Chert 106-37-10 mm Halifax Co.	MC 374 Chert 68-31-7 mm Mecklenburg Co.	MC 375 Jasper 65-27-8 mm Mecklenburg Co.	MC 376 Jasper 47-23-7 mm Nansemond Co.	MC 377 Chert 42-33-7 mm Chesterfield Co.	MC 378 Chert 68-27-6 mm Dinwiddie Co.
MC 379 Quartz 55-30-7 mm Mecklenburg Co.	Smithsonian Institution MC 380 Jasper 108-35-8 mm ???	Smithsonian Institution MC 381 Chert 106-27-8 mm ???	Smithsonian Institution MC 382 Chert 58-22-7 mm Campbell Co.	Smithsonian Institution MC 383 Chert 72-27-7 mm Orange Co.	Smithsonian Institution MC 384 Chalcedony 54-26-7 mm Charlotte Co.
MC 385 Rhyolite x-26-4 mm Halifax Co.	MC 386 Chert 54-21-6 mm Mecklenburg Co.	MC 387 Chert 120-30-7 mm Mecklenburg Co.	MC 388 Chert 57-26-8 mm Radford Co.	MC 389 Jasper 52-22-7 mm Page Co.	MC 390 Quartz 45-17-6 mm Mecklenburg Co.

MC 391 Rhyolite 73-29-8 mm Loudoun Co.	MC 392 Chert 91-33-9 mm Fauquier Co.	MC 393 Chert 50-26-6 mm Fort Eustis	MC 394 Jasper x-x-9 mm Essex Co.	MC 395 Chert x-27-6 mm Dinwiddie Co.	MC 396 Chert x-38-7 mm Dinwiddie Co.
MC 397 Chert x-30-8 mm Dinwiddie Co.	MC 398 Chert x-29-6 mm Dinwiddie Co.	MC 399 Chert 45-25-7 mm Dinwiddie Co.	MC 400 Chert x-30-x mm Augusta Co.	MC 401 Chert x-24-6 mm Dinwiddie Co.	MC 402 Quartzite x-28-6 mm Dinwiddie Co.
MC 403 Chert 36-23-9 mm Dinwiddie Co.	MC 404 Chert 35-20-5 mm Dinwiddie Co.	MC 405 Chert x-29-6 mm Dinwiddie Co.	MC 406 Jasper 55-20-7 mm Dinwiddie Co.	MC 407 Chert 57-30-6 mm Dinwiddie Co.	MC 408 Chert 32-23-6 mm Dinwiddie Co.

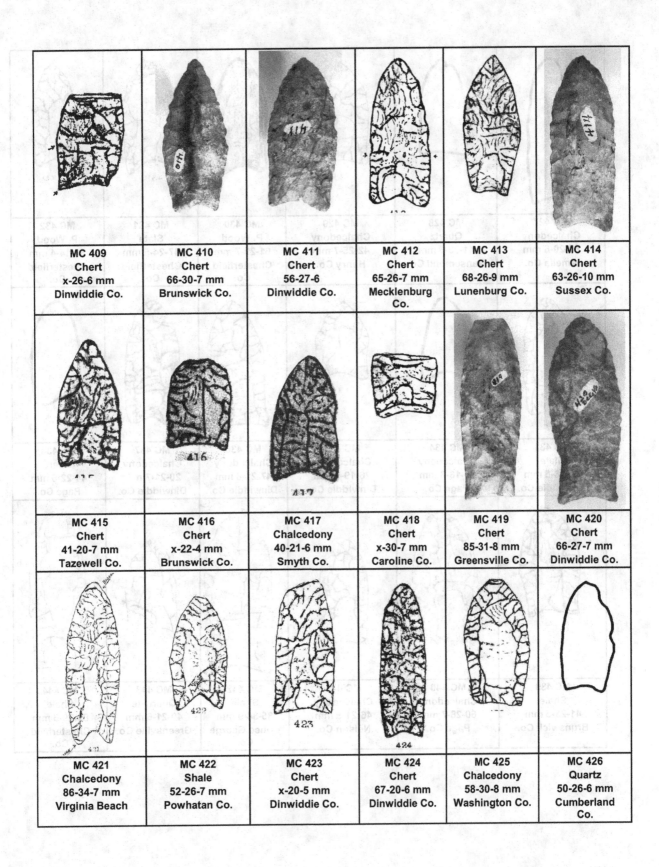

MC 409 Chert x-26-6 mm Dinwiddie Co.	MC 410 Chert 66-30-7 mm Brunswick Co.	MC 411 Chert 56-27-6 Dinwiddie Co.	MC 412 Chert 65-26-7 mm Mecklenburg Co.	MC 413 Chert 68-26-9 mm Lunenburg Co.	MC 414 Chert 63-26-10 mm Sussex Co.
MC 415 Chert 41-20-7 mm Tazewell Co.	MC 416 Chert x-22-4 mm Brunswick Co.	MC 417 Chalcedony 40-21-6 mm Smyth Co.	MC 418 Chert x-30-7 mm Caroline Co.	MC 419 Chert 85-31-8 mm Greensville Co.	MC 420 Chert 66-27-7 mm Dinwiddie Co.
MC 421 Chalcedony 86-34-7 mm Virginia Beach	MC 422 Shale 52-26-7 mm Powhatan Co.	MC 423 Chert x-20-5 mm Dinwiddie Co.	MC 424 Chert 67-20-6 mm Dinwiddie Co.	MC 425 Chalcedony 58-30-8 mm Washington Co.	MC 426 Quartz 50-26-6 mm Cumberland Co.

MC 427 Chalcedony 64-20-6 mm Amelia Co.	MC 428 Quartz 41-23-6 mm Nansemond Co.	MC 429 Chalcedony 42-25-7 mm Henry Co.	MC 430 P. Wood 61-29-7 mm Chesterfield Co.	MC 431 Slate 47-24-5 mm Chesterfield Co.	MC 432 P. Wood 32-14-4 mm Chesterfield Co.
MC 433 Slate 40-18-5 mm Dinwiddie Co.	MC 434 Chalcedony 30-18-3 mm Page Co.	MC 435 Chalcedony 26-19-5 mm Dinwiddie Co.	MC 436 Chalcedony 47-21-6 mm Dinwiddie Co.	MC 437 Chalcedony 20-21-7 mm Dinwiddie Co.	MC 438 Chert 44-22-6 mm Page Co.
MC 439 Shale 41-23-5 mm Brunswick Co.	MC 440 Chalcedony 60-28-7 mm Page Co.	MC 441 Chalcedony 46-21-5 mm Nelson Co.	MC 442 Shale 85-34-9 mm Prince George Co.	MC 443 Quartzite 40-21-6 mm Greensville Co.	MC 444 Shale 89-29-6 mm Chesterfield Co.

MC 445 Chalcedony 49-23-8 mm Prince Edward Co.	MC 446 Chalcedony x-30-6 mm Cumberland Co.	MC 447 Quartzite x-27-8 mm Virginia Beach	MC 448 Oolitic 48-24-6 mm Wythe Co.	MC 449 Chert 45=23-5 mm Pittsylvania Co.	MC 450 Jasper 46-20-6 mm Greensville Co.
MC 451 Chert 28-12-3 mm Dinwiddie Co.	MC 452 Jasper x-29-7 mm Dinwiddie Co.	MC 453 Quartzite x-20-7 mm Dinwiddie Co.	MC 454 Chert 52-23-6 mm Bedford Co.	MC 455 Slate x-25-5 mm Dinwiddie Co.	MC 456 Greenstone 33-22-7 mm ???
MC 457 Chert x-29-5 mm Dinwiddie Co.	MC 458 Chalcedony x-27-7 mm Dinwiddie Co.	MC 459 Quartz 36-25-8 mm Dinwiddie Co.	MC 460 Quartzite 56-25-10 mm Southampton Co.	MC 461 Quartzite 52-25-7 mm Virginia Beach	MC 462 Quartzite 61-25-7 mm Gloucester Co.

MC 463 Jasper 40-26-6 mm York Co.	MC 464 Quartz 40-25-6 mm Dinwiddie Co.	MC 465 Chert x-25-x mm Albermarle Co.	MC 466 Chert x-29-7 mm Isle of Wight Co.	MC 467 ? 74-26-5 mm King and Queen Co.	MC 468 Quartz x-21-7 mm Campbell Co.
MC 469 Chert 45-27-6 mm Westmoreland Co.	MC 470 Chalcedony 50-25-8 mm Rockingham Co.	MC 471 Greenstone x-22-4 mm Fairfax Co.	MC 472 Chalcedony 45-24-8 mm Mecklenburg Co.	MC 473 Jasper 62-28-8 mm Mecklenburg Co.	MC 474 Chert 50-24-7 mm Mecklenburg Co.
MC 475 Rhyolite 53-25-7 mm Mecklenburg Co.	MC 476 Quartz 39-25-8 mm Nansemond Co.	MC 477 Quartz 41-23-7 mm Dinwiddie Co.	MC 478 Jasper 47-23-7 mm Charles City Co.	MC 479 Quartz 36-31-4 mm Mecklenburg Co.	MC 480 Argillite 70-27-7 mm Halifax Co.

52

MC 481 Quartzite 61-24-7 mm Mecklenburg Co.	**MC 482** Chert 62-24-5 mm Mecklenburg Co.	**MC 483** Chert 35-20-5 mm Mecklenburg Co.	**MC 484** Quartz x-29-6 mm Mecklenburg Co.	**MC 485** Chert 76-30-6 mm Mecklenburg Co.	**MC 486** Chert 75-33-9 mm Dinwiddie Co.
MC 487 Chert 22-15-4 mm Dinwiddie Co.	**MC 488** Quartzite 27-16-6 mm Dinwiddie Co.	**MC 489** Chert x-24-5 mm Dinwiddie Co.	**MC 490** Jasper 20-22-5 mm Dinwiddie Co.	**MC 491** Rhyolite 39-22-6 mm Dinwiddie Co.	**MC 492** Chert x-33-8 mm Dinwiddie Co.
MC 493 Slate x-27-6 mm Dinwiddie Co.	**MC 494** Quartz x-27-7 mm Dinwiddie Co.	**MC 495** Jasper 48-22-7 mm Dinwiddie Co.	**MC 496** Felsite 59-23-7 mm Dinwiddie Co.	**MC 497** Quartz x-30-9 mm Dinwiddie Co.	**MC 498** Quartzite 41-20-7 mm Dinwiddie Co.
MC 499 Chert 47-25-7 mm Dinwiddie Co.	**MC 500** Jasper 42-22-7 mm Dinwiddie Co.	**MC 501** Quartz x-22-x mm Dinwiddie Co.	**MC 502** Quartz 35-22-6 mm Greensville Co.	**MC 503** Rhyolite 64-25-5 mm Greensville Co.	**MC 504** Jasper 60-25-6 mm Greensville Co.

MC 505 Jasper 48-22-7 mm Halifax Co.	**MC 506** Quartz 76-27-7 mm Pittsylvania Co.	**MC 507** Rhyolite 45-24-6 mm Hanover Co.	**MC 508** Chalcedony x-26-5 mm Powtatan Co.	**MC 509** Quartzite 46-29-10 mm Chesterfield Co.	**MC 510** Chert 72-31-6 mm Charlotte Co.
MC 511 Chert 55-22-7 mm Charlotte Co.	**MC 512** Chert 38-20-6 mm Campbell Co.	**MC 513** Chert 82-30-7 mm Prince Edward Co.	**MC 514** Chalcedony 50-22-7 mm Charlotte Co.	**MC 515** Chert x-21-5 mm Dinwiddie Co.	**MC 516** Quartz 31-20-7 mm Dinwiddie Co.
MC 517 Quartzite x-35-7 mm Dinwiddie Co.	**MC 518** Flint 93-29-x mm Smyth Co.	**MC 519** ? 40-20-x mm Tazewell Co.	**MC 520** Quartzite 41-23-8 mm Dinwiddie Co.	**MC 521** Chalcedony x-16-5 mm Dinwiddie Co.	**MC 522** Slate 75-28-8 mm Greensville Co.

MC 523 Chalcedony 77-32-7 mm Dinwiddie Co.	**MC 524** Quartzite x-28-8 mm Newport News	**MC 525** Quartz x-33-9 mm Dinwiddie Co.	**MC 526** Quartzite 39-25-7 mm Dinwiddie Co.	**MC 527** Slate x-23-6 mm Dinwiddie Co.	**MC 528** Quartz x-26-x mm Dinwiddie Co.
MC 529 Chert 49-24-x mm Petersburg City	**MC 530** Chert 51-22-x Petersburg City	**MC 531** Chalcedony 66-27-6 mm Nansemond Co.	**MC 532** ? 47-19-5 mm King George Co.	**MC 533** Chert 42-28-7 mm Smyth Co.	**MC 534** Greenstone 56-27-7 mm Dinwiddie Co.
MC 535 Chert 45-20-5 mm Lunenburg Co.	**MC 536** Chert 64-20-6 mm Lee Co.	**MC 537** Chalcedony 38-29-9 mm Greensville Co.	**MC 538** Chalcedony 76-35-9 mm Brunswick Co.	**MC 539** Jasper 62-27-8 mm Mecklenburg Co.	**MC 540** Chalcedony 51-23-6 mm Greensville Co.

MC 541 Quartz 43-24-7 mm Sussex Co.	**MC 542** Jasper 61-21-7 mm Greensville Co.	**MC 543** Quartzite 74-31-9 mm Prince George Co.	**MC 544** Quartzite 52-23-7 mm Sussex Co.	**MC 545** Jasper 58-27-8 mm Sussex Co.	**MC 546** Chert 49-23-8 mm Greensville Co.
MC 547 Chalcedony 53-21-6 mm Sussex Co.	**MC 548** Chert 69-26-10 mm Sussex Co.	**MC 549** Slate 81-38-8 mm Lunenburg Co.	**MC 550** Chert 108-31-10 mm Mathews Co.	**MC 551** Flint 47-29-7 mm Giles Co.	**MC 552** Chalcedony x-23-5 mm Giles Co.
MC 553 Chert 63-30-7 mm Hanover Co.	**MC 554** Chalcedony 55-26-8 mm Greensville Co.	**MC 555** Chalcedony 65-27-8 mm Sussex Co.	**MC 556** Slate 48-24-5 mm Suffolk Co.	**MC 557** Slate 70-31-7 mm Chesapeake City	**MC 558** Quartzite 46-32-8 mm Nansemond Co.

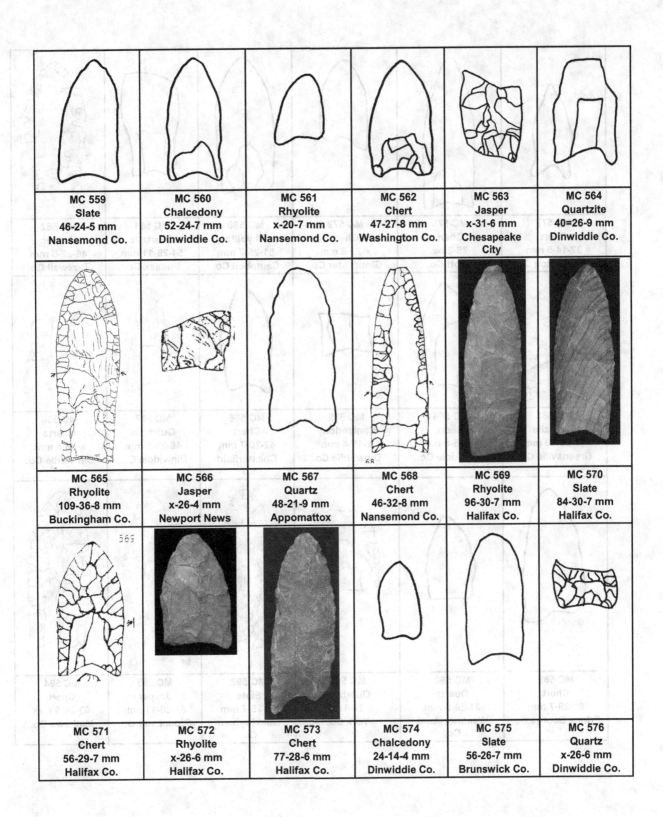

MC 559 Slate 46-24-5 mm Nansemond Co.	**MC 560** Chalcedony 52-24-7 mm Dinwiddie Co.	**MC 561** Rhyolite x-20-7 mm Nansemond Co.	**MC 562** Chert 47-27-8 mm Washington Co.	**MC 563** Jasper x-31-6 mm Chesapeake City	**MC 564** Quartzite 40=26-9 mm Dinwiddie Co.
MC 565 Rhyolite 109-36-8 mm Buckingham Co.	**MC 566** Jasper x-26-4 mm Newport News	**MC 567** Quartz 48-21-9 mm Appomattox	**MC 568** Chert 46-32-8 mm Nansemond Co.	**MC 569** Rhyolite 96-30-7 mm Halifax Co.	**MC 570** Slate 84-30-7 mm Halifax Co.
MC 571 Chert 56-29-7 mm Halifax Co.	**MC 572** Rhyolite x-26-6 mm Halifax Co.	**MC 573** Chert 77-28-6 mm Halifax Co.	**MC 574** Chalcedony 24-14-4 mm Dinwiddie Co.	**MC 575** Slate 56-26-7 mm Brunswick Co.	**MC 576** Quartz x-26-6 mm Dinwiddie Co.

57

MC 577 Chert 32-14-5 mm Washington Co.	MC 578 Chert 75-28-x Scott Co.	MC 579 Chert x-23-6 mm Gloucester Co.	MC 580 Rhyolite 61-25-7 mm Campbell Co.	MC 581 Quartzite 54-29-11 mm Sussex Co.	MC 582 Jasper 46-22-5 mm Tazewell Co.
MC 583 Quartzite 45-28-10 mm Greensville Co.	MC 584 Chert 51-25-8 mm Dinwiddie Co.	MC 585 Chalcedony x-19-4 mm Dinwiddie Co.	MC 586 Chert 42-20-7 mm Chesterfield Co.	MC 587 Quartzite 46-23-8 mm Dinwiddie Co.	MC 588 Quartz x-25-8 mm Dinwiddie Co.
MC 589 Chert 62-29-7 mm Prince George Co.	MC 590 Quartz 31-20-9 mm Westmoreland Co.	MC 591 Quartzite x-22-4 mm York Co.	MC 592 Slate 79-25-7 mm Buckingham Co.	MC 593 Jasper 87-30-11 mm Gloucester Co.	MC 594 Chert 63-24-6 mm Mathews Co.

MC 595 **Chalcedony** **83-28-6 mm** **Rockbridge Co.**	**MC 596** **Quartzite** **x-31-7 mm** **Chesapeake City**	**MC 597** **Quartzite** **41-23-7 mm** **Mecklenburg Co.**	**MC 598** **Jasper** **48-26-7 mm** **Rockingham Co.**	**MC 599** **Jasper** **90-30-10 mm** **Lancaster City**	**MC 600** **Chert** **47-24-7 mm** **Dinwiddie Co.**
MC 601 **Quartz** **41-23-6 mm** **Albermarle Co.**	**MC 602** **Chert** **60-25-6 mm** **Mecklenburg Co.**	**MC 603** **Quartz** **45-22-9 mm** **Dinwiddie Co.**	**MC 604** **Quartzite** **58-28-8 mm** **Nansemond Co.**	**MC 605** **Quartzite** **55-30-10 mm** **Sussex Co.**	**MC 606** **Quartzite** **53-37-9 mm** **Sussex Co.**
MC 607 **Quartzite** **35-26-6 mm** **Sussex Co.**	**MC 608** **Quartzite** **x-30-6 mm** **Southampton Co.**	**MC 609** **Quartzite** **x-22-9 mm** **Isle of Wight Co.**	**MC 610** **Quartzite** **50-25-14 mm** **Isle of Wight Co.**	**MC 611** **Chalcedony** **58-29-8 mm** **Chesapeake City**	**MC 612** **Slate** **68-24-7 mm** **Brunswick Co.**

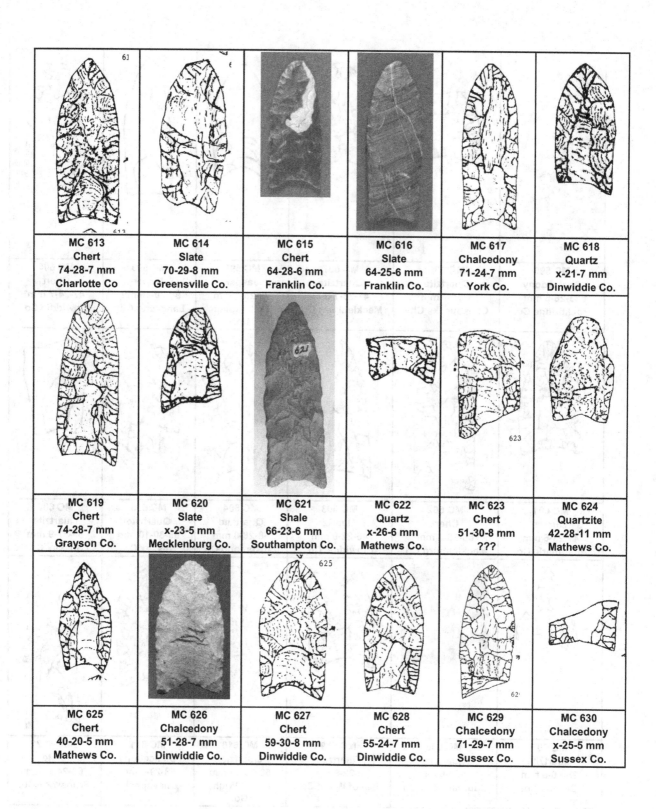

MC 613 Chert 74-28-7 mm Charlotte Co	**MC 614** Slate 70-29-8 mm Greensville Co.	**MC 615** Chert 64-28-6 mm Franklin Co.	**MC 616** Slate 64-25-6 mm Franklin Co.	**MC 617** Chalcedony 71-24-7 mm York Co.	**MC 618** Quartz x-21-7 mm Dinwiddie Co.
MC 619 Chert 74-28-7 mm Grayson Co.	**MC 620** Slate x-23-5 mm Mecklenburg Co.	**MC 621** Shale 66-23-6 mm Southampton Co.	**MC 622** Quartz x-26-6 mm Mathews Co.	**MC 623** Chert 51-30-8 mm ???	**MC 624** Quartzite 42-28-11 mm Mathews Co.
MC 625 Chert 40-20-5 mm Mathews Co.	**MC 626** Chalcedony 51-28-7 mm Dinwiddie Co.	**MC 627** Chert 59-30-8 mm Dinwiddie Co.	**MC 628** Chert 55-24-7 mm Dinwiddie Co.	**MC 629** Chalcedony 71-29-7 mm Sussex Co.	**MC 630** Chalcedony x-25-5 mm Sussex Co.

MC 631 Rhyolite 61-23-6 mm Sussex Co.	MC 632 Jasper 49-29-7 mm Shenandoah Co.	MC 633 Chert x-28-7 mm Greensville Co.	MC 634 Jasper 38-24-5 mm Gloucester Co.	MC 635 ? 91-34-7 mm Rockingham Co.	MC 636 Jasper x-22-7 mm Chesterfield Co.
MC 637 Chert x-26-5 mm Roanoke Co.	MC 638 Chalcedony 33-16-4 mm Roanoke Co.	MC 639 Chert 39-30-6 mm Orange Co.	MC 640 Slate x-23-6 mm Sussex Co.	MC 641 Chalcedony 51-23-5 mm Smyth Co.	MC 642 Quartzite x-30-8 mm Nansemond Co.
MC 643 Chalcedony x-23-6 mm Dinwiddie Co.	MC 644 Chalcedony 30-18-5 mm Dinwiddie Co.	MC 645 Chalcedony 27-14-5 mm Dinwiddie Co.	MC 646 Chalcedony 65-30-6 mm Dinwiddie Co.	MC 647 Chalcedony 85-28-8 mm Dinwiddie Co.	MC 648 Quartzite 52-30-9 mm Sussex Co.

MC 649 Quartz 45-22-8 mm Mecklenburg Co.	MC 650 Flint 54-26-6 mm Smyth Co.	MC 651 Flint 99-37-8 mm Washington Co.	MC 652 Chalcedony 55-27-7 mm Isle of Wight Co.	MC 653 Shale 51-25-5 mm Isle of Wight Co.	MC 654 Chalcedony 43-19-7 mm Isle of Wight Co.
MC 655 Quartz 43-23-6 Isle of Wight Co.	MC 656 Chrome Ore 40-24-7 mm Isle of Wight Co.	MC 657 Quartzite 35-27-10 mm Isle of Wight Co.	MC 658 Chalcedony 42-19-7 mm Isle of Wight Co.	MC 659 Chalcedony 35-25-6 mm Isle of Wight Co.	MC 660 Quartzite 33-21-8 mm Isle of Wight Co.
MC 661 Quartzite x-39-11 mm Isle of Wight Co.	MC 662 Quartz 24-17-5 mm Dinwiddie Co.	MC 663 Agate 45-22-5 mm Smyth	MC 664 Chert 33-16-4 mm Roanoke Co.	MC 665 Chert 54-30-8 mm Dinwiddie Co.	MC 666 Slate 57-21-6 mm Greensville Co.
MC 667 Slate 111-28-8 mm Brunswick Co.	MC 668 Chert 47-16-6 mm Southampton Co.	MC 669 Chert 36-19-5 mm Greensville Co.	MC 670 Chert 88-26-7 mm Botetourt Co.	MC 671 Quartzite 50-22-7 mm Nansemond Co.	MC 672 ? 98-37-8 mm Nansemond Co.

MC 673 Chalcedony 69-26-8 mm Gloucester Co.	MC 674 ? x-26-7 mm Greensville	MC 675 ? 24-18-3 mm Dinwiddie Co.	MC 676 Chert 59-26-7 mm Amherst Co.	MC 677 Chert 75-22-7 mm Mathews Co.	MC 678 Quartz 40-19-x mm Virginia Beach
MC 679 Flint 60-23-7 mm Amelia Co.	MC 680 Rhyolite x-24-6 mm Mathews Co.	MC 681 Jasper x-26-6 mm Amelia Co.	MC 682 Flint 39-21-6 mm Amelia Co.	MC 683 Chert 37-17-3 mm Dinwiddie Co.	MC 684 Chalcedony 36-19-5 mm Dinwiddie Co.
MC 685 Chalcedony 52-23-6 mm Greensville Co.	MC 686 Chalcedony x-26-6 mm Dinwiddie Co.	MC 687 Slate x-22-6 mm Greensville Co.	MC 688 Rhyolite 60-24-6 mm Fairfax Co.	MC 689 Rhyolite 41-22-6 mm Gloucester Co.	MC 690 Jasper 48-24-6 mm ???
MC 691 Quartz 35-21-8 mm Isle of Wight Co.	MC 692 Chalcedony 46-25-6 mm Sussex Co.	MC 693 Chalcedony 51-21-6 mm Greensville Co.	MC 694 Jasper 49-24-5 mm Sussex Co.	MC 695 Slate 45-36-6 mm Mecklenburg Co.	MC 696 Rhyolite x-26-7 mm Halifax Co.

MC 697 Chalcedony x-27-6 mm Halifax Co.	MC 698 Slate x-26-6 mm Halifax Co.	MC 699 Quartz x-25-7 mm Halifax Co.	MC 700 Chalcedony 62-26-6 mm Dinwiddie Co.	MC 701 Chalcedony 54-27-6 mm Dinwiddie Co.	MC 702 Rhyolite 71-25-6 mm Dinwiddie Co.
MC 703 Rhyolite 42-23-6 mm Halifax Co.	MC 704 Slate 68-32-7 mm Patrick Co.	MC 705 Quartz x-26-8 mm Accomac Co.	MC 706 Chert 57-27-7 mm Pulaski Co.	MC 707 Quartz 59-29-9 mm Mecklenburg Co.	MC 708 Quartz x-23-6 mm Mecklenburg Co.
MC 709 Chalcedony 42-20-5 mm Mecklenburg Co.	MC 710 Quartz 38-22-7 mm Mecklenburg Co.	MC 711 Chert/Chal 36-22-5 mm Mecklenburg Co.	MC 712 Chert 31-19-4 mm Mecklenburg Co.	MC 713 Chert 65-27-6 mm Mecklenburg Co.	MC 714 P. Wood 51-22-7 mm Mecklenburg Co.

64

MC 715 Chalcedony 33-20-5 mm Nansemond Co.	**MC 716** Chalcedony x-26-7 mm Nansemond Co.	**MC 717** Chalcedony x-21-5 mm Greensville Co.	**MC 718** Jasper 37-22-6 mm Nansemond Co.	**MC 719** Chert 63-27-7 mm Mecklenburg Co.	**MC 720** Quartz 37-20-6 mm Dinwiddie Co.
MC 721 Quartz 47-22-6 mm Buckingham Co.	**MC 722** Chert 86-27-7 mm Pittsylvania Co.	**MC 723** Chert 86-30-7 mm Pittsylvania Co.	**MC 724** Chert 70-27-7 mm Pittsylvania Co.	**MC 725** Chalcedony 54-30-6 mm Greensville Co.	**MC 726** Chalcedony 30-17-5 mm Greensville Co.
MC 727 Chert 30-16-5 mm Southampton Co.	**MC 728** Quartz 62-31-8 mm Sussex Co.	**MC 729** Chalcedony 55-26-7 mm Dinwiddie Co.	**MC 730** Chert 52-22-6 mm Franklin Co.	**MC 731** Jasper 108-34-10 mm Northampton Co.	**MC 732** Jasper x-22-5 mm Chesapeake City

MC 733 Quartzite 48-24-6 mm Suffolk Co.	MC 734 Chert 47-23-8 mm Dinwiddie Co.	MC 735 Chert 46-23-6 mm Halifax Co.	MC 736 Chalcedony 45=21-6 mm Amelia Co.	MC 737 Quartzite 56-24-8 mm Suffolk Co.	MC 738 Quartz 45-17-4 mm Mecklenburg Co.
MC 739 Chalcedony 35-16-4 mm Mecklenburg Co.	MC 740 Chert 70-25-7 mm Mecklenburg Co.	MC 741 Chert 83-28-7 mm Mecklenburg Co.	MC 742 Slate 62-32-5 mm Mecklenburg Co.	MC 743 Chert 38-27-7 mm Mecklenburg Co.	MC 744 Chert 46-26-8 mm Mecklenburg Co.
MC 745 Chalcedony x-21-3 mm Mecklenburg Co.	MC 746 Quartzite 57-22-7 mm Mecklenburg Co.	MC 747 Quartz 40-20-6 mm Mecklenburg Co.	MC 748 Chert 138-30-8 mm Roanoke City See Page 1	MC 749 Quartz 48-25-6 mm Mecklenburg Co.	MC 750 Quartz 45-20-8 mm Mecklenburg Co.

MC 751 Shale 35-25-8 mm Chesterfield Co.	MC 752 Chalcedony 66-31-7 mm Washington Co.	MC 753 Flint 27-18-4 mm Washington Co.	MC 754 Flint 37-25-5 mm Washington Co.	MC 755 Chalcedony 56-25-7 mm Sussex Co.	MC 756 Chalcedony 71-31-8 mm Dinwiddie Co.
MC 757 Chalcedony 59-26-7 mm Dinwiddie Co.	MC 758 Chalcedony 55-26-7 mm Dinwiddie Co.	MC 759 Chalcedony x-29-7 mm Dinwiddie Co.	MC 760 Jasper 75-24-7 mm Franklin Co.	MC 761 Jasper 63-23-8 mm Mecklenburg Co.	MC 762 Chert x-26-5 mm Washington Co.
MC 763 Flint 46-23-6 mm Washington Co.	MC 764 Flint x-25-6 mm Washington Co.	MC 765 Chalcedony 45-25-3 mm York Co.	MC 766 Chert 44-30-6 mm Surry Co.	MC 767 Jasper 37-24-4 mm Dinwiddie Co.	MC 768 Quartz 38-30-8 mm Dinwiddie Co.
MC 769 Chert x-20-3 mm Smyth Co.	MC 770 Jasper 50-25-10 mm Mecklenburg Co.	MC 771 Quartzite 59-29-8 mm Portsmouth City	MC 772 Chert(?) 38-22-8 mm Bedford Co.	MC 773 Chalcedony 47-25-7 mm Mecklenburg Co,	MC 774 Flint x-22-5 mm Giles Co.

67

MC 775 Quartzite 116-37-10 mm York Co.	MC 776 Chalcedony 62-22-7 mm Sussex Co.	MC 777 Flint x-26-4 mm Washington Co.	MC 778 Chert 36-19-5 mm Dinwiddie Co.	MC 779 Quartz 44-22-7 mm Dinwiddie Co.	MC 780 Chalcedony 42-22-6 mm Greensville Co.
MC 781 Chert 85-31-6 mm ???	MC 782 Flint 46-23-4 mm Southampton Co.	MC 783 Quartzite x-27-6 mm Isle of Wight Co.	MC 784 Chert 51-22-4 mm Lee Co.	MC 785 Chert x-16-4 mm Roanoke City	MC 786 Flint 59-32-6 mm Franklin Co.
MC 787 Chalcedony 35-24-7 mm Franklin Co.	MC 788 Quartz x-27-7 mm Bedford Co.	MC 789 Slate 46-20-6 mm Mecklenburg Co.	MC 790 Chalcedony 43-16-5 mm Jamestown	MC 791 Chert 21-16-5 mm Newport News	MC 792 Flint-Like 57-24-x mm ???

68

MC 793 Quartz 42-25-8 mm Bedford Co.	MC 794 Quartz x-23-8 mm Bedford Co.	MC 795 Quartzite 32-20-6 mm Mecklenburg Co.	MC 796 Slate 53-23-5 mm Caroline Co.	MC 797 Quartzite 59-29-10 mm Sussex Co.	MC 798 Slate 63-37-7 mm Culpeper Co.
MC 799 Slate 40-26-3 mm Greensville Co,	MC 800 Chalcedony 68-30-8 mm Dinwiddie Co.	MC 801 Chert 38-20-6 mm Nansemond Co.	MC 802 Chert x-30-6 mm Lee Co.	MC 803 Chert 57-25-7 mm Roanoke Co.	MC 804 Jasper 56-27-6 mm Northumberland Co.
MC 805 Chert 49-25-6 mm Brunswick Co.	MC 806 Quartzite x-20-7 mm Spotsylvania Co.	MC 807 Jasper 53-29-8 mm Sussex Co.	MC 808 Quartz 88-35-12 mm Surry Co.	MC 809 Chert 61-27-7 mm Carroll Co.	MC 810 Quartz 65-28-11 mm Patrick Co.

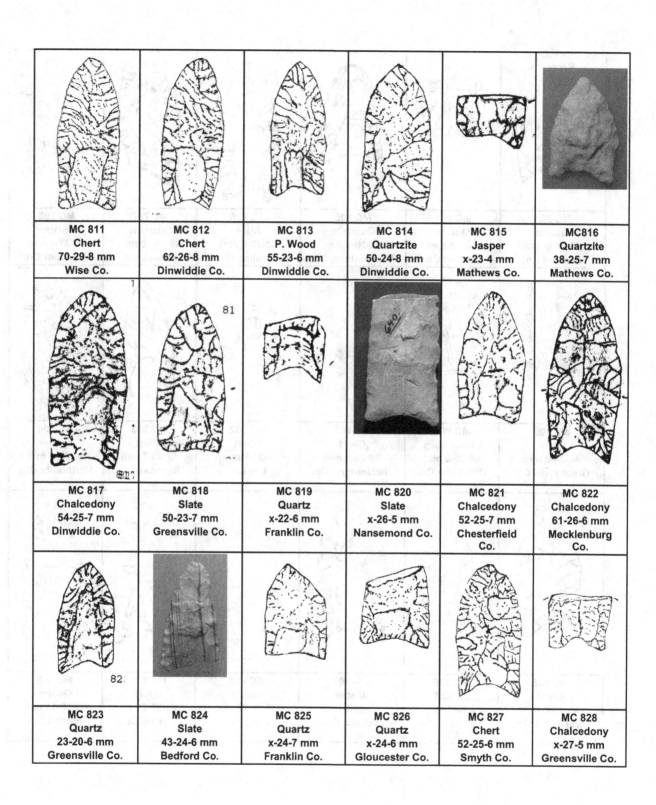

MC 811 Chert 70-29-8 mm Wise Co.	MC 812 Chert 62-26-8 mm Dinwiddie Co.	MC 813 P. Wood 55-23-6 mm Dinwiddie Co.	MC 814 Quartzite 50-24-8 mm Dinwiddie Co.	MC 815 Jasper x-23-4 mm Mathews Co.	MC816 Quartzite 38-25-7 mm Mathews Co.
MC 817 Chalcedony 54-25-7 mm Dinwiddie Co.	MC 818 Slate 50-23-7 mm Greensville Co.	MC 819 Quartz x-22-6 mm Franklin Co.	MC 820 Slate x-26-5 mm Nansemond Co.	MC 821 Chalcedony 52-25-7 mm Chesterfield Co.	MC 822 Chalcedony 61-26-6 mm Mecklenburg Co.
MC 823 Quartz 23-20-6 mm Greensville Co.	MC 824 Slate 43-24-6 mm Bedford Co.	MC 825 Quartz x-24-7 mm Franklin Co.	MC 826 Quartz x-24-6 mm Gloucester Co.	MC 827 Chert 52-25-6 mm Smyth Co.	MC 828 Chalcedony x-27-5 mm Greensville Co.

70

MC 829 Chalcedony 40-21-6 mm Southampton Co.	**MC 830** Slate 45-20-6 mm Dinwiddie Co.	**MC 831** Chalcedony 54-22-9 mm Bedford Co.	**MC 832** Flint x-22-5 mm Floyd Co.	**MC 833** Chert x-25-6 mm Greensville Co.	**MC 834** Shale 52-22-6 mm Suffolk City
MC 835 Quartzite 55-23-7 mm Charlotte Co.	**MC 836** Chalcedony 41-22-6 mm Prince Edward Co.	**MC 837** Chalcedony x-21-5 mm Powhatan Co.	**MC 838** Slate 60-22-7 mm Sussex Co.	**MC 839** Quartz 45-22-8 mm Charlotte Co.	**MC 840** Chalcedony 60-25-8 mm Sussex Co.
MC 841 Chalcedony x-16-5 mm Sussex Co.	**MC 842** Slate x-20-5 mm Suffolk City	**MC 843** Slate 45-21-7 mm Suffolk City	**MC 844** Flint 48-22-7 mm Hanover Co.	**MC 845** Quartz 76-40-10 mm Suffolk City	**MC 846** Quartzite 56-35-5 mm Campbell Co.

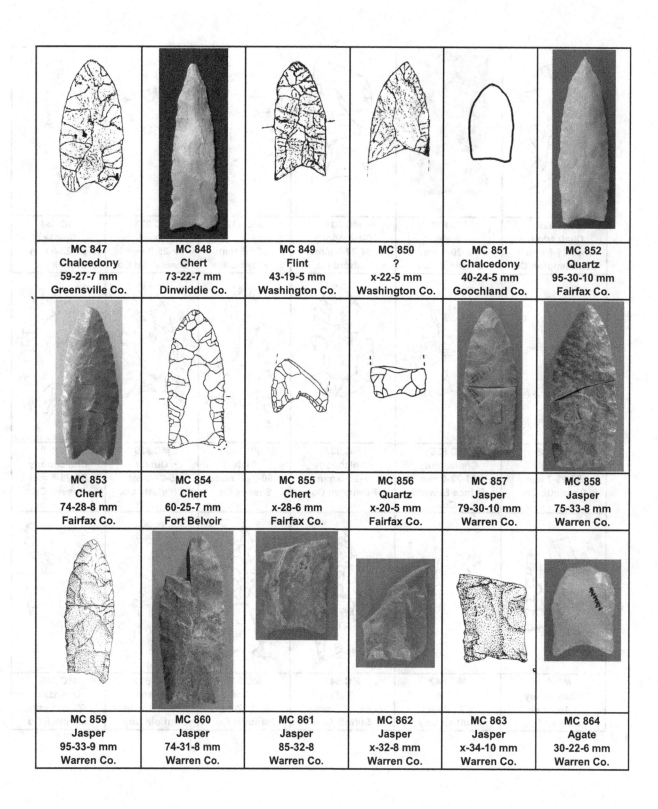

MC 847 Chalcedony 59-27-7 mm Greensville Co.	**MC 848** Chert 73-22-7 mm Dinwiddie Co.	**MC 849** Flint 43-19-5 mm Washington Co.	**MC 850** ? x-22-5 mm Washington Co.	**MC 851** Chalcedony 40-24-5 mm Goochland Co.	**MC 852** Quartz 95-30-10 mm Fairfax Co.
MC 853 Chert 74-28-8 mm Fairfax Co.	**MC 854** Chert 60-25-7 mm Fort Belvoir	**MC 855** Chert x-28-6 mm Fairfax Co.	**MC 856** Quartz x-20-5 mm Fairfax Co.	**MC 857** Jasper 79-30-10 mm Warren Co.	**MC 858** Jasper 75-33-8 mm Warren Co.
MC 859 Jasper 95-33-9 mm Warren Co.	**MC 860** Jasper 74-31-8 mm Warren Co.	**MC 861** Jasper 85-32-8 Warren Co.	**MC 862** Jasper x-32-8 mm Warren Co.	**MC 863** Jasper x-34-10 mm Warren Co.	**MC 864** Agate 30-22-6 mm Warren Co.

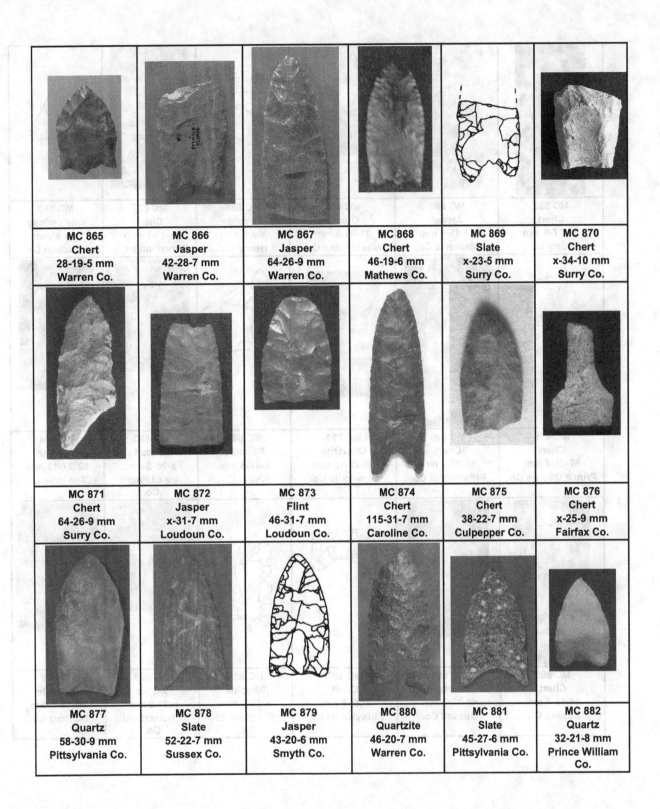

MC 865 Chert 28-19-5 mm Warren Co.	**MC 866** Jasper 42-28-7 mm Warren Co.	**MC 867** Jasper 64-26-9 mm Warren Co.	**MC 868** Chert 46-19-6 mm Mathews Co.	**MC 869** Slate x-23-5 mm Surry Co.	**MC 870** Chert x-34-10 mm Surry Co.
MC 871 Chert 64-26-9 mm Surry Co.	**MC 872** Jasper x-31-7 mm Loudoun Co.	**MC 873** Flint 46-31-7 mm Loudoun Co.	**MC 874** Chert 115-31-7 mm Caroline Co.	**MC 875** Chert 38-22-7 mm Culpepper Co.	**MC 876** Chert x-25-9 mm Fairfax Co.
MC 877 Quartz 58-30-9 mm Pittsylvania Co.	**MC 878** Slate 52-22-7 mm Sussex Co.	**MC 879** Jasper 43-20-6 mm Smyth Co.	**MC 880** Quartzite 46-20-7 mm Warren Co.	**MC 881** Slate 45-27-6 mm Pittsylvania Co.	**MC 882** Quartz 32-21-8 mm Prince William Co.

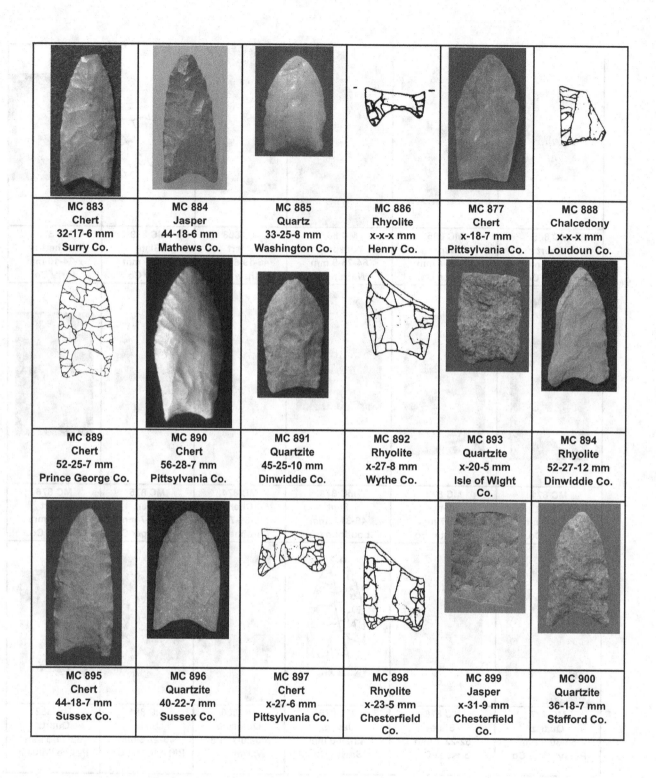

MC 883 Chert 32-17-6 mm Surry Co.	**MC 884** Jasper 44-18-6 mm Mathews Co.	**MC 885** Quartz 33-25-8 mm Washington Co.	**MC 886** Rhyolite x-x-x mm Henry Co.	**MC 877** Chert x-18-7 mm Pittsylvania Co.	**MC 888** Chalcedony x-x-x mm Loudoun Co.
MC 889 Chert 52-25-7 mm Prince George Co.	**MC 890** Chert 56-28-7 mm Pittsylvania Co.	**MC 891** Quartzite 45-25-10 mm Dinwiddie Co.	**MC 892** Rhyolite x-27-8 mm Wythe Co.	**MC 893** Quartzite x-20-5 mm Isle of Wight Co.	**MC 894** Rhyolite 52-27-12 mm Dinwiddie Co.
MC 895 Chert 44-18-7 mm Sussex Co.	**MC 896** Quartzite 40-22-7 mm Sussex Co.	**MC 897** Chert x-27-6 mm Pittsylvania Co.	**MC 898** Rhyolite x-23-5 mm Chesterfield Co.	**MC 899** Jasper x-31-9 mm Chesterfield Co.	**MC 900** Quartzite 36-18-7 mm Stafford Co.

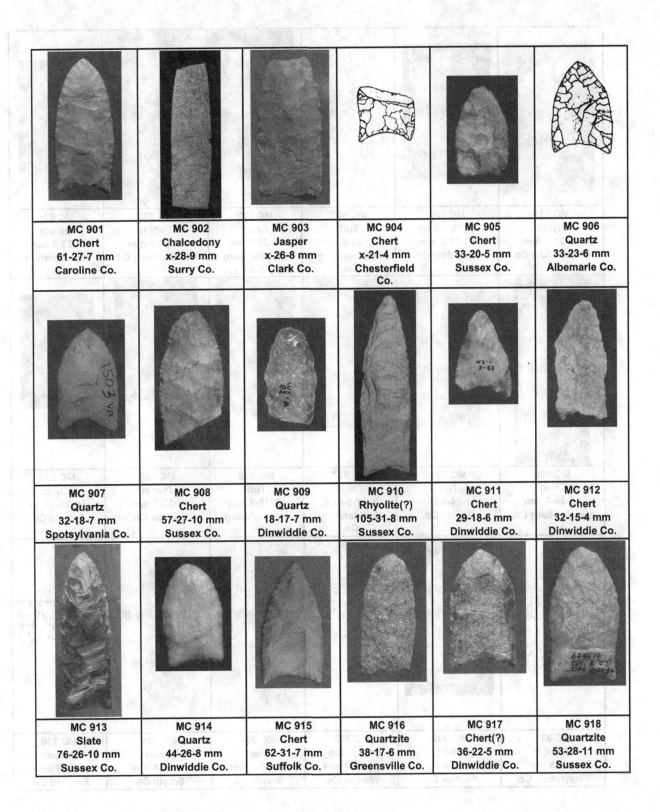

MC 901 Chert 61-27-7 mm Caroline Co.	**MC 902** Chalcedony x-28-9 mm Surry Co.	**MC 903** Jasper x-26-8 mm Clark Co.	**MC 904** Chert x-21-4 mm Chesterfield Co.	**MC 905** Chert 33-20-5 mm Sussex Co.	**MC 906** Quartz 33-23-6 mm Albemarle Co.
MC 907 Quartz 32-18-7 mm Spotsylvania Co.	**MC 908** Chert 57-27-10 mm Sussex Co.	**MC 909** Quartz 18-17-7 mm Dinwiddie Co.	**MC 910** Rhyolite(?) 105-31-8 mm Sussex Co.	**MC 911** Chert 29-18-6 mm Dinwiddie Co.	**MC 912** Chert 32-15-4 mm Dinwiddie Co.
MC 913 Slate 76-26-10 mm Sussex Co.	**MC 914** Quartz 44-26-8 mm Dinwiddie Co.	**MC 915** Chert 62-31-7 mm Suffolk Co.	**MC 916** Quartzite 38-17-6 mm Greensville Co.	**MC 917** Chert(?) 36-22-5 mm Dinwiddie Co.	**MC 918** Quartzite 53-28-11 mm Sussex Co.

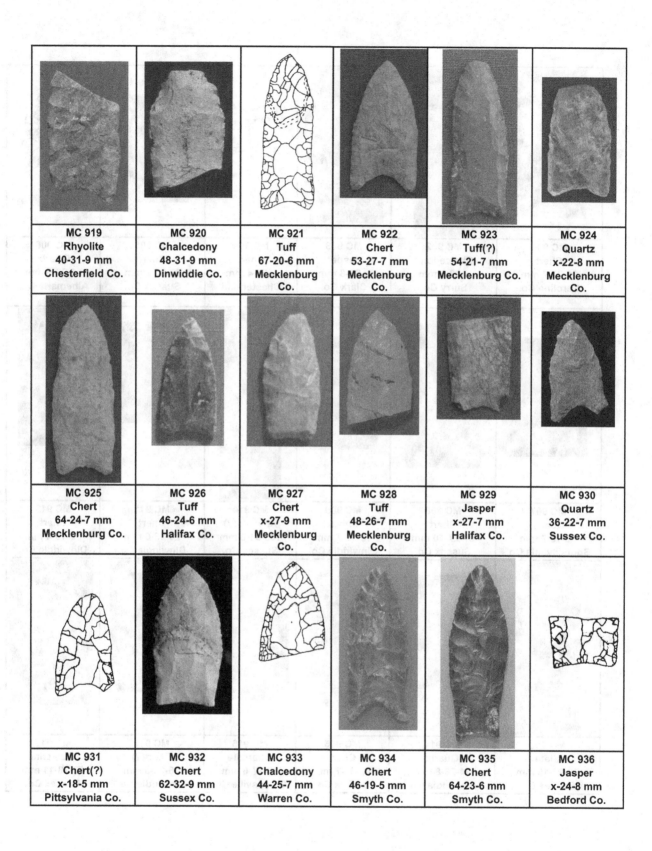

MC 919 Rhyolite 40-31-9 mm Chesterfield Co.	MC 920 Chalcedony 48-31-9 mm Dinwiddie Co.	MC 921 Tuff 67-20-6 mm Mecklenburg Co.	MC 922 Chert 53-27-7 mm Mecklenburg Co.	MC 923 Tuff(?) 54-21-7 mm Mecklenburg Co.	MC 924 Quartz x-22-8 mm Mecklenburg Co.
MC 925 Chert 64-24-7 mm Mecklenburg Co.	MC 926 Tuff 46-24-6 mm Halifax Co.	MC 927 Chert x-27-9 mm Mecklenburg Co.	MC 928 Tuff 48-26-7 mm Mecklenburg Co.	MC 929 Jasper x-27-7 mm Halifax Co.	MC 930 Quartz 36-22-7 mm Sussex Co.
MC 931 Chert(?) x-18-5 mm Pittsylvania Co.	MC 932 Chert 62-32-9 mm Sussex Co.	MC 933 Chalcedony 44-25-7 mm Warren Co.	MC 934 Chert 46-19-5 mm Smyth Co.	MC 935 Chert 64-23-6 mm Smyth Co.	MC 936 Jasper x-24-8 mm Bedford Co.

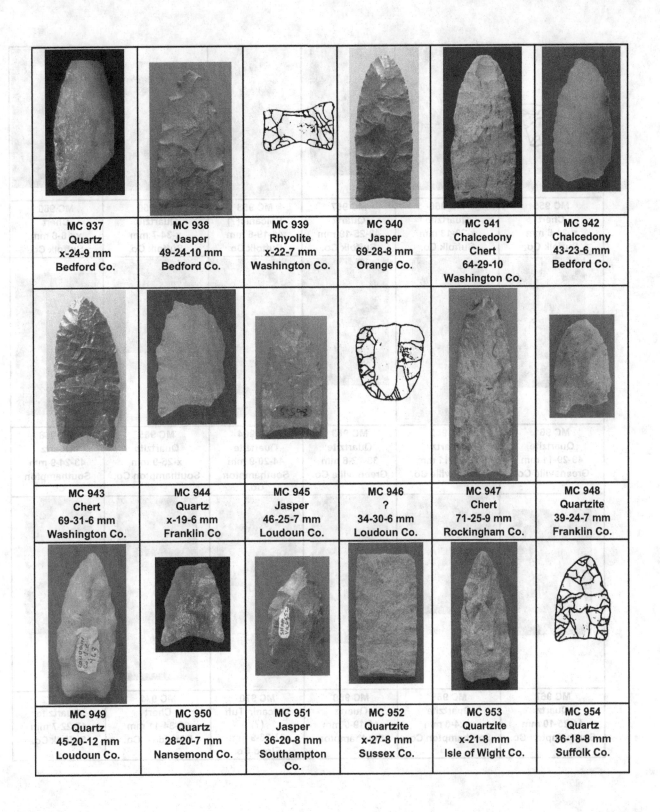

MC 937 Quartz x-24-9 mm Bedford Co.	**MC 938** Jasper 49-24-10 mm Bedford Co.	**MC 939** Rhyolite x-22-7 mm Washington Co.	**MC 940** Jasper 69-28-8 mm Orange Co.	**MC 941** Chalcedony Chert 64-29-10 Washington Co.	**MC 942** Chalcedony 43-23-6 mm Bedford Co.
MC 943 Chert 69-31-6 mm Washington Co.	**MC 944** Quartz x-19-6 mm Franklin Co	**MC 945** Jasper 46-25-7 mm Loudoun Co.	**MC 946** ? 34-30-6 mm Loudoun Co.	**MC 947** Chert 71-25-9 mm Rockingham Co.	**MC 948** Quartzite 39-24-7 mm Franklin Co.
MC 949 Quartz 45-20-12 mm Loudoun Co.	**MC 950** Quartz 28-20-7 mm Nansemond Co.	**MC 951** Jasper 36-20-8 mm Southampton Co.	**MC 952** Quartzite x-27-8 mm Sussex Co.	**MC 953** Quartzite x-21-8 mm Isle of Wight Co.	**MC 954** Quartz 36-18-8 mm Suffolk Co.

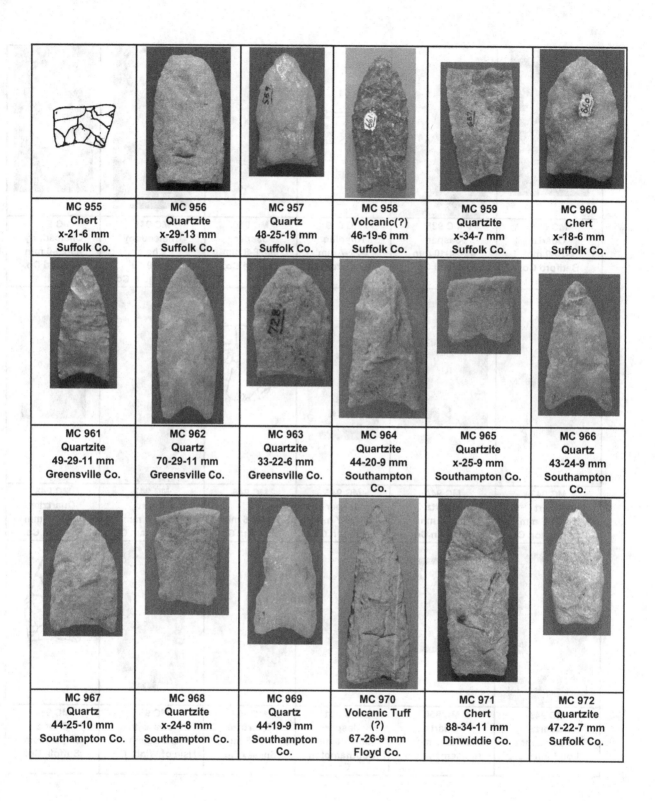

MC 955 Chert x-21-6 mm Suffolk Co.	MC 956 Quartzite x-29-13 mm Suffolk Co.	MC 957 Quartz 48-25-19 mm Suffolk Co.	MC 958 Volcanic(?) 46-19-6 mm Suffolk Co.	MC 959 Quartzite x-34-7 mm Suffolk Co.	MC 960 Chert x-18-6 mm Suffolk Co.
MC 961 Quartzite 49-29-11 mm Greensville Co.	MC 962 Quartz 70-29-11 mm Greensville Co.	MC 963 Quartzite 33-22-6 mm Greensville Co.	MC 964 Quartzite 44-20-9 mm Southampton Co.	MC 965 Quartzite x-25-9 mm Southampton Co.	MC 966 Quartz 43-24-9 mm Southampton Co.
MC 967 Quartz 44-25-10 mm Southampton Co.	MC 968 Quartzite x-24-8 mm Southampton Co.	MC 969 Quartz 44-19-9 mm Southampton Co.	MC 970 Volcanic Tuff (?) 67-26-9 mm Floyd Co.	MC 971 Chert 88-34-11 mm Dinwiddie Co.	MC 972 Quartzite 47-22-7 mm Suffolk Co.

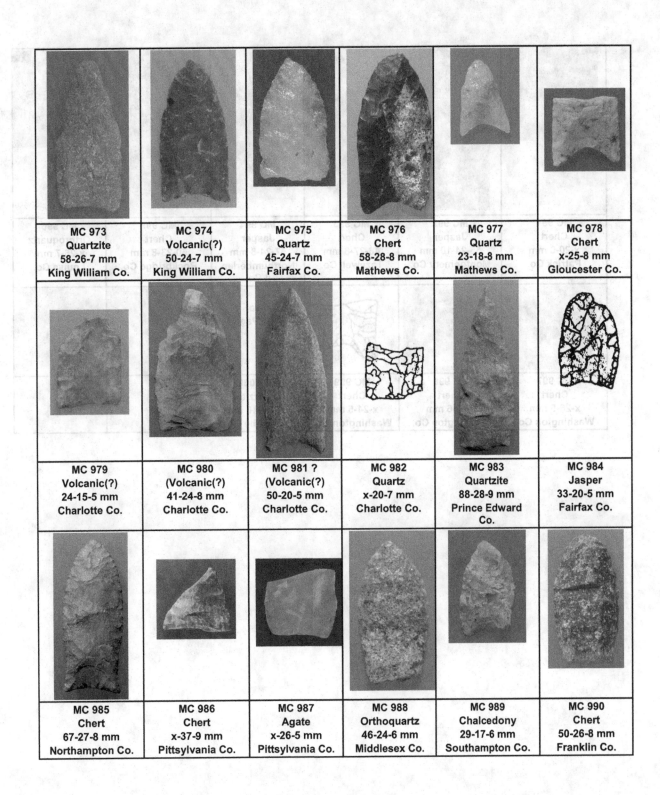

MC 973 Quartzite 58-26-7 mm King William Co.	MC 974 Volcanic(?) 50-24-7 mm King William Co.	MC 975 Quartz 45-24-7 mm Fairfax Co.	MC 976 Chert 58-28-8 mm Mathews Co.	MC 977 Quartz 23-18-8 mm Mathews Co.	MC 978 Chert x-25-8 mm Gloucester Co.
MC 979 Volcanic(?) 24-15-5 mm Charlotte Co.	MC 980 (Volcanic(?) 41-24-8 mm Charlotte Co.	MC 981 ? (Volcanic(?) 50-20-5 mm Charlotte Co.	MC 982 Quartz x-20-7 mm Charlotte Co.	MC 983 Quartzite 88-28-9 mm Prince Edward Co.	MC 984 Jasper 33-20-5 mm Fairfax Co.
MC 985 Chert 67-27-8 mm Northampton Co.	MC 986 Chert x-37-9 mm Pittsylvania Co.	MC 987 Agate x-26-5 mm Pittsylvania Co.	MC 988 Orthoquartz 46-24-6 mm Middlesex Co.	MC 989 Chalcedony 29-17-6 mm Southampton Co.	MC 990 Chert 50-26-8 mm Franklin Co.

MC 991 Chert x-20-6 mm Patrick Co.	MC 992 Jasper 55-24-10 mm Montgomery Co.	MC 993 Chert 46-27-8 mm Tazewell Co.	MC 994 Jasper 57-24-8 mm Northumberland Co.	MC 995 Chert 50-23-8 mm Rockbridge Co.	MC 996 Orthroquartz x-26-7 mm Louisa Co.
			See Title Page		
MC 997 Chert x-26-5 mm Washington Co.	MC 998 Chert x-23-6 mm Washington Co.	MC 999 Chert x-24-5 mm Washington Co.	MC 1000 Quartzite 136-37-10 mm Dinwiddie Co.		

Part Three – McCary Survey Database

POINT_NUM	LENGTH	WIDTH	THICK	FLUT_LEN_1	FLUT_LEN_2	WGT	CONDITION	MATERIAL	COUNTY_CTY	INIT_OWNER
1	58	22	4.5	58	56		Complete	?	Mecklenburg	A. Robertson
2	63	46	6.5	32	22		Broken	Quartz	Mecklenburg	A. Robertson
3	53	22	4.5	26	12		Complete	Quartz	Mecklenburg	A. Robertson
4	35	22	8.5	12	10		Complete	Quartz	Mecklenburg	A. Robertson
5	52	27	5.5	13	6		Complete	Quartz	Mecklenburg	A. Robertson
6	33	19	0	13	4		Complete	Quartz	Mecklenburg	A. Robertson
7	57	22		20	10		Complete	Flint	Mecklenburg	A. Robertson
8	47	23	4.5	27	19		Complete	Flint	Mecklenburg	A. Robertson
8.1	47.9	25.4	5.3	29	27		Complete		Mecklenburg	
9	63	29		21	4		Complete	Chalcedony	Mecklenburg	A. Robertson
10	64	24	4.5	21	10		Complete	Flint	Mecklenburg	A. Robertson
11	46	24		25	13		Complete	Quartz	Mecklenburg	A. Robertson
12	51	24		51	13		Complete	Flint	Mecklenburg	A. Robertson
13	73	24		35	16		Complete	Flint	Mecklenburg	A. Robertson
13.1	73	26	7.5	37.5	18.5		Complete			
14	65	27		32	20		Complete	Flint	Mecklenburg	A. Robertson
14.1	56.1	28.5	7.9	37	32.5		Complete		Mecklenburg	A. Robertson
15	35	17		13	4		Complete	Flint	Mecklenburg	A. Robertson
15.1	38	20	4.7	15	11.5		Complete			
16	43	21	4	11	5		Complete	Flint	Mecklenburg	A. Robertson
17	57	24		21	16		Complete	Flint	Mecklenburg	A. Robertson
17.1	61	25.1	6	19.9	12		Complete			
18	58	24	5	24	19		Complete	Flint	Mecklenburg	A. Robertson
18.1	61.8	26	6.1	35	24		Complete			

POINT_NUM	LENGTH	WIDTH	THICK	FLUT_LEN_1	FLUT_LEN_2	WGT	CONDITION	MATERIAL	COUNTY_CTY	INIT_OWNER
19	48	21		12	6		Complete	Flint	Mecklenburg	A. Robertson
20	35	21		9	3		Complete	Chalcedony	Mecklenburg	A. Robertson
21	90	30		22	0		Complete	Gneiss	Mecklenburg	A. Robertson
21.1	92.5	32.5	9	27.4	14		Complete			
22	102	26	4.5	38	8		Complete	Rhyolite	Mecklenburg	A. Robertson
22.1	104.9	29.1	7	35	21.5		Complete			
23	90	25		15	5		Complete	?	Mecklenburg	A. Robertson
23.1	89.5	28	8	15			Complete			
24	27	19		5	2		Complete	Flint	Mecklenburg	A. Robertson
24.1	30.3	29	5.5	16.3	13.2		Complete			
25	56	30		32	3		Complete	Flint	Mecklenburg	A. Robertson
25.1	89	31	8	33	24.8		Complete			
26	50	24	4.5	20	10		Complete	Flint	Mecklenburg	A. Robertson
27	67	25		23	12		Complete	Flint	Mecklenburg	A. Robertson
28	69	30		12	0		Complete	Flint	Mecklenburg	A. Robertson
28.1	73.9	30	6	12.5			Complete			
29	81	32		41	32		Broken	Flint	Mecklenburg	A. Robertson
30	86	32		30	5		Complete	Flint	Amelia	A. Robertson
30.1	91.5	33	9.5	32	27		Complete			
31	36	22		18	5		Complete	Flint	Mecklenburg	A. Robertson
32	35	21		12	0		Broken	Chalcedony	Mecklenburg	A. Robertson
33	44	22		17	0		Complete	Pertified Wood	Mecklenburg	A. Robertson
34	33	21		33	7		Complete	Flint	Mecklenburg	A. Robertson
34.1	47.5	28	7	18.5	13		Complete			
35	79	27		6	0		Complete	Flint	Mecklenburg	A. Robertson

POINT_NUM	LENGTH	WIDTH	THICK	FLUT_LEN_1	FLUT_LEN_2	WGT	CONDITION	MATERIAL	COUNTY_CTY	INIT_OWNER
36	86	28		8	4		Complete	Flint	Mecklenburg	A. Robertson
36.1	78.5	28	7	14	10		Complete			
37	33	17		5	0		Complete	Flint	Mecklenburg	A. Robertson
37.1	88	30	10	21	10		Complete			
38	42	25		10	3		Complete	Flint	Mecklenburg	A. Robertson
39	52	31		13	0		Complete	Flint	Mecklenburg	A. Robertson
40	57	22		8	3		Complete	Flint	Mecklenburg	A. Robertson
41	43	18		7	4		Complete	Flint	Mecklenburg	A. Robertson
42	56	25		19	10		Complete	Flint	Mecklenburg	A. Robertson
42.1	44.1	19	6.9	14	10		Complete			
43	47	20		17	7		Complete	Flint	Mecklenburg	A. Robertson
43.1	59.8	28	9	21.5	17.3		Complete			
44	45	21		17	9		Complete	?	Mecklenburg	A. Robertson
45	50	25	5	9	8		Complete	Flint	Amelia	S. Morefield
45.1	48	23	8	19.9	11.2		Complete			
46	44	27	8	30	28		Complete	Chert	Prince Edward	S. Morefield
46.1	65.1	27.5	8	29	20.5		Complete			
47	75	26	7	45	25		Broken	Quartz	Cumberland	S. Morefield
48	50	28	8	15	14		Complete	Chalcedony	Cumberland	S. Morefield
49	64	28	6	15	5		Complete	Flint	Charlotte	S. Morefield
50	75	28	5	75	33		Complete	Flint	Buckingham	S. Morefield
51	73	30	7	65	25		Complete	Flint	Amelia	S. Morefield
52	70	33	5	45	10		Complete	Flint	Roanoke	S. Morefield
52.1	65.2	26.8	7	30	7		Complete			
53	72	21	6	25	18		Complete	Chert	Prince Edward	S. Morefield

POINT_NUM	LENGTH	WIDTH	THICK	FLUT_LEN_1	FLUT_LEN_2	WGT	CONDITION	MATERIAL	COUNTY_CTY	INIT_OWNER
54	56	23	4.5	6	6		Complete	Flint	Amelia	S. Morefield
54.1	61	29.3	9	17.2	14.1		Complete	Chert		
55	55	19	6	25	5		Complete	Chert	Halifax	S. Morefield
56	35	25	7	16	8		Complete	Quartz	Amelia	S. Morefield
56.1	70	31.1	8	32.2	22		Complete			
57	64	25	7	17	12		Complete	Chert	Pittsylvania	S. Morefield
58	53	23	6	16	13		Complete	Flint	Amelia	S. Morefield
59	98	45	9	25	13		Complete	?	Mecklenburg	J. Rowan
60	76	32	9	12	6		Complete	?	Mecklenburg	J. Rowan
61	88	38	7	19	12		Complete	?	Dinwiddie	J. Rowan
62	44	26	6	16	12		Complete	?	Dinwiddie	J. Rowan
63	32	17	5	22	15		Complete	?	Mecklenburg	J. Rowan
64	65	22	6	25	12		Complete	?	Dinwiddie	J. Rowan
65	44	25	5	17	12		Complete	?	Mecklenburg	J. Rowan
66	41	25	5	12	6		Complete	?	Mecklenburg	J. Rowan
67	41	22	5	19	10		Complete	?	Mecklenburg	J. Rowan
68	53	21	3.5	16	12		Complete	?	Mecklenburg	J. Rowan
69	25	19	3	22	7		Complete	?	Mecklenburg	J. Rowan
70	70	32	7	14	12		Complete	?	Dinwiddie	J. Rowan
71	76	33	9	21	7		Complete	?	King William	J. Rowan
72	50	24	5	19	7		Complete	?	Mecklenburg	J. Rowan
73	63	25	6	25	22		Complete	Flint	Nansemond	B. McCary
74	45	20	4	20	12		Complete	Flint	Nansemond	B. McCary
75	66	26	5	20	15		Complete	Flint	Nansemond	B. McCary
76	29	16	4	27	27		Complete	Jasper	Shenandoah	B. McCary

POINT_NUM	LENGTH	WIDTH	THICK	FLUT_LEN_1	FLUT_LEN_2	WGT	CONDITION	MATERIAL	COUNTY_CTY	INIT_OWNER
77	47	20	4	28	28		Broken	Flint	Albermarle	B. McCary
78	70	28	5	41	30		Complete	Flint	Caroline	B. McCary
79	58	26	5.5	41	30		Complete	Flint	Scott	B. McCary
80	57	26	5.5	25	23		Complete	Chalcedony	Scott	B. McCary
81	43	27	8.5	14	10		Complete	Quartzite	Albermarle	B. McCary
82	59	21	5	16	6		Complete	Flint	James City	B. McCary
83	50	25	5	32	6		Complete	?	Bedford	G. Lindsay
84	50	27	5.5	32	32		Complete	?	Bedford	G. Lindsay
85	26	21		13	12		Complete	?	Bedford	G. Lindsay
86	44	22		20	15		Complete	?	Bedford	G. Lindsay
87	65	30	5.5	30	20		Complete	?	Bedford	G. Lindsay
88	70	25		25	19		Complete	?	Bedford	G. Lindsay
89	50	22		20	20		Complete	Flint	Mecklenburg	J. Howe
90	55	24		10			Complete	?	Amelia	J. Howe
91	60	28		15			Broken	Quartz	Virginia	J. Howe
92	40	21		35	34		Complete	Flint	Rockingham	J. Howe
93	50	20		10			Complete	Quartz	Mecklenburg	J. Howe
94	60	27	5.5	30	12		Complete	?	Mecklenburg	S. Davenport
95	74	28		5			Complete	?	Mecklenburg	S. Davenport
96	88	27	8.5	37	33		Complete	?	Mecklenburg	S. Davenport
97	115	35	8.5	31	19		Complete	?	Campbell	S. Davenport
98	137	52	7	44	30		Complete	?	Mecklenburg	S. Davenport
99	79	30	8.5	31	25		Complete	?	Mecklenburg	W. Maxey
100	50	25	5.5	45	35		Complete	Flint	Mecklenburg	W. Maxey
101	163	19	5.5	31	19		Complete	Flint	Mecklenburg	W. Maxey

POINT_NUM	LENGTH	WIDTH	THICK	FLUT_LEN_1	FLUT_LEN_2	WGT	CONDITION	MATERIAL	COUNTY_CTY	INIT_OWNER
102	44	24	5.5	16	10		Complete	?	Mecklenburg	W. Maxey
103	70	25	5.5	15	15		Complete	Chalcedony	Page	C. Finter
104	55	24	6.5	25	15		Complete	Quartz	Page	C. Finter
105	92	31	5.5		40		Broken	Chalcedony	Page	C. Finter
106	92	29	5.5	25			Complete	Flint	Prince Edward	G. Butcher
107	104	31	5.5	23			Complete	Slate	Bedford	G. Butcher
108	47	30	5.5	36	36		Complete	Flint	Prince George	R. Sturdivent
109	53	22	4.5	50	48		Complete	Flint	Prince George	R. Sturdivant
110	62	33	6.5	42	35		Complete	Jasper	Bedford	A. Drewery
111	93	50	6.5	28	27		Complete	Quartzite	Hanover	A. Drewery
112	82	28	5.5	25	19	0	Complete	Flint	Brunswick	E. Sacrey
112.1	52.1	25.8	5.2	33	33		Complete			E. Sacrey
113	44	25	3	18			Complete	Flint	Henrico	E. Sacrey
114	44	22	5	22			Complete	Conglomerate	Caroline	C. Beard
115	64	31	7	32	30		Complete	Chalcedony	Caroline	C. Beard
116	97	31	5.5	34	25		Complete	Jasper	Bedford	L. Updike
117	80	25	5.5	34			Broken	Chert	Bedford	L. Updike
118	98	32	9	36	33		Complete	?	Nelson	C. Brown
119	68	25	6.5	30	30		Complete	?	Prince George	Y. LaPrade
120	38	25	4.5	22	12		Complete	Flint	Spotsylvania	J. Nichols
121	98	33	6	78	66		Complete	Flint	Dinwiddie	C. Coffin
122	82	30	6	42	30		Complete	Flint	Mecklenburg	C. Holland
123	50	29	5.5	32	29		Complete	Chert	King and Queen	Ms W. Heister
124	30	17	4	15	13		Complete	Quartz	Caroline	W. Congdon
125	83	31	6.5	30	25		Complete	?	Amelia	A. Helwig

POINT_NUM	LENGTH	WIDTH	THICK	FLUT_LEN_1	FLUT_LEN_2	WGT	CONDITION	MATERIAL	COUNTY_CTY	INIT_OWNER
126	70	25	6	53	29		Complete	?	Mecklenburg	A. Capehart
127	40	22	5	6			Complete	?	Mecklenburg	
128	42	25	5				Broken	Quartz	Mecklenburg	
129	45	25	5				Complete	Flint	Mecklenburg	
130	85	32	6	37	29		Complete	Flint	Dinwiddie	
131	60	20	6	6	3		Complete	Flint	Mecklenburg	
132	59	22	7.5	19	13		Complete	Chert	Bedford	C. Brown
133	45	30	4	20	16		Complete	Flint	Campbell	J. Fauntleroy
134	50	27	5	27	23		Complete	Flint	Campbell	J. Fauntleroy
135	40	15	5	20	13		Complete	Quartz	Mecklenburg	J. Tisdale
136	49	25	8	30	20		Complete	Quartz	Mecklenburg	J. Tisdale
137	61	24	4.5	13	10		Complete	Flint	Bedford	C. Harris
138	109	31	5.5	23	15		Complete	Flint	Bedford	S. Morefield
139	47	23	7.5	23	12		Complete	Flint	Amherst	C. Brown
140	69	25	8	31	31		Complete	?	Alleghany	C. Browm
141	72	26		32	27		Complete	Jasper	Nelson	E. Purvis
142	36	20	3.5	28	22		Complete	?	Surry	A. Bohannan
143	53	21	4.5	20	13		Complete	?	Charlotte	A. Robertson
144	58	27	6.5	25	25		Complete	Flint	Campbell	J. Hancock
145	55	27	6	22	18		Complete	Chert	Bedford	C. Brown
146	60	27	8	25	19		Broken	?	Dinwiddie	C. Gregory
147	47	23	5	19	8	0	Complete	?	Dinwiddie	J. Williamson
148	56	21	5	8	7		Complete	?	Dinwiddie	J. Williamson
149	90	32	7	27	23		Complete	Jasper	Pittsylvania	A. Bruce
150	59	29	7	30	20		Complete	Quartz	Mecklenburg	B. McCary

POINT_NUM	LENGTH	WIDTH	THICK	FLUT_LEN_1	FLUT_LEN_2	WGT	CONDITION	MATERIAL	COUNTY_CTY	INIT_OWNER
151	75	31	7	58	25		Broken	?	Dinwiddie	
152	50	38	5.5	13	12		Complete	Flint	Sussex	H. Huffington
153	48	25	6	22	7		Complete	Chalcedony	Pittsylvania	J. McAllister
154	53	28	5	18	17		Complete	Quartz	Mecklenburg	J. McAllister
155	73	29	9	22	20		Complete	?	Dinwiddie	J. Williamson
156	77	28	7	38	28		Complete	Chert	Rockingham	H. Gibson
157	60	25	6	28	13		Broken	Flint	Rockingham	W. Gibson
158	72	26	6.5	60	42		Broken	Quartzite	Prince George	J. Lucas
159	94	27	4	26	24		Broken	Chert	Mecklenburg	W. Ward
160	58	32		27			Complete	Flint	Mecklenburg	R. Cumbee
161	90	21	4	20	18		Complete	Chalcedony	Shenandoah	
162	32	18	4	32	12		Complete	Chalcedony	Dinwiddie	
163	40	21	6	30	15		Complete	Chalcedony	Dinwiddie	
164	31	20	4	15	12		Complete	Quartz	Dinwiddie	
165	46	20	6	15	10		Complete	Chalcedony	Dinwiddie	
166	45	24	6	16	10		Complete	Chalcedony	Dinwiddie	
167	40	33	6	25	15		Broken	Chalcedony	Dinwiddie	
168	20	20	5	20	20		Broken	Chalcedony	Dinwiddie	
169	10	25	5	10	10		Broken	Chalcedony	Dinwiddie	
170	44	23	6	25	13		Complete	Jasper	Dinwiddie	E. Gilliam
171	28	12	5.5	10			Complete	Chert	Dinwiddie	
172	29	19	4	13	5		Complete	Quartz	Dinwiddie	
173	19	27	5	18	18		Broken	Chert	Dinwiddie	J. Williamson
174	40	21	3.5	13	9		Complete	Chert	Dinwiddie	J. Williamson
175	55	32	6	28	16		Complete	Chert	Dinwiddie	J. Williamson

POINT_NUM	LENGTH	WIDTH	THICK	FLUT_LEN_1	FLUT_LEN_2	WGT	CONDITION	MATERIAL	COUNTY_CTY	INIT_OWNER
176	37	18	5	12	11		Complete	Chert	Dinwiddie	J. Williamson
177	48	20	4	21	18		Complete	Chert	Hanover	R. Brockwell
178	47	26	4	27	18		Complete	Chert	Chesterfield	R. Morris
179	66	25	6	60	8		B	Chert	Dinwiddie	R. Morris
180	51	24	6	15			Complete	Chert	Chesterfield	J. Magee
181	73	33	5.5	38	30		Complete	Flint	Mathews	W. Sanders
182	69	25	5	19	14		Complete	Chert	Buchanan	W. Altemose
183	56	28	6.5	21	20		Complete	Chert	Mecklenburg	B. McCary
184	60	28	6	19	15		Complete	Flint	Smyth	J. Woolsey
185	41	16	8	9			Complete	Chert	Dinwiddie	J. Williamson
186	50	22	5	15	12		Complete	Chert	Dinwiddie	J. Williamson
187	38	27	7	36	16		Broken	Chert	Dinwiddie	J. Williamson
188	45	23	6	15			Complete	Quartzite	Dinwiddie	J. Williamson
189	26	12	6		3.5		Complete	Quartz	Dinwiddie	J. Williamson
190	63	26	8	10	8		Broken	Chert	Dinwiddie	J. Williamson
191	23	29	6	18	18		Broken	Quartz	Dinwiddie	J. Williamson
192	65	28	8	16	11		Broken	Quartzite	Dinwiddie	J. Williamson
193	56	31	8	12			Complete	Chert	Dinwiddie	J. Williamson
194	33	29	9	30	22		Broken	Chert	Dinwiddie	J. Williamson
195	57	23	6	22	11		Complete	Quartzite	Dinwiddie	J. Williamson
196	50	29	8	20	18		Broken	Quartz	Dinwiddie	J. Williamson
197	15	25	4	13	13		Broken	Chert	Dinwiddie	J. Williamson
198	55	22	4	20	18		Complete	Chert	Dinwiddie	J. Williamson
199	71	31	8	26	15		Complete	Quartzite	Dinwiddie	J. Williamson
200	42	22	5	12			Complete	Chert	Dinwiddie	J. Williamson

POINT_NUM	LENGTH	WIDTH	THICK	FLUT_LEN_1	FLUT_LEN_2	WGT	CONDITION	MATERIAL	COUNTY_CTY	INIT_OWNER
201	34	20	6	17	14		Complete	Quartz	Dinwiddie	J. Williamson
202	30	19	6	12	10		Complete	Quartz	Dinwiddie	J. Williamson
203	36	24	6	18	15		Broken	Chert	Dinwiddie	J. Willamson
204	13	24	5	12	12		Broken	Chert	Dinwiddie	J. Williamson
205	27	21	5	14	10		Broken	Chert	Dinwiddie	J. Williamson
206	15	24	4	12	12		Broken	Quartz	Dinwiddie	J. Williamson
207	42	27	5	21	20		Complete	Chert	Dinwiddie	B. McCary
208	28	20	6	20	2.5		Broken	Chert	Dinwiddie	B. McCary
209	17	25	5	16	16		Broken	Quartzite	Dinwiddie	B. McCary
210	61	24	7	20	19		Complete	Flint	Smyth	B. McCary
211	47	29	6	19	12		Complete	Chert	Dinwiddie	B. Mcary
212	16	25	5	14	14		Broken	Chert	Dinwiddie	B. McCary
213	54	27	5	29	23		Complete	Quartz	Smyth	B. McCary
214	72	31	7	28	21		Complete	Chert	Dinwiddie	J. Adkins
215	40	26	10	25	12		Broken	Quartz	Dinwiddie	C. Gilliam
216	72	31	7	16	11		Complete	Chert	Dinwiddie	J. Rowan
217	35	24	5				Complete	Chert	Dinwiddie	J. Williamson
218	52	21		32	27		Complete	Flint	Mecklenburg	
219	38	19	5	17	12		Complete	Chert	Greensville	
220	140	32	10	27	24		Complete	Jasper	Halifax	J. Guthrie
221	70	31	7	25	20		Complete	Chert	Mecklenburg	L. Carter
222	56	35	6	45	23		Complete	Chert	Mecklenburg	L. Carter
223	29	22	5	20	17		Broken	Quartz	Brunswick	L. Carter
224	93	40	6.5	36	35		Complete	Chert	Mecklenburg	L. Carter
225	46	23	6	25	23		Complete	Chert	Mecklenburg	L. Carter

POINT_NUM	LENGTH	WIDTH	THICK	FLUT_LEN_1	FLUT_LEN_2	WGT	CONDITION	MATERIAL	COUNTY_CTY	INIT_OWNER
226	71	26	5	53	40		Complete	Chert	Mecklenburg	L. Carter
227	79	29	5	20	15		Complete	Chert	Mecklenburg	L. Carter
228	69	25	4	12			Complete	Chert	Lunenburg	L. Carter
229	65	34	10	12			Complete	Chert	Mecklenburg	L. Carter
230	47	24	5	22	16		Complete	Chert	Mecklenburg	B. McCary
231	52	24	5	29	12		Complete	Chert	Dinwiddie	J. McAllister
232	72	35	6.5	40	34		Broken	Chert	Dinwiddie	J. Williamson
233	53	30	9.5	30	25		Broken	Chert	Dinwiddie	J. Williamson
234	70	27	7	17	11		Complete	Quartzite	Dinwiddie	J. Williamson
235	66	23	6.5	19	17		Complete	Chert	Dinwiddie	J. Williamson
236	57	25	5.5	26	12		Complete	Chert	Dinwiddie	J. Williamson
237	53	22	5	18	18		Complete	Chert	Dinwiddie	J. Williamson
238	46	20	5	17	14		Complete	Chert	Dinwiddie	J. Williamson
239	36	24	5	27	16		Broken	Chert	Dinwiddie	J. Williamson
240	38	28	6	36	36		Broken	Chert	Dinwiddie	J. Williamson
241	22	27	5	21	21		Broken	Chert	Dinwiddie	J. Williamson
242	46	22	4.5	10	10		Complete	Chert	Dinwiddie	J. Williamson
243	35	20	5	15	12		Complete	Quartz	Dinwiddie	J. Williamson
244	29	21	4	13	11		Broken	Chert	Dinwiddie	J. Williamson
245	38	22	5	14	12		Complete	Chert	Dinwiddie	J. Williamson
246	43	19	6	10	8		Complete	Chert	Dinwiddie	J. Williamson
247	56	22	3.5	18	13		Complete	Jasper	Nansemond	B. McCary
248	50	29	5	18	16		Complete	Quartzite	Nansemond	B. McCary
249	53	26	5	28	27		Complete	Chert	?	B. McCary
250	77	26	5	42	23		Complete	Chert	York	B. McCary

POINT_NUM	LENGTH	WIDTH	THICK	FLUT_LEN_1	FLUT_LEN_2	WGT	CONDITION	MATERIAL	COUNTY_CTY	INIT_OWNER
251	36	23	5	27	21		Complete	Chert	Dinwiddie	B. McCary
252	37	22	5	34			Complete	Chert	Dinwiddie	B. McCary
253	51	24	8.5	12	8		Complete	Quartzite	Nansemond	B. McCary
254	52	23	5	16	11		Complete	Chert	Nansemond	B. McCary
255	23	27	5	21	21		Broken	Quartz	Dinwiddie	B. McCary
256	26	17	4.5	20	20		Complete	Jasper	Dinwiddie	B. McCary
257	19	27	7	17	17		Broken	Quartz	Dinwiddie	B. McCary
258	28	16	4.5	7			Broken	Quartz	Dinwiddie	B. McCary
259	36	22	5	16	14		Complete	Quartz	Dinwiddie	B. McCary
260	82	23	7.5	38	20		Complete	Chert	Bath	M. Davis
261	58	20	5.5	5	3		Complete	Rhyolite	Mecklenburg	L. Carter
262	63	23	5.5	21	11		Complete	Chert	Mecklenburg	L. Carter
263	40	22	3.5	10	5		Complete	Chert	Mecklenburg	L. Carter
264	49	26	7	35	21		Broken	Chert	Rockbridge	R. Carroll
265	45	20	10	15	11		Complete	Quartzite	Nansemond	B. McCary
266	36	20	4	16	8		Complete	Jasper	Nansemond	J. Marsh
267	61	26	7	37	12		Complete	Chert	Northampton	W. Moseley
268	42	21	4	16	11		Complete	Pertified wood	Mecklenburg	B. McCary
269	69	25	7	28	21		Complete	Quartz	Dinwiddie	B. McCary
270	36	27	7	32	30		Broken	Quartz	Princess Anne	B. McCary
271	38	23	7	14	9		Complete	Chert	Southampton	W. Moseley
272	54	24	5	13	12		Broken	Chert	Princess Anne	W. Moseley
273	74	26	7	23	22		Complete	Quartzite	Southampton	W. Moseley
274	71	25	6	25	25		Complete	Chert	Isle of Wight	E. Siegel
275	46	20	6	31	18		Broken	Quartzite	Greensville	B. McCary

POINT_NUM	LENGTH	WIDTH	THICK	FLUT_LEN_1	FLUT_LEN_2	WGT	CONDITION	MATERIAL	COUNTY_CTY	INIT_OWNER
276	50	26	7	15	14		Complete	Chert	Dinwiddie	W. Moseley
277	32	16	5	13	7		Complete	Chert	Greensville	J. McAllister
278	42	22	7	13	8		Broken	Chert	Sussex	W. Moseley
279	90	35	8.5	24	23		Complete	Chert	Sussex	J. Melton
280	38	19	7	22	17		Complete	Chert	Southampton	J. Melton
281	50	39	7.5	23	18		Broken	Chert	Southampton	M. Vickers
282	18	22	7	15	8		Broken	Quartz	Dinwiddie	J. McAvoy
283	63	32	8	18	18		Complete	Rhyolite	Dinwiddie	B. McCary
284	41	25	7.5	16	15		Complete	Quartzite	Dinwiddie	?
285	45	22	7	20	18		Complete	Chert	Dinwiddie	?
286	55	28	7	45	45		Broken	Greenstone	Dinwiddie	B. McCary
287	78	32	5.5	36	28		Broken	Chert	Brunswick	J. Melton
288	46	21	8	29	23		Complete	Jasper	Rockbridge	R. Carroll
289	58	26	5.5	18	12		Complete	Chert	Charlotte	B. McCary
290	41	25	7	15	8		Complete	Chert	Nansemond	B. McCary
291	26	32	6	19	19		Broken	Quartzite	Hampton City	R. Daley
292	30	28	6	18	14		Broken	Chert	Charles City	D. Smith
293	105	34		52			Complete	Chert	Madison	N. Estes
294	32	28	6	31	31		Broken	Chert	Norfolk	J. Traver
295	17	26	6.5				Broken	Chert	Norfolk	J. Traver
296	63	23	6.5	21	10		Complete	Greenstone	Mecklenburg	B. McCary
297	50	28	7.5	29	13		Complete	Jasper	Isle of Wight	L. Wilson
298	45	25	6.5	20	20		Complete	Rhyolite	Nansemond	F. Wood
299	38	22	4	30	18		Complete	Jasper	Surry	A. Bohannan
300	53	28	7	26	22		Complete	Chert	Smyth	B. McCary

POINT_NUM	LENGTH	WIDTH	THICK	FLUT_LEN_1	FLUT_LEN_2	WGT	CONDITION	MATERIAL	COUNTY_CTY	INIT_OWNER
301	70	30	6.5	13	11		Complete	Chert	Dinwiddie	J. McAllister
302	21	27	7	16	12		Broken	Jasper	Surry	B. McCary
303	23	26	7	10	8		Broken	Quartz	Southampton	F. Painter
304	62	29	8.5	32	17		Complete	Chert	Mecklenburg	E. Bottoms
305	34	20	5	9	6		Complete	Quartz	Brunswick	E. Bottoms
306	27	27	8	23	13		Broken	Quartz	Nansemond	E. Bottoms
307	15	26	6	12	12		Broken	Chert	Dinwiddie	E. Bottoms
308	42	34	9	18	12		Broken	Quartzite	Nansemond	C. Hall
309	50	24	7	15	13		Complete	Chert	Greensville	H. Boney
310	71	29	6.5	22	21		Complete	Rhyolite	James City	E. Bottoms
311	28	30	5	20	15		Broken	Jasper	Halifax	D. Eggleston
312	56	28	6	21	20		Complete	Chert	Mecklenburg	J. McAvoy
313	76	25	7	20	17		Complete	Jasper	Richmond	J. McAvoy
314	32	24	6	15	3.5		?	Chert	Prince George	J. McAvoy
315	41	22	6	22	15		Complete	Quartz	Albermarle	P. Weems
316	57	28	6	20	20		Complete	Chert	Grayson	T. Matthews
317	60	23	6	7	6		Complete	Chert	Grayson	T. Matthews
318	54	32	6	50	32		Broken	Chert	?	A. Smith
319	79	33	6	17	12		Broken	Jasper	?	B. McCary
320	50	26	7	13	12		Complete	Quartzite	Pittsylvania	B. McCary
321	75	28	7	20	14		Broken	Chert	Pittsylvania	H. Beggarly
322	46	28	6	25	19		Complete	Chert	Pearsburg	D. Brown
323	54	20	6				Broken	Greenstone	Princess Anne	J. Traver
324	81	30	6	13	11		Complete	Flint	Southampton	J. Tompkins
325	22	21	6	19	19		Broken	Greenstone	Dinwiddie	J. Traver

POINT_NUM	LENGTH	WIDTH	THICK	FLUT_LEN_1	FLUT_LEN_2	WGT	CONDITION	MATERIAL	COUNTY_CTY	INIT_OWNER
326	22	27	7	15	15		Broken	Chert	Southampton	J. Traver
327	51	30	6	33	13		Broken	Chert	Sussex	J. Traver
328	49	25	6	41	36		Complete	Schist	Sussex	J. Traver
329	26	18	4	6	6		Broken	Chert	Dinwiddie	J. Traver
330	69	31	7	25	20		Complete	Chalcedony	Brunswick	L. Carter
331	52	36	8	14	13		Complete	Quartz	Nelson	E. Bottoms
332	66	26	9	14	13		Complete	Quartzite	Southampton	E. Bottoms
333	62	22	7	14	9		Complete	Chert	Mecklenburg	E. Bottoms
334	39	25	6	12	10		Broken	Chalcedony	Surry	E. Bottoms
335	56	21	6	15	15		Complete	Chert	Dinwiddie	J. McAvoy
336	33	20	6	21	19		Broken	Quartzite	?	J. McAvoy
337	75	33	7	27	22		Complete	Chert	Powhatan	J. McAvoy
338	56	28		18			Complete	Chert	Sussex	R. Twisdale
339	38	18	5	20			Complete	?	Tazewell	W. Bane
340	44	24	7	32	26		Broken	Quartzite	King George	J. McAvoy
341	56	22	7	51	20		Complete	Jasper	Chesterfield	J. McAvoy
342	26	20	6	14	13		Broken	Quartz	Chesterfield	J. McAvoy
343	22	21	6				Broken	Pertified Wood	Chesterfield	J. McAvoy
344	38	21	5	16	13		Complete	Chert	Chesterfield	J. McAvoy
345	37	19	7	6			Complete	Quartz	Chesterfield	J. McAvoy
346	33	20	6	26	19		Complete	Chert	Chesterfield	J. McAvoy
347	53	32	3	32	13		Complete	Chert	Shenandoah	P. Myers
348	35	15	4	22			Complete	Chert	Dinwiddie	F. Painter
349	37	15	5	10			Complete	Chert	Dinwiddie	F. Painter
350	32	15	4				Complete	Chert	Dinwiddie	F. Painter

POINT_ NUM	LENGTH	WIDTH	THICK	FLUT_ LEN_1	FLUT_ LEN_2	WGT	CONDITION	MATERIAL	COUNTY_CTY	INIT_OWNER
351	32	21	5	18	8		Complete	Chert	Dinwiddie	F. Painter
352	24	18	5	8	6		Broken	Chert	Dinwiddie	F. Painter
353	61	29	7	16	13		Complete	Chert	Dinwiddie	R. Peck
354	50	30	8	16	9		Broken	Quartzite	Sussex	R. Peck
355	43	25	6	30	17		Complete	Quartzite	Sussex	R. Peck
356	22	25	5	19	13		Broken	Jasper	Sussex	R. Peck
357	31	32	7	28	28		Broken	Chert	Bedford	R. Peck
358	74	28		26	23		Complete	Chalcedony	?	Ms E. Palmore
359	64	27	7	52	0		Broken	Chert	Tazewell	Ms M. Rich
360	75	30	7				Complete	Chert	Tazewell	C. Bell
361	30	15		28	22		Complete	Chert	Scott	W. Hicks
362	47	25	6	30	17		Complete	Slate	Nansemond	E. Bottoms
363	79	34	8	30	14		Broken	Quartzite	Isle of Wight	E. Bottoms
364	36	21	6	20	17		Broken	Chalcedony	Princess Anne	J. Pritchard
365	62	31	8	25	18		Complete	Chert	Hanover	T. Lipscombe
366	47	23	6	20	12		Complete	Chert	Amherst	L. East
367	15	25	6	7	7		Broken	Chert	Virginia Beach	Ms J. Tyler
368	32	19	6	11	10		Complete	Quartzite	Dinwiddie	J. McAvoy
369	51	25	7	19	14		Broken	Quartzite	Norfolk	J. Traver
370	30	17	5	8	7		Complete	Chert	Dinwiddie	R. Peck
371	18	22	6	15	14		Complete	Jasper	Henrico	J. Strass
372	56	24	7	18	13		Complete	Chert	Brunswick	J. Stotesbury
373	106	37	10	20	18		Complete	Chert	Halifax	T. Stevens
374	68	31	7	30	25		Complete	Chert	Mecklenburg	B. McCary
375	65	27	8	18	17		Complete	Jasper	Mecklenburg	B. McCary

POINT_NUM	LENGTH	WIDTH	THICK	FLUT_LEN_1	FLUT_LEN_2	WGT	CONDITION	MATERIAL	COUNTY_CTY	INIT_OWNER
376	47	23	7	19	14		Complete	Jasper	Nansemond	B. McCary
377	42	33	7	33	23		Broken	Chert	Chesterfield	B. McCary
378	68	27	6	32	14		Complete	Chert	Dinwiddie	B. McCary
379	55	30	7	32	19		Complete	Quartz	Mecklenburg	B. McCary
380	108	35	8	19			Complete	Jasper	Virginia	S. Potter
381	106	27	8				Complete	Chert	Virginia	S. Potter
382	58	22	7	17	14		Complete	Chert	Campbell	S. Potter
383	72	27	7	28			Complete	Chert	Orange	S. Potter
384	54	26	7	37	33		Complete	Chalcedony ?	Charlotte	S. Potter
385	23	26	4	19	18		Broken	Rhyolite	Halifax	Ms R. Stevens
386	54	21	6	11	0		Complete	Chert	Mecklenburg	J. Wells
387	120	39	7	20	0		Complete	Chert	Mecklenburg	J. Wells
388	57	26	8	30	10		Broken	Chert	Radford	M. Hubble
389	52	22	7	16	12		Complete	Jasper	Page	J. Powell
390	45	17	6	20	10		Complete	Quartz	Mecklenburg	L. Carter
391	73	29	8	17	0		Complete	Rhyolite	Loudoun	S. Silsby
392	91	33	9	15	14		Broken	Chert	Fauquier	H. Pearson
393	50	26	6	29	15		Broken	Chert	Fort Eustis	A. Dippre
394	37	35	9				Broken	Jasper	Essex	J. O'Dell
395	19	27	6	16	16		Broken	Chert	Dinwiddie	B. McCary
396	33	28	7	27	11		Broken	Chert	Dinwiddie	B. McCary
397	28	30	8	23	21		Broken	Chert	Dinwiddie	B. McCary
398	25	29	6	18	15		Broken	Chert	Dinwiddie	B. McCary
399	45	25	7	18	13		Broken	Chert	Dinwiddie	B. McCary
400	30	30		28	28	2	Broken	Chert	Augusta	J. Rusmiselle

POINT_NUM	LENGTH	WIDTH	THICK	FLUT_LEN_1	FLUT_LEN_2	WGT	CONDITION	MATERIAL	COUNTY_CTY	INIT_OWNER
401	32	24	6	16	16		Broken	Chert	Dinwiddie	J. Williamson
402	17	28	6	14	13		Broken	Quartzite	Dinwiddie	J. Williamson
403	36	23	9	8	5		Complete	Chert	Dinwiddie	J. Williamson
404	35	20	5	0	0	0	Complete	Chert	Dinwiddie	J. Williamson
405	18	29	6	16	16		Broken	Chert	Dinwiddie	J. Williamson
406	55	20	7	17	6		Complete	Jasper	Dinwiddie	J. Williamson
407	57	30	6	8	7		Broken	Chert	Dinwiddie	J. Williamson
408	32	23	6	11	8		Broken	Chert	Dinwiddie	J. Williamson
409	39	26	6	19	18		Broken	Chert	Dinwiddie	J. Williamson
410	66	30	7	10	7		Complete	Chert	Brunswick	J. Melton
411	56	27	6	10	10		Complete	Chert	Dinwiddie	J. Melton
412	65	26	7	14	11		Complete	Chert	Mecklenburg	J. Melton
413	68	26	9	16	10		Complete	Chert	Lunenburg	J. Melton
414	63	26	10	20	15		Complete	Chert	Sussex	J. Melton
415	41	20	7	16	13		Complete	Chert	Tazewell	J. Melton
416	30	22	4	22	0		Broken	Chert	Brunswick	J. Melton
417	40	21	6	20	12		Complete	Chalcedony	Smyth	J. Melton
418	30	30	7	13	11		Broken	Chert	Caroline	J. Melton
419	85	31	8	21	21		Broken	Chert	Greensville	J. Melton
420	66	27	7	10	10		Complete	Chert	Dinwiddie	J. Melton
421	86	34	7	42	25		Broken	Chalcedony	Virginia Beach	J. McAvoy
422	52	26	7	28	20		Complete	Shale	Powhatan	J. McAvoy
423	50	20	5	24	20		Broken	Chert	Dinwiddie	J. McAvoy
424	67	20	6	18	18		Complete	Chert	Dinwiddie	J. McAvoy
425	58	30	8	42	23		Broken	Chalcedony	Washington	J. McAvoy

POINT_NUM	LENGTH	WIDTH	THICK	FLUT_LEN_1	FLUT_LEN_2	WGT	CONDITION	MATERIAL	COUNTY_CTY	INIT_OWNER
426	50	26	6	23	15		Complete	Quartz	Cumberland	J. McAvoy
427	64	20	6	20	6		Complete	Chalcedony	Amelia	J. McAvoy
428	41	23	6	22	12		Complete	Quartz	Nansemond	J. McAvoy
429	42	25	7	17	9		Complete	Chalcedony	Henry	J. McAvoy
430	61	29	7	15	0		Complete	Petrified Wood	Chesterfield	J. McAvoy
431	47	24	5	20	16		Complete	Slate	Chesterfield	J. McAvoy
432	32	14	4	20	7		Complete	Petrified Wood	Chesterfield	J. McAvoy
433	40	18	5	32	8		Complete	Slate	Dinwiddie	J. McAvoy
434	30	18	3	9	6		Complete	Chalcedony	Page	L. McAvoy
435	26	19	5	16	14		Complete	Chalcedony	Dinwiddie	J. McAvoy
436	47	21	6	16	15		Complete	Chalcedony	Dinwiddie	J. McAvoy
437	20	21	7	16	8		Complete	Chalcedony	Dinwiddie	J. McAvoy
438	44	22	6	22	16		Complete	Chert	Page	J. McAvoy
439	41	23	5	17	10		Complete	Shale	Brunswick	J. McAvoy
440	60	28	7	25	17		Broken	Chalcedony	Page	J. McAvoy
441	46	21	5	20	13		Broken	Chalcedony	Nelson	J. McAvoy
442	85	34	9	29	25		Complete	Shale	Prince George	J. McAvoy
443	40	21	6	30	16		Broken	Quartzite	Greensville	J. McAvoy
444	89	29	6	17	17		Complete	Shale	Chesterfield	J. McAvoy
445	49	23	8	17	11		Complete	Chalcedony	Prince Edward	J. McAvoy
446	62	30	6	25	22		Broken	Chalcedony	Cumberland	J. McAvoy
447	62	27	8	17	15		Broken	Quartzite	Virginia Beach	J. McAvoy
448	48	24	6	15	9		?	Oolitic rock	Wythe	P. Perkinson
449	45	23	5	20	15		Broken	Chert	Pittsylvania	P. Perkinson

POINT_NUM	LENGTH	WIDTH	THICK	FLUT_LEN_1	FLUT_LEN_2	WGT	CONDITION	MATERIAL	COUNTY_CTY	INIT_OWNER
450	46	20	6	17	16		Complete	Jasper	Greensville	L. Carter
451	28	12	3	0	0		Complete	Chert	Dinwiddie	J. Williamson
452	21	29	7	18	18		Broken	Jasper	Dinwiddie	J. Williamson
453	35	20	7	16	13		Broken	Quartzite	Dinwiddie	J. Williamson
454	52	23	6	20	17		Complete	Chert	Bedford	A. Gulley
455	29	25	5	25	25		Broken	Slate	Dinwiddie	J. McAvoy
456	33	22	7	20	9		Complete	Greenstone	?	F. Painter
457	15	29	5	12	12		Broken	Chert	Dinwiddie	F. Painter
458	18	27	7	15	15		Broken	Chalcedony	Dinwiddie	F. Painter
459	36	25	8	26	25		Complete	Quartz	Dinwiddie	F. Painter
460	56	25	10	21	8		Complete	Quartzite	Dinwiddie	F. Painter
461	52	25	7	16	13		Complete	Quartzite	Virginia Beach	R. Parron
462	61	25	7	0	0		Complete	Quartzite	Gloucester	P. Moore
463	40	26	6	29	17		Broken	Jasper	York	G. Bittner
464	40	25	6	26	13		Broken	Quartz	Dinwiddie	B. McCary
465	66	25	7	25	20		Complete	Chert	Albermarle	L. Lindberg
466	59	29	5	24	16		Broken	Chert	Isle of Wight	J. Dixon
467	74	26	7	31	19		Complete	?	King and Queen	M. Kerby
468	22	21	7	18	8		Broken	Quartz	Campbell	P. Perkinson
469	45	27	6	12	7		Complete	Chert	Westmoreland	J. Johnson
470	50	25	8	24	14		Complete	Chalcedony	Rockingham	J. Harter
471	25	22	4	16	14		Broken	Greenstone	Fairfax	R. Collier
472	45	24	8	19	14		Complete	Chalcedony	Mecklenburg	?
473	62	28	8	23	14		Complete	Jasper	Mecklenburg	E. Hecht
474	50	24	7	13	11		Complete	Chert	Mecklenburg	G. Griffin

POINT_NUM	LENGTH	WIDTH	THICK	FLUT_LEN_1	FLUT_LEN_2	WGT	CONDITION	MATERIAL	COUNTY_CTY	INIT_OWNER
475	53	25	7	15	8		Complete	Rhyolite	Mecklenburg	J. Melton
476	39	25	8	20	6		Complete	Quartz	Nansemond	J. Byrd
477	41	23	7	9	7		Complete	Quartz	Dinwiddie	J. Traver
478	47	23	7	19	19		Broken	Jasper	Charles City	P. Perkinson
479	36	31	4	15	8		Broken	Quartz	Mecklenburg	P. Lewis
480	70	27	7	35	27		Complete	Argillite	Halifax	P. Lewis
481	61	24	7	25	22		Complete	Quartzite	Mecklenburg	T. Stevens
482	62	24	5	19	16		Complete	Chert	Mecklenburg	T. Stevens
483	35	20	5	19	10		Complete	Chert	Mecklenburg	G. Poteat
484	49	29	6	32	16		Broken	Quartz	Mecklenburg	G. Poteat
485	76	30	6	25	17		Complete	Chert	Mecklenburg	G. Poteat
486	75	33	9	37	25		Complete	Chert	Dinwiddie	J. Williamson
487	22	15	4	0	0		Complete	Chert	Dinwiddie	J. Williamson
488	27	16	6	11	0	0	Complete	Quartzite	Dinwiddie	J. Williamson
489	27	24	5	15	12		Broken	Chert	Dinwiddie	J. Williamson
490	20	22	5	16	11		Complete	Jasper	Dinwiddie	J. Williamson
491	39	22	6	23	15		Complete	Rhyolite	Dinwiddie	J. Wyatt
492	30	33	8	32	25		Broken	Chert	Dinwiddie	J. Williamson
493	42	27	6	30	30		Broken	Slate	Dinwiddie	F. Painter
494	22	27	7	30	30		Broken	Quartz	Dinwiddie	F. Painter
495	48	22	7	10	9		Complete	Jasper	Dinwiddie	J. Ampy
496	59	23	7	20	16		Complete	Felsite	Dinwiddie	J. Ampy
497	52	30	9	14	3		Broken	Quartz	Dinwiddie	J. Ampy
498	41	20	7	11	7		Complete	Quartzite	Dinwiddie	J. Ampy
499	47	25	7	5	0		Complete	Chert	Dinwiddie	J. Ampy

POINT_NUM	LENGTH	WIDTH	THICK	FLUT_LEN_1	FLUT_LEN_2	WGT	CONDITION	MATERIAL	COUNTY_CTY	INIT_OWNER
500	42	22	7	15	14		Complete	Jasper	Dinwiddie	C. Gilliam
501	15	22	0	13	13	2	Broken	Quartz	Dinwiddie	J. McAvoy
502	35	22	6	9	5		Complete	Quartz	Greensville	J. McAvoy
503	64	25	5	51	40		Complete	Rhyolite	Greensville	J. McAvoy
504	60	25	6	13	9		Complete	Chalcedony	Greensville	J. McAvoy
505	48	22	7	10	6		Broken	Jasper	Halifax	T. Stevens
506	76	27	7	57	51		Broken	Quartz	Pittsylvania	P. Perkinson
507	45	24	6	35	28		Complete	Rhyolite	Hanover	B. McCary
508	16	26	5	8	8		Broken	Chalcedony	Powhatan	R. Porter
509	46	29	10	17	10		Complete	Quartzite	Chesterfield	R. Gwinn
510	72	31	6	20	17		Complete	Chert	Charlotte	H. Mason
511	55	22	7	30	12		Complete	Chert	Charlotte	H. Mason
512	38	20	6	20	15		Complete	Chert	Campbell	H. Mason
513	82	30	7	41	35		Complete	Chert	Prince Edward	G. Clark
514	50	22	7	22	13		Broken	Chalcedony	Charlotte	G. Clark
515	24	21	5	11	10		Broken	Chert	Dinwiddie	B. McCary
516	31	20	7	9	0		Complete	Quartz	Dinwiddie	F. Painter
517	37	35	7	17	15		Broken	Quartzite	Dinwiddie	Ms J. Williamson
518	93	29		32	24		Broken	Flint	Smyth	J. Creer
519	40	20		25	14		Complete	?	Tazewell	T. George
520	41	23	8	18	16		Complete	Quartzite	Dinwiddie	G. Stanford
521	31	16	5	15	14		Broken	Chalcedony	Dinwiddie	P. Hearne
522	75	28	8	30	20		Complete	Slate	Greensville	H. Bowney
523	77	32	7	20	15		Broken	Chalcedony	Dinwiddie	J. McAvoy
524	44	28	8	12	0		Broken	Quartzite	Newport News	R. Becker

POINT_NUM	LENGTH	WIDTH	THICK	FLUT_LEN_1	FLUT_LEN_2	WGT	CONDITION	MATERIAL	COUNTY_CTY	INIT_OWNER
525	34	33	9	20	20		Broken	Quartz	Dinwiddie	P. Perkinson
526	39	25	7	6	0		Broken	Quartzite	Dinwiddie	Phil Perkinson
527	39	23	6	17	4		Broken	Slate	Dinwiddie	P. Perkinson
528	42	26		12	9		Broken	Quartz	Dinwiddie	VMI
529	49	24		16	16		Complete	Chert	Petersburg	VMI
530	51	22		22	14		Complete	Chert	Petersburg	VMI
531	66	27	6	27	17		Complete	Chalcedony	Nansemond	J. McAvoy
532	47	19	5	11			Complete	?	King George	M. Hastings
533	42	28	7	15	13		Complete	Chert	Smyth	B. McCary
534	56	27	7	15	15		Complete	Greenstone	Dinwiddie	B. McCary
535	45	20	5	24	22		Complete	Chert	Lunenburg	B. McCary
536	64	20	6	33	32		Complete	Chert	Lee	B. McCary
537	38	29	9	22	20		Broken	Chalcedony	Greensville	W. Allgood
538	76	35	9	29	27		Broken	Chalcedony	Brunswick	W. Allgood
539	62	27	8	20	10		Complete	Jasper	Mecklenburg	W. Allgood
540	51	23	6	13	7		Complete	Chalcedony	Greensville	W. Allgood
541	43	24	7	14	9		Complete	Quartz	Sussex	W. Allgood
542	61	21	7	20	15		Complete	Jasper	Greensville	W. Allgood
543	74	31	9	15	13		Complete	Quartzite	Prince George	W. Allgood
544	52	23	7	13	8		Complete	Quartzite	Sussex	W. Allgood
545	58	27	8	19	18		Complete	Jasper	Sussex	W. Allgood
546	49	23	8	17	14		Complete	Chert	Greensville	W. Allgood
547	53	21	6	19	9		Complete	Chalcedony	Sussex	W. Allgood
548	69	26	10	19	15		Complete	Chert	Sussex	W. Allgood
549	81	38	8	21	11		Broken	Slate	Lunenburg	W. Allgood

POINT_NUM	LENGTH	WIDTH	THICK	FLUT_LEN_1	FLUT_LEN_2	WGT	CONDITION	MATERIAL	COUNTY_CTY	INIT_OWNER
550	108	31	10	35	17		Complete	Chert	Mathews	B. McCary
551	47	29	7	25	13		Complete	Flint	Giles	B. McCary
552	13	23	4.5	11	11		Broken	Chalcedony	Giles	B. McCary
553	63	30	7	25	17		Complete	Chert	Hanover	T. Lipscome
554	55	26	8	31	24		Complete	Chalcedony	Greensville	W. Jarratt
555	65	27	8	30	21		Complete	Chalcedony	Sussex	W. Rae
556	48	24	5	40	40		Broken	Slate	Suffolk	E. Bottoms
557	70	31	7	20	13		Complete	Slate	Chesapeake	E. Bottoms
558	46	32	8	29	9		Broken	Quartzite	Nansemond	E. Bottoms
559	46	24	5	12	11		Complete	Slate	Nansemond	E. Bottoms
560	52	24	7	17	13		Complete	Chalcedony	Dinwiddie	E. Bottoms
561	30	20	7	13	7		Broken	Rhyolite	Nansemond	E. Bottoms
562	47	27	8	10	0		Complete	Chert	Washington	E. Bottoms
563	44	31	6	12	11		Broken	Jasper	Chesapeake	E. Bottoms
564	40	26	9	25	23		Broken	Quartzite	Dinwiddie	E. Bottoms
565	109	36	7.5	34	18		Complete	Rhyolite	Buckingham	J. McAvoy
566	22	26	3.5	18	14	0	Broken	Jasper	Newport News	T. Barnes
567	48	21	9	18	16		Complete	Quartz	Appomattox	D. Merkey/J. Rigby
568	98	31	9	19	12		Broken	Chert	Halifax	S. Brooks
569	96	30	7	35	14		Broken	Rhyolite	Halifax	S. Brooks
570	84	30	7	31	20		Complete	Slate	Halifax	S. Brooks
571	56	29	7	21	11		Complete	Chert	Halifax	S. Brooks
572	44	26	6	29	20		Broken	Rhyolite	Halifax	S. Brooks
573	77	28	6	27	14		Broken	Chert	Halifax	S. Brooks
574	24	14	4	22	0		Complete	Chalcedony	Dinwiddie	J. Melchor

POINT_NUM	LENGTH	WIDTH	THICK	FLUT_LEN_1	FLUT_LEN_2	WGT	CONDITION	MATERIAL	COUNTY_CTY	INIT_OWNER
575	56	26	7	22	18		Complete	Slate	Brunswick	J. Melchor
576	20	26	6	10	9		Broken	Quartz	Dinwiddie	B. McCary/ J Melchor
577	32	14	5	11	10		Complete	Chert	Washington	T. Merrihue
578	75	28		46	44		Complete	Chert	Scott	H. Price
579	42	23	6	23	17		Broken	Chert	Gloucester	G. Hall
580	61	25	6.5	31	26		Broken	Rhyolite	Campbell	J. McAvoy
581	54	29	11	21	14		Broken	Quartzite	Sussex	J. McAvoy
582	46	22	5	40	40		Complete	Jasper	Tazewell	J. McAvoy
583	45	28	10	27	20		Broken	Quartzite	Greensville	J. McAvoy
584	51	25	7.5	30	26		Complete	Chert	Dinwiddie	J. McAvoy
585	15	19	3.5	13	0		Broken	Chalcedony	Dinwiddie	J. McAvoy
586	42	20	7	0	0		Complete	Chert	Chesterfield	R. Gwinn
587	46	23	8	17	12		Complete	Quartzite	Dinwiddie	Col Wm & Mary
588	19	25	8	18	16		Broken	Quartz	Dinwiddie	Col Wm & Mary
589	62	29	7	14	0		Broken	Chert	Prince George	Col Wm & Mary
590	31	20	9	14	11		Complete	Quartz	Westmoreland	J. Curts
591	30	22	4	8	3		Broken	Quartzite	York	G. Bittner
592	79	25	7	15	15		Broken	Slate	Buckingham	E. Callahan
593	87	30	11	17	15		Complete	Jasper	Gloucester	G. Sally
594	63	24	6	25	25		Complete	Chert	Mathews	Ms A. Tanner
595	83	28	6	16	13		Complete	Chalcedony	Rockbridge	Ms W. Rorrer
596	32	31	7	20	19		Broken	Qyartzite	Chesapeake	E. Bottoms
597	41	23	7	19	12		Complete	Quartzite	Mecklenburg	E. Bottoms
598	48	26	7	26	24		Complete	Jasper	Rockingham	R. Barnes
599	90	30	9.8	34	27		Complete	Jasper	Lancaster	I. Kellam

POINT_NUM	LENGTH	WIDTH	THICK	FLUT_LEN_1	FLUT_LEN_2	WGT	CONDITION	MATERIAL	COUNTY_CTY	INIT_OWNER
600	47	24	7	15	15		Broken	Chert	Dinwiddie	G. Stanford
601	41	23	6	17	17		Complete	Quartz	Albermarle	B. McCary
602	60	25	6	33	13		Complete	Chert	Mecklenburg	B. McCary
603	45	22	9	19	12		Complete	Quartz	Dinwiddie	B. McCary
604	58	28	8	12	9		Broken	Quartzite	Nasemond	E. Bottoms
605	55	30	10	14	6		Broken	Quartzite	Sussex	E. Bottoms
606	53	37	9	32	6		Broken	Quartzite	Sussex	E. Bottoms
607	35	26	6	11	9		Complete	Quartzite	Sussex	E. Bottoms
608	32	30	6	17	9		Broken	Quartzite	Southampton	E. Bottoms
609	34	22	9	13	11		Broken	Quartzite	Isle of Wight	E. Bottoms
610	50	25	14	15	14		Complete	Quartzite	Isle of Wight	E. Bottoms
611	58	29	8	21	10		Broken	Chalcedony	Chesapeake City	A. Halstead
612	68	24	7	27	23		Complete	Slate	Brunswick	H. Bowney
613	74	28	7	22	19		Complete	Chert	Charlotte	H. Bowney
614	70	29	8	22	7		Broken	Slate	Greensville	J. Simmons
615	64	28	6	26	15		Complete	Chert	Franklin	W. Brooks
616	64	25	6	13	10		Complete	Slate	Franklin	W. Brooks
617	71	24	7	24	12		Complete	Chalcedony	York	B. McCary
618	44	21	7	24	14		Broken	Quartz	Dinwiddie	B. McCary
619	74	28	7	45	31		Broken	Chert	Grayson	B. McCary
620	36	23	5	21	18		Broken	Slate	Mecklenburg	J. Pritchard
621	66	23	6	13	6		Complete	Shale	Southampton	J. Pritchard
622	17	26	6	11	11		Broken	Quartz	Mathews	K. Bergdoll
623	51	30	8	20	20		Broken	Chert	?	R. Hertzler
624	42	28	11	8	0		Complete	Quartzite	Mathews	R. Carmean

POINT_NUM	LENGTH	WIDTH	THICK	FLUT_LEN_1	FLUT_LEN_2	WGT	CONDITION	MATERIAL	COUNTY_CTY	INIT_OWNER
625	40	20	5	29	24		Complete	Chert	Mathews	W. Carmean
626	51	28	7	23	21		Complete	Chalcedony	Dinwiddie	H. Conover
627	59	30	8	19	17		Complete	Chert	Dinwiddie	G. Stanford
628	55	24	6.5	22	14		Complete	Chert	Dinwiddie	G. Stanford
629	71	29	7	8	7		Broken	Chalcedony	Sussex	J. McAvoy
630	20	25	5	18	18		Broken	Chalcedony	Sussex	J. McAvoy
631	61	23	6	12	0		Complete	Rhyolite	Sussex	J. McAvoy
632	49	29	7	28	19		Complete	Jasper	Shennandoah	J. Crawford
633	35	28	7	20	20		Broken	Chert	Greensville	W. Boney
634	38	24	5	27	22		Complete	Jasper	Gloucester	J. Lewandowski
635	91	34	7	26	13		Complete	?	Rockingham	J. Harter
636	33	22	7	21	19		Broken	Jasper	Chesterfield	J. Livesay
637	16	26	5	13	8		Broken	Chert	Roanoke	J. Coffey
638	33	16	4	8	6		Complete	Chalcedony	Roanoke	D. Vogt
639	39	30	6	23			Broken	Chert	Orange	J. Hale
640	44	23	6	21	20		Broken	Slate	Sussex	J. Pritchard
641	51	23	5	19	18		Complete	Chalcedony	Smyth	R. Peck
642	35	30	8	22	13		Broken	Quartzite	Nansemond	R. Peck
643	32	23	6	23	12		Broken	Chalcedony	Dinwiddie	R. Peck
644	30	18	5	8	17		Complete	Chalcedony	Dinwiddie	R. Peck
645	27	14	5	14	0		Complete	Chalcedony	Dinwiddie	R. Peck
646	65	30	6	23	24		Complete	Chalcedony	Dinwiddie	R. Peck
647	85	28	8	25	25		Broken	Chalcedony	Dinwiddie	R. Peck
648	52	30	9	16	17		Broken	Quartzite	Sussex	B. Peck
649	45	22	8	20	17		Complete	Quartz	Mecklenburg	R. Peck/Capehart

POINT_NUM	LENGTH	WIDTH	THICK	FLUT_LEN_1	FLUT_LEN_2	WGT	CONDITION	MATERIAL	COUNTY_CTY	INIT_OWNER
650	54	26	6	24	18		Complete	Flint	Smyth	R. Peck
651	99	37	8	13	13		Complete	Flint	Washington	R. Peck
652	55	27	7	16	14		Complete	Chalcedony	Isle of Wight	R. Peck
653	51	25	5	27	9		Broken	Shale	Isle of Wight	R. Peck
654	43	19	7	12	18		Complete	Chalcedony	Isle of Wight	R. Peck
655	43	23	6	0	9		Complete	Quartz	Isle of Wight	R. Peck
656	40	24	7	15	13		Complete	Chrome ore	Isle of Wight	R. Peck
657	35	27	10	14	12		Complete	Quartzite	Isle of Wight	R. Peck
658	42	19	7	20	0		Complete	Chalcedony	Isle of Wight	R. Peck
659	35	25	6	15	15		Complete	Chalcedony	Isle of Wight	R. Peck
660	33	21	8	0	6		Broken	Quartzite	Isle of Wight	R. Peck
661	39	39	11	18	5		Broken	Quartzite	Isle of Wight	R. Peck\ F. Lane
662	24	17	5	10	11		Complete	Quartz	Dinwiddie	R. Peck
663	45	22	5	37	37		Complete	Agate	Smyth	E. Callicutt
664	33	16	4	9	9		Broken	Chert	Roanoke	J. Gilliam
665	54	30	8	17	15		Complete	Chert	Dinwiddie	G. Mason
666	57	21	6	20	14		Broken	Slate	Greensville	W. Stone
666.1	57.5	22	7	22	15			Slate		Will Stone
667	111	28	8	35	31		Complete	Slate	Brunswick	S. Wall
668	47	16	6	15	13		Broken	Chert	Southampton	G. Callaway
669	36	19	5	10	6		Complete	Chert	Greensville	G. Callaway
670	88	26	7	21	8		Broken	Chert	Botetourt	Ms J. Wilson
671	50	22	7	11	0		Complete	Quartzite	Nansemond	J. Pritchard
672	98	37	8	14	11		Broken	?	Nansemond	P. Perkinson
673	69	26	8	27	23		Broken	Chalcedony	Gloucester	E. Bottoms

POINT_NUM	LENGTH	WIDTH	THICK	FLUT_LEN_1	FLUT_LEN_2	WGT	CONDITION	MATERIAL	COUNTY_CTY	INIT_OWNER
674	18	26	7	15	15		Broken	?	Greensville	D. Price
675	24	18	3	0	0		Broken	?	Dinwiddie	Ms J. Williamson
676	59	26	7	43	32		Broken	Chert	Amherst	J. McAvoy
677	75	22	7	25	17		Broken	Chert	Mathews	G. Morgan
678	40	19		18	15		Complete	Quartz	Virginia Beach	Annoynous
679	60	23	7	22	12		Broken	Flint	Amelia	T. Barnard
680	46	24	6	23	15		Broken	Rhyolite	Mathews	W. Gerald
681	48	26	6	17	17		Broken	Jasper	Amelia	B. Arrington
682	39	21	6	20		1	Complete	Flint	Amelia	T. Barnard
683	37	17	3	12	11		Complete	Chert	Dinwiddie	Ms J. Moncure
684	36	19	5	19	13		Complete	Chalcedony	Dinwiddie	M. Parson
685	52	23	6	20	17		Complete	Chalcedony	Greensville	M. Parson
686	21	26	6	16	16		Broken	Chalcedony	Dinwiddie	M. Lilley
687	30	22	6	14	13		Broken	Slate	Greensville	H. Bowney
688	60	24	6	22	19		Complete	Rhyolite	Fairfax	H. Bowney
689	41	22	6	27	26		Complete	Rhyolite	Gloucester	R. Sindle
690	48	24	5.5	8	10		Complete	Jasper	?	VRCA
691	35	21	8	12	9		Complete	Quartz	Isle of Wight	C. Thomas
692	46	25	6	23	20		Complete	Chalcedony	Sussex	C. Owen
693	51	21	6	21	6		Complete	Chalcedony	Greensville	E. Starke
694	49	24	5	41	20		Complete	Jasper	Sussex	E. Starke
695	45	36	6	20	11		Complete	Slate	Mecklenburg	L. Kindley
696	32	26	7	15	14		Broken	Rhyolite	Halifax	R. Dabbs
697	32	27	5.5	16	12		Broken	Chalcedony	Halifax	R. Dabbs
698	23	26	6	16	16		Broken	Slate	Halifax	R. Dabbs

POINT_NUM	LENGTH	WIDTH	THICK	FLUT_LEN_1	FLUT_LEN_2	WGT	CONDITION	MATERIAL	COUNTY_CTY	INIT_OWNER
699	19	25	7	13	13		Broken	Quartz	Halifax	R. Dabbs
700	62	26	6	12	10		Complete	Chalcedony	Dinwiddie	M. Lilley
701	54	27	6	19	15		Broken	Chalcedony	Dinwiddie	B. McCary
702	71	25	6	15	15		Complete	Rhyolite	Dinwiddie	R. Dabbs
703	42	23	6	27	14		Complete	Rhyolite	Halifax	R. Dabbs
704	68	32	7	19	14		Complete	Slate	Patrick	R. Dabbs
705	35	26	7.5	28	12	2	Broken	Quartz	Accomac	VRCA
706	57	27	7	27	13		Broken	Chert	Pulaski	H. Hubble
707	59	29	9	26	13		Complete	Quartz	Mecklenburg	W. Hudgins
708	40	23	6	19			Broken	Quartz	Mecklenburg	W. Hudgins
709	42	20	5	12	9		Complete	Chalcedony	Mecklenburg	W. Hudgins
710	38	22	7	16	11		Complete	Quartz	Mecklenburg	W. Hudgins
711	36	22	5	17	11		Complete	Chert/chalcedony	Mecklenburg	W. Hudgins
712	31	19	4	19	9		Complete	Chert	Mecklenburg	W. Hudgins
713	65	27	6	31	18		Complete	Chert	Mecklenburg	W. Hudgins
714	51	22	7	30	25		Complete	Pertified wood	Mecklenburg	W. Hudgins
715	33	20	5	18	9		Broken	Chalcedony	Nansemond	J. Pritchard
716	23	26	7	21	12		Broken	Chalcedony	Nansemond	J. Pritchard
717	21	21	5	11	10	2.5	Broken	Chalcedony	Greensville	H. Bowney
718	37	22	6	27	26		Complete	Jasper	Nansemond	C. Thomas
719	63	27	7	28	26		Complete	Chert	Mecklenburg	H. Bowney
720	37	20	6	24	18		Complete	Quartz	Dinwiddie	H. Bowney
721	47	22	6	20	14		Complete	Quartz	Buckingham	G. Lightfoot
722	86	27	7	21	19		Complete	Chert	Pittsylvania	R. Dabbs
723	86	30	7	30	25		Broken	Chert	Pittsylvania	R. Dabbs

POINT_NUM	LENGTH	WIDTH	THICK	FLUT_LEN_1	FLUT_LEN_2	WGT	CONDITION	MATERIAL	COUNTY_CTY	INIT_OWNER
724	70	27	7	33	25		Broken	Chert	Pittsylvania	R. Dabbs
725	54	30	6	20	17		Complete	Chalcedony	Greensville	H. Bowney
726	30	17	5	12	10		Complete	Chalcedony	Greensville	H. Bowney
727	30	18	5	14	9		Complete	Chert	Southampton	H. Bowney
728	62	31	8	28	23		Broken	Quartz	Sussex	M. Lilley
729	55	26	7	15	12		Complete	Chalcedony	Dinwiddie	H. Conover
730	52	22	6	21	16		Complete	Chert	Franklin	J. Childs
731	108	34	10	53	51		Broken	Jasper	Northampton	J. Cowan
732	31	22	5	19	17		Broken	Jasper	Chesapeake	J. Pritchard
733	48	24	6	48	37		Broken	Quartzite	Suffolk	Ms F. Gaddis
734	47	23	8	9	6		Complete	Chert	Dinwiddie	H. Bowney
735	46	23	5.5	15	12		Complete	Chert	Halifax	H. Boney
736	45	21	6	20	18		Complete	Chalcedony	Amelia	H. Bowney
737	56	24	8	12	12		Complete	Quartzite	Suffolk	J. Pritchard
738	45	17	4	20	10		Complete	Quartz	Mecklenburg	L. Carter
739	35	16	3.5	12	10		Broken	Chalcedony	Mecklenburg	L. Carter
740	70	25	6.5	25			Broken	Chert	Mecklenburg	L. Carter
741	83	28	7	23	16		Complete	Chert	Mecklenburg	L. Carter
742	62	32	5	11	0		Broken	Slate	Mecklenburg	L. Carter
743	38	27	7	10	10		Complete	Chert	Mecklenburg	L. Carter
744	46	26	8	41	39		Broken	Chert	Mecklenburg	L. Carter
745	39	21	3	7	6		Broken	Chalcedony	Mecklenburg	L. Carter
746	57	22	7	14	13		Broken	Quartzite	Mecklenburg	L. Carter
747	40	20	6	8	7		Complete	Quartz	Mecklenburg	L. Carter
748	138.5	30	8	53	46		Complete	Chert	Roanoke	L. Carter

POINT_NUM	LENGTH	WIDTH	THICK	FLUT_LEN_1	FLUT_LEN_2	WGT	CONDITION	MATERIAL	COUNTY_CTY	INIT_OWNER
749	48	25	5.5	12	0		Complete	Quartz	Mecklenburg	L. Carter
750	45	20	8	23	0		Complete	Quartz	Mecklenburg	J. Pittard
751	35	25	8	21	0		Complete	Shale	Chesterfield	D. Pond
752	66	31	7	17	17		Complete	Chalcedony	Washington	R. Peck
753	27	18	4	9	7		Complete	Flint	Washington	R. Peck
754	37	25	5	16	0		Complete	Flint	Washington	R. Peck
755	56	25	7	33	26		Broken	Chalcedony	Sussex	R. Peck
756	71	31	8	39	15		Complete	Chalcedony	Dinwiddie	R. Peck
757	59	26	7	16	7		Complete	Chalcedony	Dinwiddie	R. Peck
758	55	26	7	25	25		Complete	Chalcedony	Dinwiddie	R. Peck
759	23	29	7	20	20		Broken	Chalcedony	Dinwiddie	R. Peck
760	75	24	7	16	15		Complete	Jasper	Franklin	R. Peck
761	63	23	8	17.5	16		Complete	Jasper/Chert	Mecklenburg	C. Talley
762	35	26	5	15	9		Broken	Chert	Washington	Z. Weatherly
763	46	23	5.5	8	6		Complete	Flint	Washington	C. Bartlett
764	23	25	6				Broken	Flint	Washington	C. Herndon
765	45	25	3	12.5	10.5		Complete	Chalcedony	York	J. Melchor
766	44	30	6	25	12		Complete	Chert	Surry	J. Melchor
767	37	24	3.5	15	10		Complete	Jasper	Dinwiddie	B. McCary
768	38	30	8	22	12		Complete	Quartz	Dinwiddie	B. McCary
769	10	20	3	9			Broken	Chert	Smyth	J McDonald
770	50	25	10	25	14		Complete	Jasper	Mecklenburg	L. Carter
771	59	29	8	15	10		Complete	Quartzite	Portsmouth	E. Bottoms
772	38	22	8	14	13		Complete	Chert ?	Bedford	W. Childress
773	47	25	7	18	12		Broken	Chalcedony	Mecklenburg	R. Densmore

POINT_NUM	LENGTH	WIDTH	THICK	FLUT_LEN_1	FLUT_LEN_2	WGT	CONDITION	MATERIAL	COUNTY_CTY	INIT_OWNER
774	21	22	4.5	9	0		Broken	Flint	Giles	R. Stables
775	116	37	10	52	42		Complete	Quartzite	York	W. Gusler
776	62	21.5	6.5	19	19		Broken	Chalcedony	Sussex	J. Lilley
777	20	26	4	14	14		Broken	Flint	Washington	C. Bartlett
778	36	19	5	34	14		Complete	Chert	Dinwiddie	M. Conover
779	44	22	7	26	12		Complete	Quartz	Dinwiddie	W. Boney
780	42	22	6	26	21		Complete	Chalcedony	Greensville	H. Boney
781	85	31	6	47	43		Complete	Chert	Virginia	D. Rose
782	46	23	3.5	10	9		Broken	Flint	Southampton	H. Bowney
783	20	27	6	14	9		Broken	Quartzite	Isle of Wight	E. Bottoms
784	51	22	4	15	13		Complete	Chert	Lee	D. Harless
785	19	16	4	14	10		Broken	Chert	Roanoke	D. Coffey
786	59	32	6	15	0		Broken	Flint	Franklin	H. Smith
787	35	24	7	14	8		Complete	Chalcedony	Franklin	H. Smith
788	33	27	7	10	0		Broken	Quartz	Bedford	H. Smith
789	46	20	5.5	15	0		Complete	Slate	Mecklenburg	W. Allgood
790	43	16	5	19	10		Complete	Chalcedony	Jamestown	W. Eggleston
791	21	16	5	9	9		Broken mplete	Chert	Newport News	W. Eggleston
792	57	24					Complete	Flint-like	?	Amer Mus of Nat Hist
793	42	25	8	10	10		Broken	Quartz	Bedford	T. Smith
794	23	23	7.5	14	12		Broken	Quartz	Bedford	H. Smith
795	32	20	6	14	6		Complete	Quartzite	Mecklenburg	B. McCary
796	53	23	4.5	34	24		Complete	Slate	Caroline	J. Pritchard
797	59	29	10	13	13		Broken	Quartzite	Sussex	E. Bottoms
798	63	37	6.5	54	54		Broken	Slate	Culpeper	C. Norton

POINT_NUM	LENGTH	WIDTH	THICK	FLUT_LEN_1	FLUT_LEN_2	WGT	CONDITION	MATERIAL	COUNTY_CTY	INIT_OWNER
799	40	26	3	35	25		Broken	Slate	Greensville	E. Conner
800	68	30	8	19	18		Complete	Chalcedony	Dinwiddie	R. Adkins
801	38	20	6	21	15		Complete	Chert	Nansemond	G. Ramsey
802	25	30	6	19			Broken	Chert	Lee	J. Griffith
803	57	25	6.5	10			Complete	Chert	Roanoke	J. Crockett
804	56	27	6	30	6		Complete	Jasper	Northumberland	Anonymous
805	49	25	6	39	30		Complete	Chert	Brunswick	H. Bowney
806	39	20	7	11	6		B	Quartzite	Spotslyvania	T. Scott
807	53	29	8	26	14		Complete	Jasper	Sussex	J. Goldbery
808	88	35	12	28	25		Complete	Quartz	Surry	J. Goldberg
809	61	27	7	37	27		Complete	Chert	Carroll	J. Goldberg
810	65	28	11	20	20		Complete	Quartz	Patrick	J. Goldberg
811	70	29	8	25	21		Complete	Chert	Wise	J. Goldberg
812	62	26	8	22	22		Complete	Chert	Dinwiddie	J. Goldberg
813	55	23	6	12	12		Complete	Petrified wood	Dinwiddie	J. Goldberg
814	50	24	8	10			Complete	Quartzite	Dinwiddie	J. Goldberg
815	17	23	4	12	12		Broken	Jasper	Mathews	G. Bittner
816	38	25	6.5	15	11		Complete	Quartzite	Mathews	D. Hooley
817	54	25	7	25	18		Complete	Chalcedony	Dinwiddie	R. Adkins
818	50	23	7	26	21		Complete	Slate	Greensville	H. Bowney
819	21	22	6	15	14		Broken	Quartz	Franklin	W. Brooks
820	45	26	5	27	22		Broken	Slate	Nansemond	J. Byrd
821	52	25	7	15	12		Complete	Chalcedony	Chesterfield	G. Blankenship
822	61	26	6	16	16		Complete	Chalcedony	Mecklenburg	R. Worley
823	23	20	5.5	25	10		Complete	Quartz	Greensville	H. Boney

POINT_NUM	LENGTH	WIDTH	THICK	FLUT_LEN_1	FLUT_LEN_2	WGT	CONDITION	MATERIAL	COUNTY_CTY	INIT_OWNER
824	43	24	6	11	11		Broken	Slate	Bedford	T. Carwie
825	32	24	7	15	15		Broken	Quartz	Franklin	H. Smith
826	30	24	6	11	11		Broken	Quartz	Gloucester	L. Wass
827	52	25	6	20	12		Complete	Chert	Smyth	S. Hambrick
828	24	27	5	17	17		Broken	Chalcedony	Greensville	H. Boney
829	40	21	6	15	12		Complete	Chalcedony	Southampton	W. Stone
830	45	20	6	20	8		Complete	Slate	Dinwiddie	H. Conover
831	54	22	9	21	15		Complete	Chalcedony	Bedford	R. Key
832	40	22	4.5	15	0		Broken	Flint	Floyd	D. Quesenberry
833	20	25	6	15	17		Broken	Chert	Greensville	H. MacCord
834	52	22	6	14	14		Broken	Shale	Suffolk	J. Pritchard
835	55	23	7	13	10		Complete	Quartzite	Charlotte	G. Clark
836	41	22	5.5	18	8		Complete	Chalcedony	Prince Edward	F. Nunnally
837	38	21	5	21	14		Broken	Chalcedony	Powhatan	H. Boney
838	60	22	7	27	25		Complete	Slate	Sussex	H. Boney
839	45	22	8	14	8		Complete	Quartz	Charlotte	L. Perkins
840	60	25	8	18	17		Complete	Chalcedony	Sussex	M. Jones
841	27	16	5	19	11		Broken	Chalcedony	Sussex	E. Bottoms
842	16	20	5	12	7		Broken	Slate	Suffolk	E. Bottoms
843	45	21	7	22	20		Complete	Slate	Suffolk	E. Bottoms
844	48	22	7	17	12		Complete	Flint	Hanover	E. Bottoms
845	76	40	10	19	14		Complete	Quartz	Suffolk	E. Bottoms
846	56	35	5	25	12		Broken	quartzite	Campbell	B. Newman
847	59	27	7	15	12		Complete	Chalcedony	Greensville	H. Boney
848	73	22	7	32	21		Complete	Chert	Dinwiddie	D. Collins

POINT_NUM	LENGTH	WIDTH	THICK	FLUT_LEN_1	FLUT_LEN_2	WGT	CONDITION	MATERIAL	COUNTY_CTY	INIT_OWNER
849	43	19	5	27	15		Complete	Flint	Washington	P. Baker
850	30	22	5	30	30		Broken	?	Washington	P. Baker
851	40	24	5	18	12		Complete	Chalcedony	Goochland	P. Turpin
852	95	30	10	22.5	9		Complete	Quartz	Fairfax	D. Rubis
853	74	28	8	35	40		Complete	Chert	Fairfax	J. Brazier
854	60	25	7	50	36		Complete	Chert	Fort Belvoir	Fairfax County
855	26	28	6	22	13		Broken	Chert	Fairfax	Fairfax County
856	12	20	5	12	11		Broken	Quartz	Fairfax	Fairfax County
857	79	29.5	10	20	0		Broken	Jasper	Warren	Thunderbird Res
858	74.5	33	8	29	20		Broken	Jasper	Warren	Thunderbird Res
859	94.5	33	9	28	26		Broken	Jasper	Warren	Thunderbird Res
860	74	31	8	25	23		Broken	Jasper	Warren	Tunderbird Res
861	84.5	32	7.5	33	31		Broken	Jasper	Warren	Thunderbird Res
862	43	32	7.5	40	33		Broken	Jasper	Warren	Tunderbird Res
863	42	34	10	38	0		Broken	Jasper	Warren	Tunderbird Res
864	30	22	6	13	12		Broken	Chalcedony	Warren	Tunderbird Res
865	27.5	19	5	24	22		Complete	Chert	Warren	Tunderbirs Res
866	42	27.5	7	18	17		Broken	Jasper	Warren	Thunderbird Res
867	64	26	8.5	22.5	19		Broken	Jasper	Warren	Tunderbird Res
868	46	19	6		15		Complete	Chert	Mathews	M. Small
869	29	23	5	18	11		Broken	Slate	Surry	VFAR
870	41	34	10	35	40		Broken	Chert	Surry	VFAR
871	64	25.5	8.5				Broken	Chert	Surry	VFAR
872	46	31	6.5		0		Broken	Jasper	Loudoun	American

POINT_NUM	LENGTH	WIDTH	THICK	FLUT_LEN_1	FLUT_LEN_2	WGT	CONDITION	MATERIAL	COUNTY_CTY	INIT_OWNER
873	46	31	6.5				Broken	Brown	Loudoun	American University
874	115	31	7	48	24		Broken	Chert	Caroline	S. Hall
875	38	21.5	6.5	32	19		Broken	Chert	Culpepper	H. Crouch
876		25	8.5			8.5	Broken	Chert	Fairfax	G. DeMarr
877	58	30	9	23	23		Complete	Quartz	Pittsylvania	K. White
878	52	22	6.5	20	24		Complete	Slate	Sussex	R. Joyner
879	42.9	20	6	16		5.4	Complete	Jasper	Smyth	K. Hayden
880	45.5	20	7	12	8	7.6	Broken	Quartzite	Warren	E. Wilkison
881	45	27	6	11	17		Complete	Slate	Pittsylvania	M. Haley
882	32	21	8	14	12	5.1	Complete	Quartz	Prince William	J. Hall
883	32	16.5	5.5	22	21	0	Broken	Chert	Surry	L. Gregory - VFAR
884	44	17.5	6	19	1.7	0	Complete	Jasper	Mathews	M. Small
885	33	24.5	7.5	9	14	6.1	Complete	Quartz	Washington	L. Price
886		0	0		0	4	Broken	Rhyolite	Henry	J Childs
887		18	7		15	4.7	Broken	Chert	Smyth	H. Hayes
888							Broken	Chalcedony	Loudoun	P. Keefe
889	51.1	25	7	21	20	10.9	Complete	Chert	Prince George	S. Speedy
890	56	28	7	17	16		Complete	Chert	Pittsylvania	L. Powell
891	44.5	25	10	15	24		Complete	Quartzite	Dinwiddie	E. Ellington
892	27.5	27	7.5	17	12	4.9	Broken	Rhyolite	Wythe	E. Branham
893	27.5	20	4.5	24	6	2.8	Broken	Quartzite-ortho	Isle of Wight	VDHR
894	52	27	11.5	10	13		Complete	Rhyolite	Dinwiddie	D. Collins
895	44	18	7	20	19		Complete	Chert	Sussex	J. McAvoy
896	40	22	6.5	22	17	5.8	Complete	Quartzite	Sussex	J. McAvoy

POINT_NUM	LENGTH	WIDTH	THICK	FLUT_LEN_1	FLUT_LEN_2	WGT	CONDITION	MATERIAL	COUNTY_CTY	INIT_OWNER
897	20	27	5.5	12.5	12.5	3.5	Broken	Chert	Pittsylvania	B. Childress
898	34	23	4.5	22	7		Broken	Rhyolite	Chesterfield	J. McAvoy
899	40.5	31	9	10	0	10.7	Broken	Jasper	Chesterfield	VDHR
900	35.5	18	7	16	16	4.6	Complete	Quartzite-ortho	Stafford	VDHR
901	61	27	7	23	16	14.1	Complete	Chert	Caroline	VDHR
902	97	27.5	9	30	16		Broken	Chalcedony	Surry	VFAR
903	54	25.5	8	31	19	14.5	Broken	Jasper	Clark	Clark Historic Soc
904	17	20.5	4	12	6.5		Broken	Chert	Chesterfield	J. McAvoy
905	33	20	5	15	8.5		Complete	Chert	Sussex	J. McAvoy
906	32.5	23	6	14	25		Complete	Quartz	Albemarle	J. Hranicky
907	32	18	7	12	11		Complete	Quartz	Spotsylvania	J. Hranicky
908	57	27	10	0	9		Broken	Chert	Sussex	J. McAvoy
909	28	16.5	7	12	14		Broken	Quartz	Dinwiddie	J. McAvoy
910	105	31	8	34	0		Complete	Rhyolite (?)	Sussex	J. McAvoy
911	29	18	5.5	16	19.5		Complete	Chert	Dinwiddie	J. McAvoy
912	31.5	15	4	0	0		Complete	Chert	Dinwiddie	J. McAvoy
913	76	25.5	10	36	19.5		Complete	Silicified wood	Sussex	J. McAvoy
914	44	25.5	8	11.5	12		Complete	Quartz	Dinwiddie	J. McAvoy
914	64	29	10	12	18	19.6	Broken	Ool. Chert	Washington	Jane Noonkester
915	62	31	7	45	25	15.4	Complete	Chert	Suffolk	D. Sweet
916	37.5	17	5.5	6.5	11		Broken	Quartzite-ortho	Greenville	J. McAvoy
917	36	22	5	25.5	29		Complete	Chert (?)	Dinwiddie	J. McAvoy
918	52.5	28	11	27	20.5		Complete	Quartzite	Sussex	J. McAvoy
919	40	31	8.5	20	30		Broken	Rhyolite	Chesterfield	J. McAvoy

POINT_NUM	LENGTH	WIDTH	THICK	FLUT_LEN_1	FLUT_LEN_2	WGT	CONDITION	MATERIAL	COUNTY_CTY	INIT_OWNER
920	48	31	8.5	20	30		Broken	Chalcedony	Dinwiddie	J. McAvoy
921	67	20	6	10	29	12.7	Complete	Sil. Tuff	Mecklenburg	Steve Pool
922	53	27	7	21	16	10.4	Complete	Chert	Mecklenburg	Thomas Pool
923	54	20.5	6.5	22	11	9	Complete	Sil. Tuff?	Mecklenburg	Jerry Pool
924	38	22	8	18	21	8.5	Broken	Crystal Quartz	Mecklenburg	Jerry Pool
925	64	24	7	18	8	11.5	Complete	Chert	Mecklenburg	Joe Pool
926	47	24	6	38	37	7.3	Complete	Sil Tuff	Halifax	Hilton Hudson
927	42	27	8.5	18.5	14.5	14.5	Broken	Chert	Mecklenburg	Loy Carter
928	48	26	7	17	11	8.5	Complete	Sil. Tuff	Mecklenburg	Allen Bass
929	38	27	7	15	26	10.1	Broken	Jasper	Halifax	Jerry Pool
930	36	22	7	17	21.5	4.9	Complete	Othroquartz	Sussex	Bill Barr
931	11	18.5	5	10	9	1.6	Broken	Chert?	Pittsylvania	Bil Childress
932	62	32	9	23.5	28	18	Complete	Chert	Sussex	Annette Bar
933	44	25	7	4	7	8.7	Broken	Chalcedony	Warren	T'Bird Assc.
934	45.5	19	5	12	38	5.1	Complete	Chert	Smyth	Frank Detweiler
935	64	23	6	27	33.5	9.5	Complete	Chert	Smyth	Frank Detweiler
936	19	24	7.5	16	17	3.9	Broken	Jasper	Bedford	Jesse Fifer
937	44.5	24	8.5	12	18	9.4	Broken	Quartz	Bedford	Jesse Fifer
938	49	24	9.5	11	14	9.1	Broken	Jasper	Bedford	Jesse Fifer
939	17	22	7	10	8	3.1	Broken	Rhyolite	Washington	Charles Herndon
940	69	28	8	14	15.5	19.3	Complete	Jasper	Orange	Charles Johnson
941	64	29	10	12	18		Broken	Chert	Washington	J. Noonkester
942	43	22.5	6	8	8	7	Broken	Chalcedony	Bedford	Jesse Fifer
943	69	31	5.5	26	23	15.5	Complete	Chert	Washington	C. Nelson
944	31	19	6			4	Broken	Quartz	Franklin	Jesse Fifer
945	46	24.5	7	12	20	8.3	Complete	Jasper	Loudoun	Ada Conrad

POINT_NUM	LENGTH	WIDTH	THICK	FLUT_LEN_1	FLUT_LEN_2	WGT	CONDITION	MATERIAL	COUNTY_CTY	INIT_OWNER
946	34	30	5.5			9.4			Loudoun	Ada Conrad
947	71	24.5	9	35.5		16.5	Complete	Chert	Rockingham	Anoymous
948	38.5	24	7	13		6	Broken	Quartzite	Franklin	Leon Dudley
949	45	20	12		14.5	9.7	Complete	Quartz	Loudoun	J. Hranicky
950	28	20	6.5	20	19	4.2	Broken	Quartz	Nansemond	J. Hranicky
951	35.5	20	8	15	16	5	Complete	Jasper	Southampton	J. Hranicky
952	52	27	8			18.6	Broken	Quartzite	Sussex	Ed Bottoms
953	51.5	21	7.5	7	12.5	8.3	Broken	Quartzite	Isle of Wight	Ed Bottoms
954	35.5	17.5	7.5	10.5	13	4.6	Complete	Quartz	Suffolk	Ed Bottoms
955	16.5	21	5.5			2.1	Broken	Chert	Suffolk	Ed Bottoms
956	52	29	12.5		18	21.5	Broken	Quartzite	Suffolk	Ed Bottoms
957	47.5	25	19	17	17	11.1	Broken	Quartz	Suffolk	Ed Bottoms
958	46	19	6		23	6	Complete	Metavolcanic	Suffolk	Ed Bottoms
959	58	33.5	7	18	29	15.5	Broken	Quartzite	Suffolk	Ed Bottoms
960	42.5	18	6	20	28	5.2	Broken	Chert	Suffolk	Ed Bottoms
961	48.5	29	11	24	18.5	17.1	Complete	Quartzite	Greenville	Ed Bottoms
962	70	28.5	10.5			23.8	Complete	Quartz	Greenville	Ed Bottoms
963	32.5	21.5	6			4.8	Complete	Quartzite	Greenville	Ed Bottoms
964	43.5	20	9	14	14	6.6	Complete	Quartzite	Southampton	Ed Bottoms
965	23.5	24.5	8.5	18		5.2	Broken	Quartzite	Southampton	Ed Bottoms
966	42.5	23.5	9	15	15	8.2	Broken	Quartz	Southampton	Ed Bottoms
967	44	25	10	15	18	10.2	Complete	Quartz	Southampton	Ed Bottoms
968	34.5	24	8	12	28	9.1	Broken	Quartzite	Southampton	Ed Bottoms
969	44	19	8.5	11	9	7.3	Complete	Quartz	Southampton	Ed Bottoms
970	66.5	25.5	8.5	11	16	15	Complete	Metavolcanic	Floyd	Ed Bottoms
971	87.5	34	11		37	34.1	Complete	Chert	Dinwiddie	Ed Bottoms

POINT_NUM	LENGTH	WIDTH	THICK	FLUT_LEN_1	FLUT_LEN_2	WGT	CONDITION	MATERIAL	COUNTY_CTY	INIT_OWNER
972	46.5	22	6.5	13		7.8	Complete	Quartzite	Suffolk	George Ransey
973	58.5	26	6.5	22.5	22	10.1	Broken	Quartzite	King William	Dave Johnson
975	44.5	23.5	6.5			8.1	Broken	Quartz	Fairfax	Bob Blackwell
975	49.5	23.5	6.5	30	28	28	Complete	Metavolcani	King William	Dave Johnson
976	57.5	27.5	8	12.5	13	14.4	Complete	Chert	Mathews	Mark Small
977	23	17.5	7.5	10		4.1	Complete	Quartz	Mathews	Mark Small
978	24.5	25	7.5	16	14.5	4.7	Complete	Chert	Gloucester	Mark Small
979	23.5	15	4.5	11.5	18	1.6	Complete	Metavolcanic	Charlotte	L. D. Phaup
980	41	24	8	13.5	18.5	8.1	Complete	Metavolcanic	Charlotte	L. D. Phaup
981	50	20	4.5	39	21	5	Complete	Metavolcanic	Charlotte	L. D. Phaup
982	19.5	18	6.5	9.5	14	3.4	Broken	Quartz	Charlotte	L. D. Phaup
983	88	28	9	18		25.2	Broken	Quartzite	Prince Edward	L. D. Phaup
984	33	19.5	5	9.5	19	19	Complete	Jasper	Fairfax	Pk Authority
985	66.5	26.5	8	46.5	45	45	Complete	Chert	Northampton	David Freeney
986	33.5	37	8.5			9.6	Broken	Chert	Pittsylvania	Bill Childress
987	23.5	26	4.5			3.5	Broken	Agate-like	Pittsylvania	Bill Childress
988	46	23.5	6	19.5		8	Complete	Orthoquartz	Middlesex	Art Ensley
989	29	17	6	15	19	2.5	Complete	Chalcedony	Southampton	Russell Darden
990	49.5	25.5	8	30		13.5	Broken	Chert	Franklin	Harry Smith
991	19	20	5.5	14	12	12	Broken	Chert	Patrick	James Gregson
992	55	24	9.5	16.5	16.5	13.2	Complete	Jasper	Montgomery	Mr. Keister
993	45.5	26.5	7.5	24.5	21.5	10	Complete	Chert	Tazewell	Ralph Hilt
994	57	24	7.5	22.5	24	10.9	Complete	Jasper	Northumberland	Valnora Leister
995	49.5	23	7.5	24	19	8.6	Complete	Chert	Rockbridge	Anonymous
996	24	26	7	18	22.5	5.2	Broken	Orthoquartz	Louisa	Martha Wils
997	27	26	5		20	4.6	Broken	Chert	Washington	Freddie Caudill
998	24.5	23	6	11.5	13.5	3.7	Broken	Chert	Washington	Freddie Caudill

POINT_NUM	LENGTH	WIDTH	THICK	FLUT_LEN_1	FLUT_LEN_2	WGT	CONDITION	MATERIAL	COUNTY_CTY	INIT_OWNER
999	21	23.5	5	15.5	9	3.1	Broken	Chert	Washington	Freddie Caudill
1000	136	36.5	9.5	24	26		Complete	Quartzite	Dinwiddie	Ben McCary

Part Four – McCary Survey Points 1001 to 1055

McCary Fluted Point Survey of Virginia

Wm Jack Hranicky RPA
Survey Director

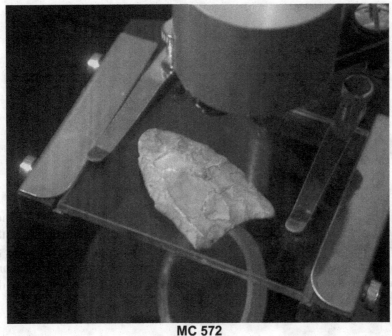

MC 572

Points 1001 to 1055
Special Publication Number 2

31 December 2007

McCary Fluted Point Survey
www.archeology.org
Post Office Box 11256
Alexandria, Virginia 22312
USA

Public Notice: The McCary Fluted Point Survey® of Virginia is an independent nonprofit organization that is not affiliated with any state or federal agency, academic institution, or special interest group or society. It conforms to all state/federal laws concerning prehistoric antiquities. All data, images, and drawings collected by the Survey are part of the public domain and can be used freely. The current Survey director is Wm Jack Hranicky, RPA. The next Survey director will be determined by the Survey Review Committee.

McCary Survey Introduction

Special Publication Number 2 from the McCary Fluted Point Survey of Virginia provides information, data, and metrics for Survey points 1001 to 1054. Each Survey point is described and illustrated. All point data is presented in tables at the end of this publication. Special Publication Number 1 contains points from 1 to 1000 (Hranicky 2008), which represents 60+ years of continuous recording and publishing paleopoints from Virginia. The Survey is an ongoing effort to discover, record, and publish Paleoindian artifacts in Virginia. Survey operational practices, procedures, and practices are published in *A Model for a Paleoindian Fluted Point Survey* (Hranicky 2005). Copies are available from the Survey or on the Survey's website.

The entire McCary Survey is available at: **www.archeology.org**

Survey Purpose

Several amateur and professional archaeologists in Virginia have commented that the McCary Survey should be stopped at 1000 points, and there was no need to continue recording paleopoint data. Perhaps the only comment – this is absolute nonsense. A major objective in American archaeology is to keep searching for more information about the indigenous populations who preceded the Europeans. First case in point, the *classic* study – Louis Brennan's call for all eastern states to report their fluted points (Brennan 1982). Second local case in "point" is the reporting of MC 1040 which establishes a culture in Virginia which was unknown, but suspected, until this publication. These "stop recording" individuals are a joke in American archaeology. The Survey will continue adding data to the national paleopoint database at the University of Tennessee (**Paleoindian Databases of the Americas - PBDA**); its director welcomes Virginia paleopoint data (http://pidba.utk.edu). The release contains:

- Newly-discovered information about the Cumberland point type
- More information about Virginia paleopoint lithic distribution
- Continued morphological studies concerning Virginia paleopoints
- More information about blade technology in Virginia's Paleoindian Period
- Obtaining a Clovis point for the public realm - to be given to the DHR
- Updating L/W*T ratio for Virginia paleopoints
- Blade edge sharpness is introduced to Survey recording and recordkeeping
- Patination evaluation is added
- And importantly, continue the recording tradition of Ben McCary.

Survey Review Committee

The Survey has in place a review committee that determines the acceptability of a paleopoint that was submitted. They are professional and amateur archaeologists, experienced collectors and, sometimes, just interested lay people. Collectively, their opinions are evaluated and a point's acceptance is usually by vote. If you would like to serve on the committee, contact the director.

Submitting Paleopoints

Everyone is invited to submit points which they believe are of Paleoindian origin. The Survey will analyze all submissions and advise owners of what the point represents in prehistory. Only Virginia points are accepted. Hand-to-hand delivery is the best way to submit a point; the same is true for its return. Otherwise, use an insured public carries, such as the Post Office, FedEx, or United Parcel Service. It is not necessary to provide return postage. Figure 1 shows a recent submittal. Please include a written statement telling the Survey everything that you know about the point's discovery and history.

Figure 1 - Recent Survey Submission by B. Perry

Database Applications

The McCary Survey database serves numerous interests in American archaeology. The Survey is among other state surveys, for example, Missouri (Anderson and O'Brian 1998), Florida (Carter, Dunbar, and Anderson 1998), and Iowa (Morrow and Morrow 1994). It is one of the few data acquisition projects in archaeology that transcends numerous activities from collectors to professional archaeologists to historic planners, and to museum personnel. All activities interact among the historic efforts of each activity. While their roles and requirements vary, the Survey is a cornerstone for Paleoindian research in Virginia. It provides:

- Physical artifact evidence for the Paleoindian Period
- Research data for the Paleoindian Period
- Point type distribution
- Lithic curation and sources
- Paleopoint morphological studies
- Interfaces between prehistoric cultures and technology
- Migration and occupation patterns
- Basic model for Paleoindian technology in Virginia.

As the Survey database grows, it provides:
- Users with greater access to increased paleopoint information
- New discoveries leading to updating the archaeological knowledge base
- Greater understanding of the complexity of Paleoindian lifeways
- Interstate relational database studies and research

Fluting vs. Basal Thinning Criteria for Paleopoints

The term fluted may be attributed to H. C. Shetrone of the Ohio State Museum to the late 1930s. Over the years, fluting has become synonymous with Clovis technology, even to become an absolute requirement for the type. The Survey depends on the definition in order to classify points. Hranicky (2004) defines it as:

A channel that extends from the base of a point upwards to the distal end; does not have to be the entire length of the point. Basically, it is a knapping procedure of producing a long narrow flake scar on the long axis of a tool. The flake can be removed by punch, pressure, or percussion flaking.

And, according to Collins (1999):

...an elongate flake scar on the face of certain types of projectile points, usually emanating from, and resulting in, the thinning of the base (examples of fluted point types include Clovis, Cumberland, Folsom Fells Cave Stemmed, and Gainey); also referred to as a channel scar.

The study of the fluting process can be found in Crabtree (1972) and Callahan (1979). Based on these references, the term fluting is used throughout this publication as a basis for selecting paleopoints for Survey numbers.

While common, basal modifications on paleopoints vary. The classic Clovis point tends to have single-to-multiple flutes which extend up through the blade. Narrow paleopoints tend to have single percussion thinning flakes. The bases are frequently indented to facilitate hafting. For both, after the basal flakes are removed, the lower side margins and base are usually smoothed.

There are three basic ways to thin the base: pressure flaking, using a punch technique, or striking it with a percussor (flaker). Each technique produces distinctive flake scars. If basal thinning were unique to paleopoints, then the decision to record them would be easy. However, the Early Archaic Period in Virginia also has fluted points. The cutoff for the Survey: Is the implement assignable to the Paleoindian era? And, whose criteria are used?

Assuming a reasonable expertise with paleomaterials, the questions are answered by the researcher. The Survey has several people who have considerable experience in archaeology from which to draw opinions on various submitted paleopoints. Essentially, an acceptable paleopoint meets written standards, policies, and follows practices that meet professional archaeological standards.

For example, Figure 2 shows a fluted flint biface from Alabama. Clearly, the flutes would qualify it for inclusion in a survey. However, the tool was not placed into service. Also, it probably could not have been finished into a lanceolate Clovis point. A fluted point survey is an ongoing research activity into Paleoindian studies. All recorded data and information about material culture contribute to the "whole" of our understanding about the ancient people in Virginia.

Based on this discussion, paleopoints will be included in the Survey if they:
- Show evidence of basal thinning or fluting
- Show evidence of having been used or were ready for service
- Show reasonable conformance to Paleoindian pointmaking styles
- And, pass a review committee that certifies the point meets these criteria.

Figure 2 – Alabama Flint Biface which is Fluted

Paleopoints have the following types of basal modifications:
- No fluting
- Shallow, wide, and short thinning
- Hinged attempts at fluting (usually stacked)
- Single channel flake scar
- Multiple, side-by-side flutes
- Composite or overlapping fluting flakes.

Figure 3 shows these basal modifications for Virginia paleopoints. Length (height), width, and depth vary depending on knapper's skill and type of material. Length appears to be culturally determined, such as full-face fluting on Cumberland points. There are three basic flaking methods used for basal thinning: percussion, pressure, and punch techniques. The depth of a flute scar in the Survey is usually referred to as shallow or bold. It is rarely measured in archaeology. See MC 1037 (this paper) for an example. See Ahler and Geile (2000) for Why Flute?

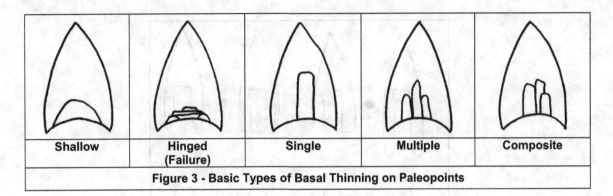

Figure 3 - Basic Types of Basal Thinning on Paleopoints

Shallow | Hinged (Failure) | Single | Multiple | Composite

Modified Paleopoints

Few, if any, Clovis points were static. They were "never changed" is some archaeologists view them. No, they were dynamic tools with multiple users on multiple tasks. All of which caused lithic wearouts and as a consequence, the point was discarded, or more likely, the point was reworked, resharpened, retrofitting, or reshaped back into a tool. These processes were used for normal paleopoint usage. There were point usage that cause breaks, which in some cases, the point could be repaired back into service. With the varieties of Clovis styles, skills in making them, type of usage, and durability of various stones, paleopoints are found in almost an infinite variety of shapes. Bearing these conditions in mind, this class of paleopoints can be identified and analyzed by professional archaeologists. The following definitions apply to the Survey:

- Resharpening – process of creating a new cutting edge on the lateral margins of the point. It involves flaking the edge on alternate faces with the removal of small flakes. Flake removal can be random or systematic such as parallel flaking.
- Reshaping – process of restructuring a point's shape into a form that is not the same as its original form, such as knife to a scraper or drill.
- Reworking – process of reforming a broken or damage point into its original shape or into a form that places the point back into service.
- Retrofitting – process of repairing a broken point back into a useable tool.

The study of modified paleopoints as a single subject/topic is found in Ellis (2004). One problem is modified paleopoint are not generally found in site contexts; thus, placing broken but repaired points is not possible. The only premise that can be used is any repairing causes a reduction in point size and shape. Generally, the major structural change is from a lanceolate form into a triangle form. As such, it is up to a survey to identify and record any type of paleopoint modification. Figure 4 shows and example of point modifications.

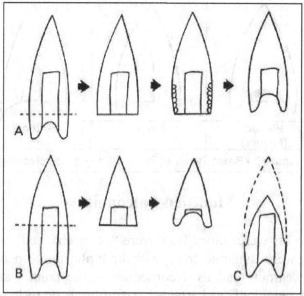

Figure 4 - Examples of Repairing Paleopoints (as in Ellis 2004)
(A = broken at base, refitted, B = broken top of flute, refitted, C = damaged, cannot be refitted)

Field vs. Laboratory Point Recording

The survey director has traveled all over the Middle Atlantic area to examine paleopoints that have been reported as being found in Virginia, which includes collectors' homes, professional meetings, and artifact shows. As such, recording points has not always been under ideal conditions. Thus, points are noted in the Survey as having field or laboratory recording, the difference in data collecting should be obvious. One problem is measuring lithic specific gravity in the field; it usually is not performed by the Survey in the field (see Figure 5). For all points after MC 1050, videos are made of point surfaces, material (color), and principal attributes (see Figure 5).

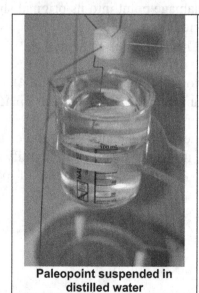

| Paleopoint suspended in distilled water | Video camera recording flake scars |

Figure 5 – Left: Measuring Specific Gravity for MC 1036; Right:

New Survey Measurement

Patination on a projectile point is the key to its history, but unfortunately, it is a poor indicator of artifact age (Hranicky 1992). Patination is both stone- and environment-specific; each having time constraints, for an example, see Figure 6. No single attribute causes more confusion in classifying Clovis points. Hranicky (2004) and Purdy (1974 and 1975) and others have suggested that patination can be analyzed and correlated to age.

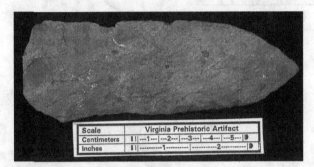

Figure 6 - Heavily Patinated Knife Found on the Potomac River

For comparison studies on patination classification, Goodwin (1960) argued for five types of patination. His first type was bleaching that is caused by the leaching out of silica and replacement with lime salts. The second is induration of exposed surfaces that is caused by the leaching out of soluble silica and redeposition of it at the surface forming a substance called silcrete. The third is limonite penetration and staining that involves limonite clays and salts in the soil being absorbed by stone artifacts. The fourth is desert varnish that is the condition of extreme dryness and intense solar radiation affecting artifacts. Finally, crust is the formation caused by leaching out iron salts and redeposition at the surface. Patination is observed using ultraviolet lighting to study point surface.

This early patination classification schema offers a starting place for this topic. Until patination is scientifically verified, using it for dating remains speculative. Patination dating may become the radiocarbon of stone – especially if patination analyses can generate the point's environmental information (Hranicky 2004). Patination depth can be measured; the Survey is not capable of the measurement. Starting with MC 1050, patination will be evaluated subjectively as:

- Light
- Moderate
- Heavy.

Paleopoint Population Dynamics

The McCary Survey data represents a statistical distribution of human material-culture movement and locations in prehistoric Virginia. While the Survey sample size is large, viewing data by county as McCary (1947) did is still inadequate. For example, viewing point distribution by material is beginning to show lithic territories which can be examined by curation practices of Early Americans. Figure 7 shows probable lithic territories for paleostone curation and usage in Virginia (Hranicky 2008).

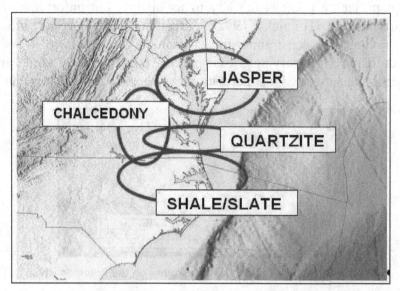

Figure 7 - Map Showing Survey Distribution of Stone Contributions

Flint distribution is currently being studied and will be presented in the next release of Survey points, This distribution is based on lithic determinism (as in Gardner 1974) and called lithic territories (as in Hranicky 2008).

By performing metric calculations by county, river basin, material, and distributional patterns emerge – which led to research investigations and paleopoint histories. For example, most researchers have a working knowledge of chalcedony point distribution in Virginia, but what are the other lithic distributions?

Gardner (1974) was among early archaeologists to use the term lithic determinism. He comments:

> It is by now well established that there was a strong to nearly exclusive preference on the part of Late Pleistocene-Early Holocene populations for a restricted range of lithic raw materials. This is a pan-continental phenomenon and the limits to which these populations would go to adhere to this is an interesting study in itself. (Gardner 1989).

Hranicky and McCary (1995) maintained that the average expended, discarded, or otherwise abandoned paleopoint was approximately 50.00 mm in length. Blade resharpening to its final width form was 25.00. The quality of a paleopoint as measured by its thickness is approximately 6.00 mm. The flute is skewed because of missing or not recorded flutes, but tends to average 15.00 mm in length/height on the blade. Variation is highest on length and flute lengths. Figure 8 shows these metrics which are based on 1054 points. Point L/W*T ratio is now listed for each point. The higher the ratio, the better quality should be obvious; MC 1000 is used as the quality standard. Thus, notice the high ratio for MC 1000; number should indicate why it was named after Ben C. McCary.

Figure 8 - Basic Metrics from the Survey Points MC 1 to MC 1054				
Point Form	Average mm	Variance	SD	Maximum
Length	50.612	406.683	20.166	140.
Width	25.114	23.983	4.897	52.0
Thickness	6.539	2.871	1.694	19.0
Flute	15.512	79.043	8.890	66.0
L/W Ratio	2.015			
L/W*T Ratio *	13.103 to 1			
MC 1000 Ratio	35.397 to 1			

* Modified from Hranicky and McCary 1995)

Statistical models are used to analyze the correlation between the population density and various factors that change in time and/or in space, e.g., material, size, county, morphology, etc. These models can be used to predict population numbers in the future or in unsampled spatial locations in Virginia.

Data may be of three types:

1. Time series - a sequence of measurements at the same point (site) in space
2. Spatial series - a set of measurements made (simultaneously or not) at different point locations in space
3. Mixed series - a set of time series obtained from different point locations in space.

Statistical models are usually represented by linear or polynomial equations:

$$Y = B_0 + B_1X_1 + B_2X_2 + B_nX_n \quad \text{Linear Model}$$
$$Y = B_0 + B_1X + B_2X^2 + B_NX^N \quad \text{Polynomial Model}$$
$$Y = B_0 + B_1X_1 + B_2X_2 + B_3X_1X_2 + B_4X_1^2 + B_5X_2^2 \quad \text{Multifactor Polynomial Model}$$

Whereas:

Y is the predicted variable (e.g., population density); X_i are factors; and B_i are parameters which can be found using regression analysis.

These models were used in Hranicky and McCary (1995), namely estimating point lengths (statistically). They illustrate numerous mathematical models that can be created to analyze and interpret Survey data. The Survey database is becoming large enough so that the horizontal (ground) and vertical (chronology) predictive models can be created.

Unfluted Paleopoints

On the Virginia paleoscene. There are lanceolate paleopoints that are not fluted (Figure 9). By definition, they cannot be included in the Survey. The cutoff for fluted points is after the Paleoindian Period, These later points are not generally included in the Survey, namely fluted Dalton and Hardaway points. See MC 1055 (this paper).

137

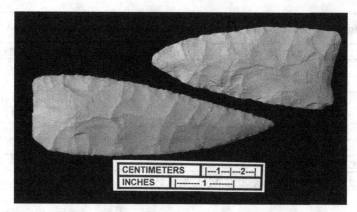

Figure 9 – Unfluted, slate Virginia Paleopoints (Mecklenburg County, Virginia) – Both are 6 mm in Thickness

The base is worth mentioning. It varies from straight to deeply indented; many archaeologists use the concavity to type "Clovis" points. The Survey rarely types paleopoints. As shown below (MC 1054), the straight-base paleopoint is included in the Survey, if fluted. Kraft (1973) found them on the Plenge paleosite in New Jersey.

Survey Points

If you find or have a fluted Virginia paleopoint, we trust you will have it recorded in the Survey. Your contribution adds to the archaeological knowledge of the Commonwealth. In many cases around the U.S., reporting Clovis points has led to the archaeological investigation of a Paleoindian site. See Anderson and Faught (1998) for national palepoint distributions. This type of reporting led to the investigation of Virginia's famous Thunderbird Plaleoindian complex in Warren County, Virginia.

The following pages describe several well known Clovis points in Virginia. Not illustrated but mentioned, the Gaulden Clovis point is another named point (Carroll 1986). The named points are: McCary (MC 1000), Wilkison, Carter (MC 748), Painter (MC 1010) and Merry points. These people made contributions to the study of paleomaterials in Virginia.

McCary Survey Point Number 1000

MC 1000 is named in honor of Ben McCary's 40+ years with the Survey. The point is in the McCary collection and has not been available for study for several years. However, Michael Johnson and Joyce Pearsall did record it. McCary never wanted to publish it because he told its former owner, Pompey Beines, that it was a Paleoindian point, which the owner did not want to accept. He did not want to embarrass him by publishing it as Clovis, so it was never published. McCary did purchase the point from the finder. Additionally, the author studied the point in the 1990s and determined that it was an excellent example of Paleoindian quartzite pointmaking. The point was published as title page artwork in Hranicky (2001) and briefly described in Hranicky (2003) as an example in fluted point surveys. Johnson (2003) calls this point *the smoking quartz point of prehistory*. And, based on what McCary was seeing during his time, he was not very receptive to "large points" being Clovis points. See MC 1033. Many archaeologists still have this size viewpoint.

Size is indicative of function, such as large knife vs. small knife. This function applies to butchering methods, such as large game vs. small game. This size difference may be a division in the Paleoindian era, namely Early vs. Late Paleoindian.

The McCary point has an unusual cross section which suggests to the author that the point may have been made of a core (spall) blade rather than the normal bifacial reduction technique. Face A has a slight medial ridge; whereas, Face B is convex. Flutes are short and were probably struck off with a soft percussor. The pointmaker used a natural ridge for Face A.

Note: Johnson and Pearsall refer to a point face as 1 and 2. A and B are used here so that fluting channels can be numbered, such as A1, A2, or B1, etc.

Quartzite is an extremely difficult material on which to perform fine flaking needed to make Clovis points. This point is a superior specimen and reflects a skilled prehistoric flintknapper. Agreeing with Johnson (2003), it ranks as one of the finest points ever made in Virginia. Again, it is privately owned, but the point's biography has been made public – and as a tribute to Ben C. McCary, the founder of the McCary Fluted Point Survey of Virginia. A tribute to McCary's work appears in Hranicky (1989 and 2003). Another tribute to McCary's overall work in Virginia archaeology is found in Egloff and McAvoy (1998). Figure 10, Figure 11, and Figure 12 show this point. Table 1 at the end of this document provides the point's metrics.

Note: A casual overview of this point has been published in Hranicky (2003), but its official report is presented in Hranicky (2004).

Basic Metrics of MC 1000

Length: 136.0 mm
Width: 36.5 mm
Thickness: 9.5 mm
L/W*T = 35.397
Flute A: 24.0 x 20.0 mm
Flute B: 26.o x 17.0 mm
Concavity: 32.0 x 2.5 mm
Color: Tan
Material: Quartzite
Provenance: Dinwiddie.

Figure 10 - Face A of MC 1000

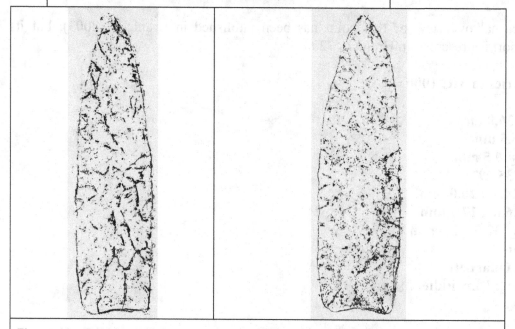

Figure 11 - Rubbings of Faces A and B of MC 1000 by Michael Johnson and Joyce Pearsall

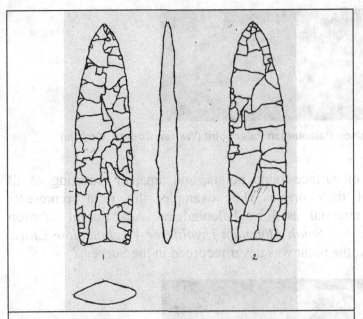

Figure 12 - Drawings of MC 1000 Faces A and B by Johnson and Pearsall. Because flake scars are shallow, drawings may not show every detail (Johnson 2003).

The point rubbings of MC 1000 argue what McCary told Johnson and the author. He said the rubbings come closest to recording the point's (topography) than any other method. Drawings are very subjective and difficult to perform. Johnson and Pearsall made rubbings and used it to create a drawing. This author creates a digital image, enlarges it, and increases its contrast, then makes the drawing. Both approaches create fairly accurate flake scar drawings. For the current Survey, however, rubbings are only made on large points.

Wilkison Paleoindian Point

Elizabeth Wilkison collected artifacts, did fieldwork, and studied the prehistory of Warren and surrounding counties in Northern Virginia during which she discovered the Thunderbird Paleoindian site. She was the first to publish on the site (Wilkison 1965 and 1966). Also, she showed the site to William Gardner of Catholic University in Washington, DC, which started years of Paleoindian investigations in the county. She had five to ten Clovis points from the area which she displayed in a Front Royal museum. Unfortunately, these points disappeared from the display. The author photographed one point at her home and in her honor is calling it the Wilkison Paleoindian point (Figure 13). However, the location of the point is not known to the Survey, but assumed to be 44WC3. It has been published as being associated with Thunderbird site materials in Wilkison (1986). Figure 14 shows a rhyolite blade knife that she said was associated with the point (same field?). Material is the same for both specimens. The toolset when viewed with the Charles Merry toolset (below) is an interesting coincidence in prehistory?

141

Figure 13 - The Elizabeth Wilkison Paleoindian Paleopoint (Warren County, Virginia)

The Wilkison point is symbolic of surface-found points, and amateur reporting of all recovered artifacts regardless of their origins. For example, this point represents distribution of a specific lithic material used by Paleoindians. As Michael Johnson comments on this point, *there are few South Mountain rhyolite or Virginia slate Clovis points in the Surve*y. Unfortunately, the point was never recorded in the Survey.

Figure 14 - Warren County Blade Rhyolite Knife Associated with Wilkison Point

Loy Carter Point

In honor of his 50 years of involvement in prehistoric Virginia's prehistoric artifacts, this point was named the Loy Carter point by Floyd Painter in the Chesaopiean Archaeological Journal (Carter 1986). The point was found in Salt Lick (now Roanoke) in the 1860s and is among the first recovered and maintained artifacts in Virginia. The point was originally in the collection of Franklin Terry who was president of the Bank of Big Lick. In 1928, it was displayed in the Virginia Museum of Natural History at Roanoke. Loy Carter acquired the point from the Terry family in 1946, and later, he sold it to Ben McCary. This point is now in the McCary collection in Virginia and its curation is definitely satifactory from the Survey viewpoint. Figure 15 shows this Survey point. Its L/W*T ratio is similar to MC 1000 and has the highest ratio of any paleopoint recovered in Virginia.

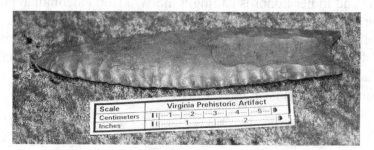

Figure 15 - Loy Carter Point Survey Number 748

Basic Metrics of MC 748

Length: 138.5 mm
Width: 30 mm
Thickness: 8 mm
L/W*T = 36.933
Flute A: 53 mm
Flute B: 46 mm
Color: Brown
Material: Chert
Provenance: Roanoke

Charlie Merry Knife and Point

The Merry Paleoindian knife and point was discovered on the Maryland side of the Potomac River at Seneca Creek in Montgomery County, Maryland by Charles Merry in the 1960s. It was first published by Merry (1988) and later in Hranicky (2002). The author examined the exact find location and found no other evidence of Paleoindian occupation; the assumption is – the site was a temporary camp site and the tools were either forgotten or abandoned. Figure 16 shows the toolset.

Figure 16 - Merry Paleotools, Montgomery County, Maryland

Charles Merry died several years ago and his son did not attempt to preserve any part of the Merry collection; thus, the collection was auctioned – piece-by-piece, and scattered to the winds of the relic world. Fortunately, a Virginia collector now has the toolset and is preserving them. He fully understands their importance to Potomac River archaeology and is curating them professionally.

Metrics:

Point:
Length: 69 mm

143

Width: 30 mm
Thickness: 8 mm
L/W*T = 18.400
Flute A: 22 x 16 mm
Flute B: 23 x 12 mm

Knife:
Length: 90 mm
Width: 40 mm
Thickness: 14 mm

Arthur Robertson Point

McCary Survey point number 22 is named here after Arthur Robertson of Chase City Virginia. He was a past ASV president and was a local historian for Chase City, Mecklenburg County, Virginia. His paleopoints were the first points that Ben McCary used for the Survey. Robertson's collection is preserved at the MacCallum More Museum in Chase City. Figure 17 shows the point.

Figure 17 - Arthur Robertson Point (MC 22)

Point:
Length: 104.9 mm
Width: 29.1 mm
Thickness: 7 mm
L/W*T = 18.400
Flute A: 35 mm
Flute B: 21.5 mm
Material: Rhyolite
Provenance: Mecklenburg County

Survey Model

The author started many years ago studying Clovis technology with the publication Hranicky (1987). After 30 years, the study is still ongoing, which includes explaining distributions, point morphologies, and numerous attributes on Virginia paleopoints. One only has to examine the points in the McCary Survey to see major morphological differences. Hranicky (2008) points out – there is Clovis; then, there is not Clovis. In other words, there are numerous point varieties, some of which are not assigned to Clovis, but still appear to be Paleoindian. As a consequence of prehistory, the term paleopoint is frequently used to mean any projectile point from the Paleoindian Period. While most paleopoints were used as knives, some were used as projectile points; thus, the tern "point" is used for any projectile point/knife in Virginia. It can be either a biface or blade (uniface) point.

Even with widely varying opinions in professional archaeology and from collectors, there is a semblance of points that can be called Clovis. Since four Survey Directors (McCary, Johnson and Pearsall, Hranicky) have been controlling the Survey's input, there has been an overly consistent range for acceptable paleopoints. Survey acceptance that is based on years of observing, examining, and studying paleopoints in Virginia. The Survey contains numerous specimens, such as MC 7, MC 9, MC 25, MC 30, Mc 36 MC 42, MC 43, MC 73, and MC 79, (a few early Survey points) that can be called "classic" Clovis points. These points can be used to define the Clovis type in Virginia.

Over the years, there have been several paper Survey Record Forms, but now a computer form is used. As the Survey grew, more data fields were added to ensure better descriptions of the point. Figure shows a current quick-lookup program window that the Survey director uses in the field.[5] The Survey maintains for comparative purposes, data calculations, such as length, width, and thickness ratios, flute length percentages, material percentages, county percentages, etc.

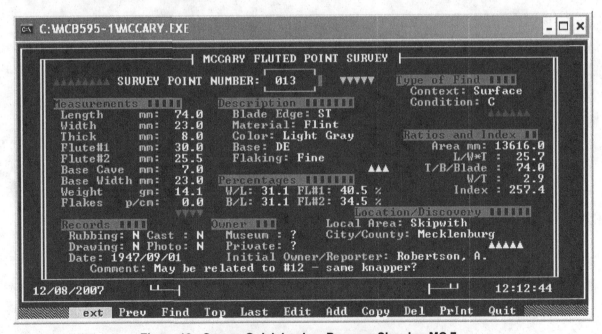

Figure 18 - Survey Quick Lookup Program Showing MC 7

Since the early days of keeping Survey points on 3x5 in. index cards, the entire Survey has been computerized and is now available in Microsoft's Access, Excel, and Word programs.

---

[5] This program was written by the author's early days in the computer sciences as a C++ programmer; thus, it is maintained.

As always, the Survey database is free to any scholar studying Paleoindians. Figure 19 shows the current Survey Recording Form. Figure 20 show one of the basic models used for identifying paleopoints. Other sources are used, namely Collins (1999), Crabtree (1972), and Callahan (1979).

As in Hranicky (2008), there are essentially no limits on the type of data and information that can be recorded about a paleopoint. The Survey uses Hranicky (2005) for its data recording philosophy.

Figure 19 - McCary Survey® Point Record Form

Record Date:	Recorder:	Location:	Finder:	Owner:
Find Type:	Discovery Date:	County:	River Basin:	Artifact Number:

Site: Yes: ____ No: _____ VA Number: 44 ____ _____	Condition: Complete: _____ Broken: _____ Damaged: _____ Rechip: _____	Manufacture: Biface: _____ Flake: _____ Uniface: _____ Tool: _____	Basic Shape: Lanceolate: _____ Triangular: ____ Pentagonal: ___ Other: _____	Flakes/cm Face #1 _____ Face #2 _____ Average: _____
Length: _____ mm Width: _____mm Thick: _____mm C to C: _____ mm Tip Angle: _____ °	Material: Grain: Source: Weight: _____ grams Specific Gravity:_____	Color: Munsell: Recording Temp: _____ °	Face #1 Flute: Single: _____ Multiple: ____ Width: _____ mm Height: ____ mm Type: _____ Ending: _____	Face #2 Flute: Single: _____ Multiple: ____ Width: _____ mm Height: _____mm Type: _____ Ending: _____
Bevel: _____ Face(s): _____	Flaking Quality: Hinges:	Serrations: Fine Retouch:	Cross Section:	Lateral Thinning:
Blade, Left: Straight:____ Incurve: ____ Excurve: ____	Blade, Right: Straight:____ Incurve: ____ Excurve: ____	Concavity: Width: _____mm Height: ____mm Ground: _____	Grinding: Stem:____ Base: _____ Degree:	D/P Tip: _____ mm Base: ____mm
Photo Nrs: Film: _____ Digital: _____	Rubbings: Made: _____ Both Faces: _____	Drawings: Made: _____ Both Faces: ____	Water Sample: Nr: _____ pH: _____	Heat Treatment: Yes: _____ No: _____

General Observations: Patination: _____ Field ___ or Laboratory ____ Recording	Map Attached: Yes ____, No ____ Discovery witness: Yes ____, No ____

Owner's address:

City, State, Zip

Phone: **Email:**

Miscellaneous Notes:

Ver: 7 – 2007

Figure 20 - Morphological Shapes found at the Plenge Site in New Jersey (Kraft 1973)

Type 1 Tapered, mildly excurvate or parallel sided, fluted point	 Deep Base	 Shallow Base	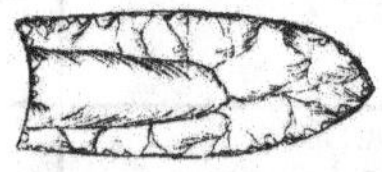 Abrupt Base
Type 2 Recurved, waisted and eared fluted point	 Long Point	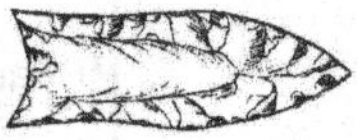 Medium Point	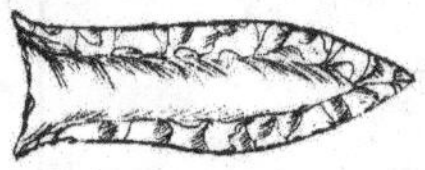 Eared Point
Type 3 "Stubby" fluted point	  Waisted / Straight	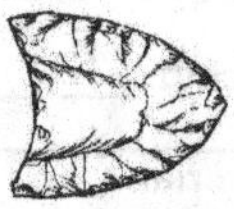 Rounded	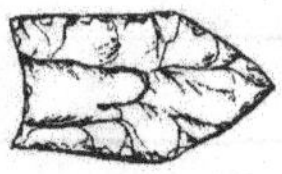 Pentagonal
Type 4 Convex sided fluted point	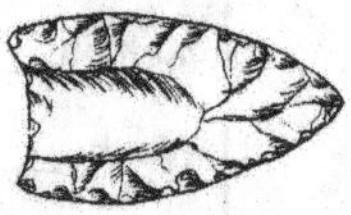 Excurvate		
Type 5 Contracted stem fluted point	 Mild Taper	 Pumpkin Seed	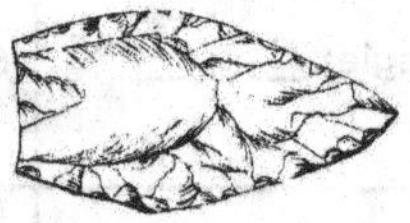 Pentagonal
Type 6 Triangular straight-sided point	 Triangle		
Type 7 Reworked fluted point (knife/scraper, drill)	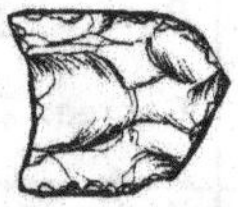 Knife	 Scraper	Not shown. Drill
Type 10 Unfluted lanceolate point	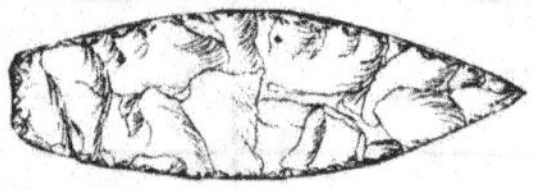 Contracting Stem	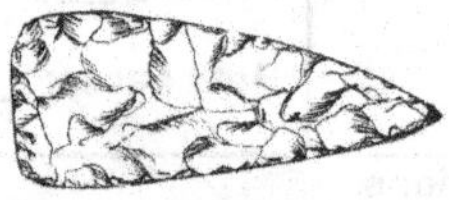 Broad Base	
Type 11 Unfluted trianguloid point	 Excurvate Sides	 Pentagonal	
Type 12 Blade point* * Added this paper.	 Parallel Sides		

The Baby, Toy, or Miniature Clovis Point

Ben McCary and Floyd Painter called this point a Baby or Toy Clovis point. There is no proof that the point is a paleopoint; however, the specimens shown were found in fields which produced Clovis points (Figure 21). Until classified otherwise, it will be classified as a paleopoint in Virginia. It has a state-wide distribution and is usually made from quartzite and quartz. Hranicky and McCary (1995) also published small points from the Williamson site and called them miniature points (Figure 22).

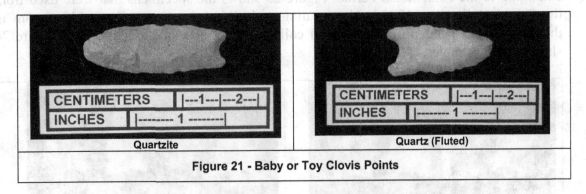

Figure 21 - Baby or Toy Clovis Points

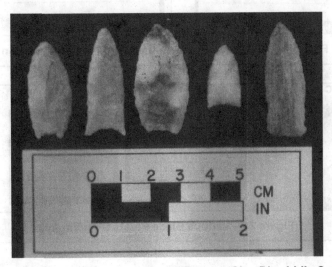

Figure 22 - Miniature Paleopoints from the Williamson Site, Dinwiddie County, Virginia

Blade Paleopoints

In a previous Survey report (Hranicky 2006), the Survey published a blade paleopoint. For most classic Clovis typologists, it was considered an out-of-range inclusion in the Survey – to say the least about it. Many archaeologists do not accept Cactus Hill as a pre-Clovis (term should be Before Clovis) site; therefore, there is no such point for them. The Survey has published these points, namely the jasper MC 767 found in Dinwiddie County, Virginia. MC 1016 in this publication shows an associated chalcedony blade point found with the Clovis point.

Both Williamson and Thunderbird sites have the thin blade points which are assumed to be knives. These observations were made years ago by the author but were not documented. They escaped archaeology until the so-called Cactus Hill point was discovered. This point is made from chalcedony, which is probably the Cattailed Creek variety at the Williamson site. The material of the Cactus Hill point presents serious doubts about Cactus Hill being pre-Clovis. However, there are blade points on Virginia's piedmont that suggest a non-Clovis technology; this point is the Elys Ford point as named by Bushnell (1935). This point was brought into popular usage by Hranicky and Painter (1988); they classified it as belonging to the Paleoindian Period. Figure 23 shows the specimens that were used from the Painter collection (1980s). Note fluting and all specimens average under 5 mm in thickness. After Painter's death, a local collector sold most of this collection. Figure 24 shows other examples.

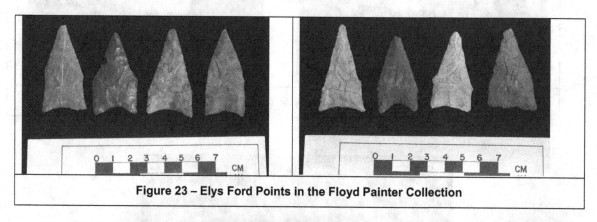

Figure 23 – Elys Ford Points in the Floyd Painter Collection

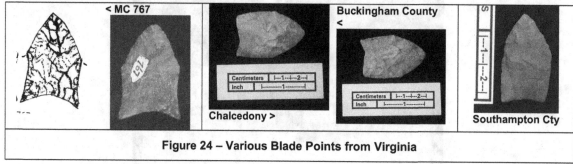

Figure 24 – Various Blade Points from Virginia

The Classic Clovis

For many archaeologists and collectors in Virginia, the only paleopoints that should go into a survey are classic Clovis points. This is simply a relic collector's philosophy, and its implementation never would reach the reality of the Paleoindian world. The author's – ***The Classic Clovis Point: Can It Be Defined?*** – was published in 1987. The author is still attempting to answer the question. For these so-called professionals and amateur/collectors, there is no place in archaeology for this attitude; archaeology is a knowledge-based science – not the science of collecting artifacts. See Archeological Society of Virginia Newsletter No. 186. Figure 25 shows various Clovis points? And, another example is shown in Figure 26. There is more work in Virginia to be done! For most of these attitudinal archaeologists, they generally fail to recognize resharpened or reworked points; few have the skill-set or experience to analyze Clovis technology, and many of their actions cause great damage to American archaeology. This is a final word for critics of the McCary Fluted Point Survey of Virginia, who suggest we stop publishing Virginia paleopoint information and data.

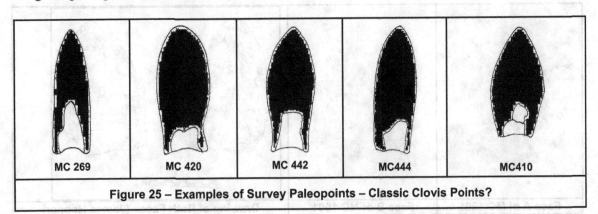

MC 269 | MC 420 | MC 442 | MC444 | MC410

Figure 25 – Examples of Survey Paleopoints – Classic Clovis Points?

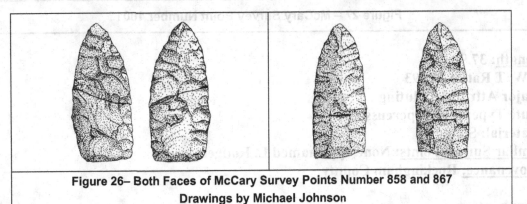

Figure 26– Both Faces of McCary Survey Points Number 858 and 867
Drawings by Michael Johnson

McCary Survey Point Number 1001

MC 1001 is an expended jasper point which is credited to 44BR402. It may have been resharpened until the blade was completely exhausted; however, as discussed below, this may not be the case. Base and lower lateral margins are lightly ground. Face A has multiple flutes (A1 and A2). Face B has a single flute (B1). No patination testing was performed as the point's source was academia. Point was recorded, photographed and drawn by James Hepner. Johnson (2003) suggests that this point could be from a later period in prehistory; the author has data on other points which merit further study as a variety of Virginia fluted points. What haunts its analysis is the slight lateral indentation. The Survey committee was apprehensive about its being numbered. When the point came in, the author issued a number without committee review. The figure shows the reason, but is it Paleoindian? The date is suggested as being Late Paleoindian. Overall, it could be a heavily reworked point which is outside of Clovis technology. Figure 27 shows point photographs and drawings. Table 1 provides the metrics for this point.

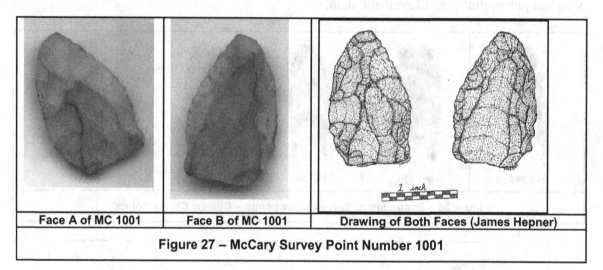

| Face A of MC 1001 | Face B of MC 1001 | Drawing of Both Faces (James Hepner) |

Figure 27 – McCary Survey Point Number 1001

Length: 37.9
L/W*T Ratio: 11.993
Major Attribute: Fluting
Flute Type: Single, percussion
Material: Slate
Similar Survey Points: None, type named L. Rodgers point.
Provenance: Rockingham County

Comment:

This style point has been named by the author. It is called the L. Rodges type in honor of Lanier Rodgers work at the Thunderbird site in Warren County (Hranicky 2008). The type is generally fluted, but most lack the length of fluting on MC 1001. On Face A, note the round corner and straight base. The opposite margin's corner is indented, but suggests an abnormality with this specimen. Figure 28 shows examples. Again, these points may be reworked Clovis points.

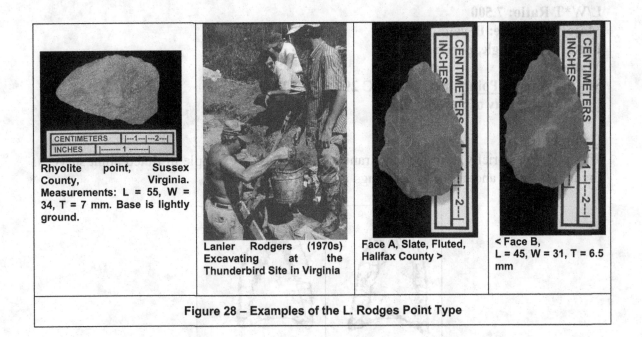

Rhyolite point, Sussex County, Virginia. Measurements: L = 55, W = 34, T = 7 mm. Base is lightly ground.

Lanier Rodgers (1970s) Excavating at the Thunderbird Site in Virginia

Face A, Slate, Fluted, Halifax County >

< Face B, L = 45, W = 31, T = 6.5 mm

Figure 28 – Examples of the L. Rodges Point Type

McCary Survey Point Number 1002

MC 1002 was field recorded and is an expended blackish flint point. It has bold, single channel flutes (A1 and B1). Base and lower lateral margins are ground. Point has excellent lateral base (parallel) thinning. Left margin is beveled, or raised due to fluting. Point passed the ultraviolet test (as in Hranicky 2004). Water sample for chemical testing was not performed (as in Hranicky 2004) as the point has excellent finder credentials. A water sample from the point is used to test the point's surface for elements that might not be part of the normal patination process (as in Hranicky 2003). Figure 29 shows point photographs and drawings. Figure 30 shows point rubbings. Table 1 provides the metrics for this point.

Note: A casual overview of this point has been published in Hranicky (2003), but its official report is presented here.

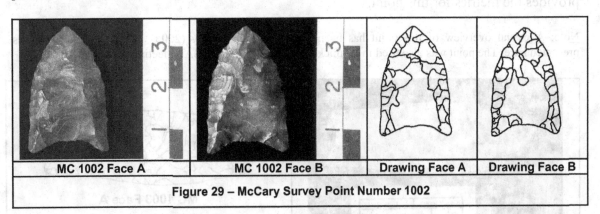

| MC 1002 Face A | MC 1002 Face B | Drawing Face A | Drawing Face B |

Figure 29 – McCary Survey Point Number 1002

<u>Length</u>: 30 mm

L/W*T Ratio: 7.500
Major Attribute: Beveling
Flute Type: Single, percussion
Material: Flint
Similar Survey Points: MC 164, MC 297, MC 120, MC 256
Provenance: City of Suffolk

Comment:
This point was briefly described in Hranicky (2003) as an example in fluted point surveys. Figure 30 shows another set of rubbings for MC 1002.

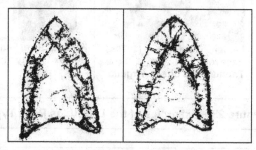

Figure 30 – Rubbings of Faces A and B of MC 1002 by Edward Bottoms and George Helmintoller

McCary Survey Point Number 1003

MC 1003 is a field-recorded point and is an excellent rhyolite point that was probably used as a knife. It is classified as a large paleopoint. One blade margin has extensive retouching. While not obvious, the flutes are larger than the general Clovis population for this size point. Flute A1 is a wide, probably percussion, single flute. Flute B1 has a lateral flake scar going through it. Base and lower lateral margins are ground. This point appears on the cover of Hranicky's (2003) *Projectile Point Types Found along the Atlantic Coastal Plain*. Point manufacture was probably the standard Clovis biface reduction method as defined in Callahan (1979). Figure 31 shows point photographs and drawings. Table 1 provides the metrics for this point.

Note: A casual overview of this point has been published in Hranicky (2003), but its official report is presented here. The point was also used in Hranicky's (2003) ASV and ESAF meeting papers.

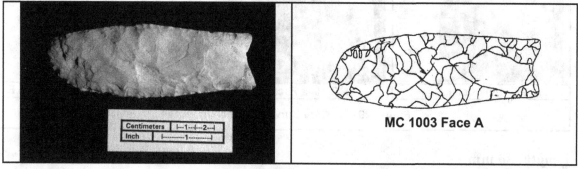

MC 1003 Face A

154

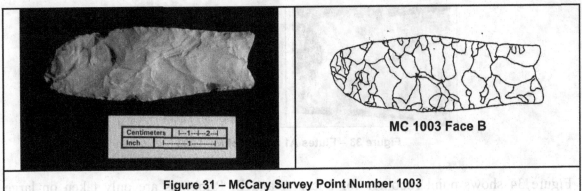

MC 1003 Face B

Figure 31 – McCary Survey Point Number 1003

Length: 96 mm
L/W*T Ratio: 23.289
Major Attributes: Size, fluting
Flute Type: Single, percussion
Material: Rhyolite
Similar Survey Points: MC 269, MC 220, MC 97, MC 149, MC 250, MC 269, MC 324, MC 419, MC 510
Provenance: Brunswick County

Comment:
Using the Hranicky and McCary's (1995) length algorithm, the point's original length was 118.68 mm (statistically). Figure 32 shows the point as compared to: all Virginia fluted points in the Survey, the Williamson Paleoindian site, and the Thunderbird site. As tabulated, the point is an exceptional point. The point has W/T ratio of 1:4.121 which falls within norm of the Survey population. This ratio further argues for the well-made property of the point. The greatest frank angle for the point is 18 degrees; it easily is classified as a knife. Point edge sharpness is described below and in Hranicky (2006). Figure 33 shows flute close-ups.

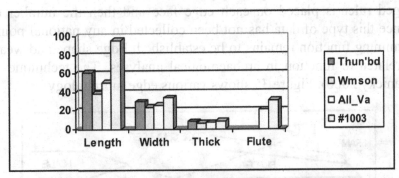

Figure 32 – Survey Comparison with Point Number 1003

Note: Flute length is only compared to the total Virginia population.

155

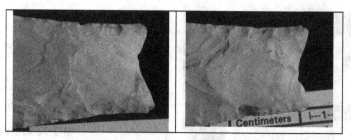

Figure 33 – Flutes A1 and B1 of MC 1003

Figure 34 shows point rubbings for Faces A and B. Rubbings are only taken on large paleopoints.

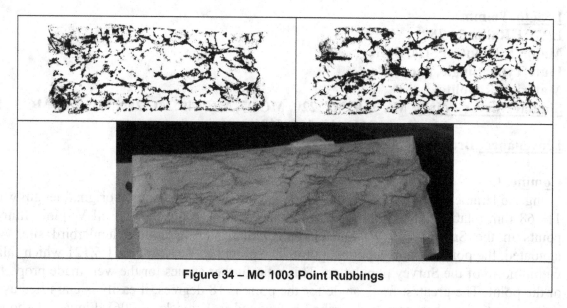

Figure 34 – MC 1003 Point Rubbings

Franking is a method of recording the cutting edge on a paleopoint blade margin. It is only a practical measurement on non-expended points or on any point that has a beveled edge. A straight-edged ruler is placed on each edge face and then the number of degrees is calculated. Since this type of data has not been collected in any national point surveys, its usage in determining function remains to be established. Edge shape and wear patterns are generally correlated to function in archaeological analyses. The technique is difficult to apply (see Hranicky 2006). Figure 35 shows various edge morphology.

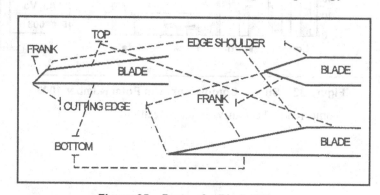

Figure 35 – Parts of a Blade Edge

156

McCary Survey Point Number 1004

MC 1004 was laboratory recorded and is an expended, small jasper point. It was resharpened until the blade was completely exhausted. Its blade reduction form suggests that it was a knife. One lateral basal margin has serriations worked into it which suggest that it was hand held in the final stage of the point lifecycle. Flute A1 is shallow, and B1 is bold. Base is ground. Water sample for chemical testing was not performed. Johnson (2003) notes that the point's shiney surface makes it an excellent example of thermal alteration. Figure 36 shows point photographs and drawings. Table 1 provides the metrics for this point.

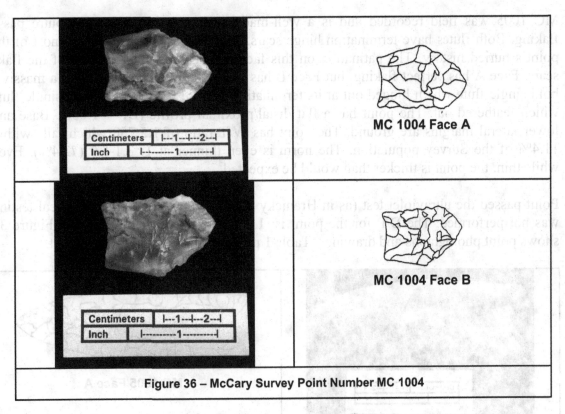

Figure 36 – McCary Survey Point Number MC 1004

<u>Length</u>: 35.9 mm
L/W*T Ratio: N/A
Major Attribute: None
Flute Type: Single, percussion
Material: Flint
<u>Similar Survey Points</u>: MC 174, MC 280, MC 396
<u>Provenance</u>: Mecklenburg County

Comment:

In this paper, point numbers 1001, 1002, and 1004 are expended points. Their length is far below the average in the McCary database which is 50.69 mm (discard length). The average falls within 32.7% (largest group) of the total Survey population. The lifecycle of a Clovis point starts when the Native American put it into service. At some time during its usage, the user decided that the point was no longer serviceable and discarded it. Hranicky (2002) suggests that this process is culturally determined. It is called the expention process (Hranicky 2004). The Survey is a good source for determining the length-mm for Native discard points.

McCary Survey Point Number 1005

MC 1005 was field recorded and is a well-made slate point. It has some outré passé flaking. Both flutes have termination hinge scars. Face B was the up face for most of the point's buried history. The patination on this face has nearly removed most of the flake scars. Face A has perfect flaking, but Face B has two flake hinges. Flute A1 is a massive, bold single flute which hinged out at its terminating point. Flute B1 is a light, single flute which feathered out. The point has a flat distal/proximal profile (DP = 1.036). Base and lower lateral margins are ground. The point has W/T ratio of 1:5.758 which falls within 11.4% of the Survey population. The norm is even thinner at 1: 3.1-5.0 (72.4%). Even while thin, the point is thicker than would be expected.

Point passed the ultraviolet test (as in Hranicky 2004). Water sample for chemical testing was not performed. The D/P for the point is: 1.038. Point was field recorded. Figure 37 shows point photographs and drawings. Table 1 provides the metrics for this point.

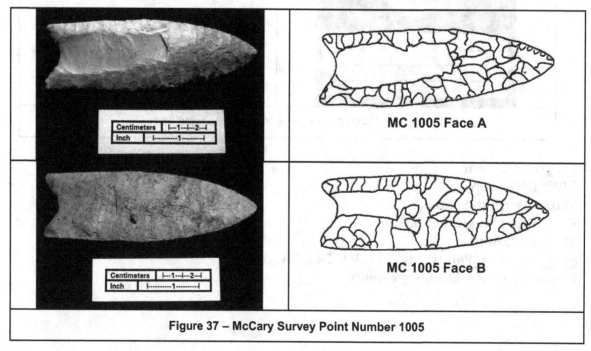

Figure 37 – McCary Survey Point Number 1005

Length: 109 mm
L/W*T Ratio: 18.644
Major Attribute: Fluting, flat/thinness
Flute Type: Single, punch?
Material: Flint
Similar Survey Points: MC 18, MC 29, MC 293, MC 296, MC 522, MC 556, MC 617
Provenance: Mecklenburg County

Comment:
It may be a Virginia/North Carolina "which" border point but was included in the Survey. Figure 38 shows point profile.

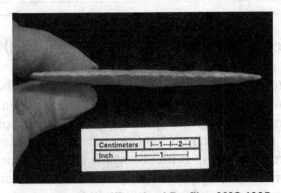

Figure 38 – Distal/Proximal Profile of MC 1005

Survey Directors, Michael Johnson and Joyce Persall, recorded and drew paleopoint profiles. This technique for recordkeeping is not currently maintained in the Survey for McCary points above 1000.

The D/P ratio is called the Johnson Index which is named after the Survey's former director. It is a measure of taper or flatness profile of a paleopoint (Figure 39). All paleopoints have one of these profiles, with the exception of curved points. None of the curved points have been reported in Virginia. The index is produced by measuring point thickness at 5 mm on each end. Then, distal measurement is divided by the proximal measurement (Figure 40).

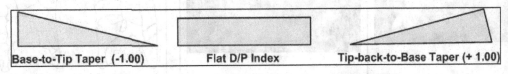

Base-to-Tip Taper (-1.00)   Flat D/P Index   Tip-back-to-Base Taper (+ 1.00)

Figure 39 – Three Types of D/P Indices (Side Views)

Figure 40 – Example of Tip Measurement

McCary Survey Point Number 1006

MC 1006 was a laboratory-recorded specimen and may not have been placed into service by the Paleoindian. However, it has pronounced flutes and is assigned a Survey number. It is a small point that is made from rhyolite, probably from Mt Jackson area. The pointmaker attempted to remove a medial hump on Face A, but the flute hinged on him. Base and lower lateral margins are ground. Tip is broken which does not appear to have been caused during manufacture. Point is heavily patinated and flake scars are difficult to discern. Base was broken during manufacture, and it was ground afterwards. Face A has two side-by-side flutes (A1 and A2. Face B has a wide shallow thinning flake (B1). Infrared images were made which show flute scars. This method is generally used on heavily patinated points. The point's original length was 98.88 mm (statistically). Johnson (2003) suggests that the damage and stepping on Face A are the result of extended use life and reworking. The frank angle is 28.5 degrees which suggests a heavy duty function. Flute A1 overlaps flute A1.1 as it was an attempt to remove a stacked flake near the medial axis. Figure 41 shows point photographs and drawings. Table 1 provides the metrics for this point.

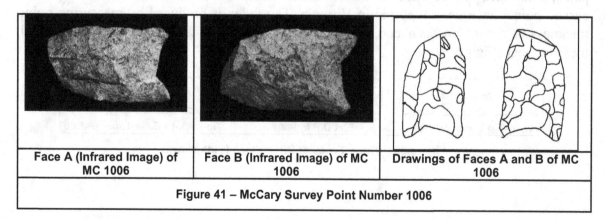

Face A (Infrared Image) of MC 1006	Face B (Infrared Image) of MC 1006	Drawings of Faces A and B of MC 1006

Figure 41 – McCary Survey Point Number 1006

Length: 43.0 mm
L/W*T Ratio: 18.192
Major Attribute: None

Flute Type: Single, percussion
Material: Rhyolite
Similar Survey Points: MC 517
Provenance: Mecklenburg County

Comment:
As with any technology, practitioners need to learn methods and procedures; all of which improve their skill with the technology. This is probably the case here. This point is probably the ugliest point in the Survey. Or, see MC 1038 (this paper).

McCary Survey Point Number 1007

MC 1007 is a broken rhyolite point. The lithic source is probably the Uwharrie Mountains of North Carolina. The break was caused by an impact with a soft target, such as bone, wood, etc. It argues for Clovis projectiling. Breakage occurs at the top of the flutes, suggesting a hafting margin (chassis area) for the point. No study has been made on Virginia data to determine the causation (tensel strength) of the Clovis hafting technology. Flutes A1 and B1 are wide and bold. The W/T ratio is 3.857 to 1; it is not close to the Survey average. However, casually-speaking, the location of this break was common. The exact topographic provenance is known for this point, and the area will be investigated by the Survey. Figure 42 shows point photographs and drawings. Table 1 provides the metrics for this point.

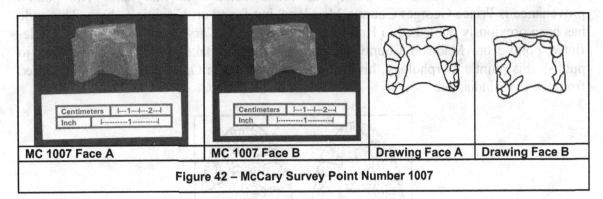

| MC 1007 Face A | MC 1007 Face B | Drawing Face A | Drawing Face B |

Figure 42 – McCary Survey Point Number 1007

Length: 23.5 mm
L/W*T Ratio: N/A
Major Attribute: None
Flute Type: Single, percussion
Material: Rhyolite
Similar Survey Points: MC 622, MC 458, MC 398, MC 402, MC 397
Provenance: Smyth County

Comment:

Breakage on paleopoints has two high fracture areas: the tip and the area above the hafting. Figure 43 shows a generalized breakage chart for Virginia paleopoints. Quartzite has the highest breakage rate in the Survey.

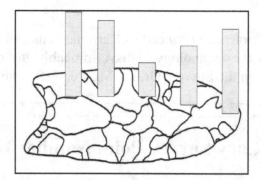

Figure 43 - Breakage for Virginia Paleopoints (boxes show relative breakage frequencies).

McCary Survey Point Number 1008

MC 1008 was field-recorded and published in Hranicky (2004); it was re-recorded and published here. It is another border point in that it was found in the Potomac River waters just east of the Woodrow Wilson bridge. The bridge is technically in Washington, DC and the Potomac River where the point was found belongs to Maryland. The point's provenance is Prince Georges County, Maryland, but found on Virginia's shore. This style has been previously published in Hranicky (2001), and McCary (1982) published a single-fluted point from Madison County (Figure 44). Mayer-Oakes (1955) was the first to publish this point's morphology; his specimen was found in Ohio. This point is classified from the Paleoindian era.

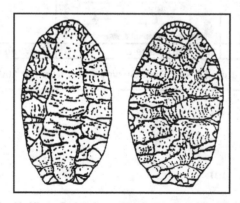

Figure 44 – Uniflute Point from Madison County (McCary 1982)

It is a thin point with bold diagonal resharpening flake scars. It has one face fluting, and the reverse face does not show an attempt to flute it. Flute A1 (40 x 13 mm) is a single flute channel. The point's material remains to be determined. This point would have had full-face fluting which is a basic trait for the type, but the stone had a seam running diagonally across the midsection. This seam stopped the flute from carrying out to the distal end. The flute was well-developed and would have traveled down the full face. This flute was performed by a punch and is the same method used on the full-face Cumberland points. The W/T ratio is 3.914 to 1; defines a well-made point. The D/P ratio is 1.078 to 1; a strong hafting area. The flute channel is bold and well defined. Type was named the Northumberland type after specimens found in Pennsylvania by Hranicky and Fogelman (1994). Figure 45 shows point photographs and drawings. Table 1 provides the metrics for this point.

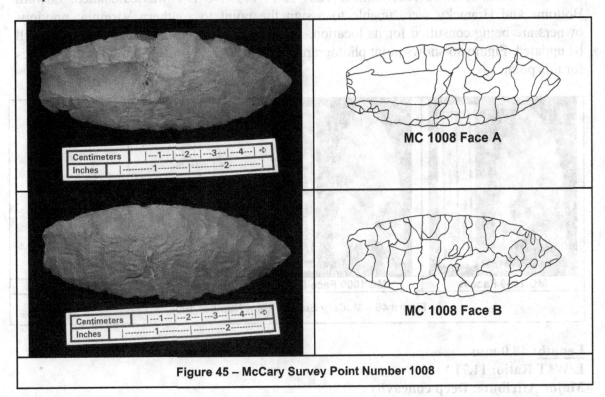

MC 1008 Face A

MC 1008 Face B

Figure 45 – McCary Survey Point Number 1008

Length: 100.5 mm
L/W*T Ratio: 24.366
Major Attribute: Single face fluting
Flute Type: Single, punch
Material: Jasper
Similar Survey Points: McCary's unrecorded point
Provenance: Alexandria City, Virginia

Comment:
This type is called the Northumberland type, named after specimens in Pennsylvania. However, some archaeologists attempt to call it the Crowfield type. Deller and Ellis (1984) never showed this form when they named the Crowfield type. Blade resharpening may still be a factor in identifying the type.

McCary Survey Point Number 1009

MC 1009 is no longer in Virginia; the author traveled to Pennsylvania to field record it. It is heavily patinated and made from quarried rhyolite. The point has a deep concavity, and the base has finalizing thinning flakes. Both faces have hinges, but overall, it is a well-made point. Flute A1 has over scar chipping; it is a single flute. Flute B1 is a wide, shallow flute which hinged on termination. The blade edges have minor retouching. The Survey LW*T benchmark is: 13.103; number 1009 is 11.719. No D/P was calculated. Edward Bottoms and Hranicky were unable to assign the point to southern Virginia; previous owners are being consulted for its location. If located precisely, the Survey database will be updated. Figure 46 shows point photographs and drawings. Table 2 provides the metrics for this point.

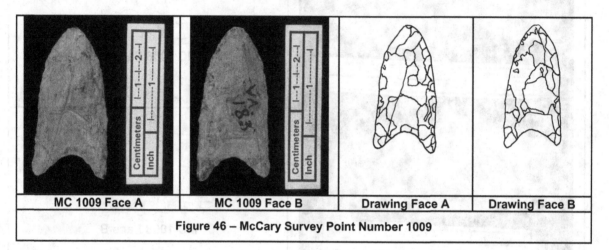

| MC 1009 Face A | MC 1009 Face B | Drawing Face A | Drawing Face B |

Figure 46 – McCary Survey Point Number 1009

Length: **48.0 mm**
L/W*T Ratio: 11.719
Major Attribute: Deep concavity
Flute Type: Single, percussion
Material: Rhyolite
Similar Survey Points: MC 8, MC 305, MC 710, MC 749, MC 827
Provenance: ?

McCary Survey Point Number 1010

MC 1010 was laboratory recorded; it has an interesting history. Like Survey point number 1000 (McCary Point) and number 748 (Loy Carter Point), this point is being named here after a collector-archaeologist in Virginia – Floyd Painter who published the Chesopiean for many years. This point is quite similar to Point 1000 but is made from flint as opposed to quartzite. Its material does not appear to be from Virginia; sourcing it is difficult because of the heavy patination on the point. It has several bold percussion flake scars (A1 and A2, and B1 and B2) which were left over from its initial biface reduction. The distal end has fine retouch. The base also has fine basal thinning. Base and lower margins are lightly ground. The dorsal face has a shallow flute which was overlaid with a second attempt. Both faces had the setup for lengthy fluting, but the knapper seems to have been unable to complete them. The ventral face has a narrow flute and a diagonal flute. The base is straight which is fairly common for large narrow Clovis points. The Survey L/W*T benchmark is: 13.103; number 1010 is 36.660. Its D/P is .947; flatness. Figure 47 shows point photographs and drawings. Table 2 provides the metrics for this point.

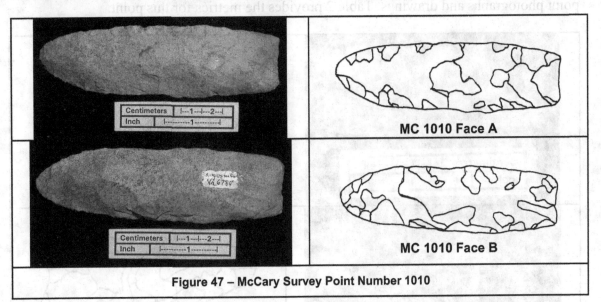

Figure 47 – McCary Survey Point Number 1010

Length: 100.0 mm
L/W*T Ratio: 36.666
Major Attribute: Straight base
Flute Type: Multiple, pressure
Material: Flint
Similar Survey Points: MC 971, MC 727
Provenance: Augusta County

Comment:
This point is from Augusta County and will be returned there to the historical society – in Painter's name.

McCary Survey Point Number 1011

MC 1011 was laboratory recorded; it exemplifies distances that Paleoindians traveled in pursuit of lithic materials and following game herds. It is made from coral which is found in Florida and Georgia. However, Flint Creek material from northwest Alabama is a dark brown stone also and could be the point's source. It is an expended point. The dorsal face has a bold, wide, shallow flute (A1); the ventral face has two small parallel flute scars (B1 and B2). The base is lightly ground. The blade margins have systematic flaking, but overall, the point has bold percussion flaking. The ventral face has a flat area with weathering giving an impression that it has remaining cortex. This area has a long fracture that was probably caused by excessive usage. Johnson suggests that the stone appears to have been heat-treated, but only on the distal end. This may have been caused by subsequent environment. The ventral blade could be classified as being beveled, but the raised flat area probably dictated the edge formation. The Survey L/W*T benchmark is: 13.103; number 1011 is 21.000. Its D/P is .632; point tapers to point. Figure 48 shows point photographs and drawings. Table 2 provides the metrics for this point.

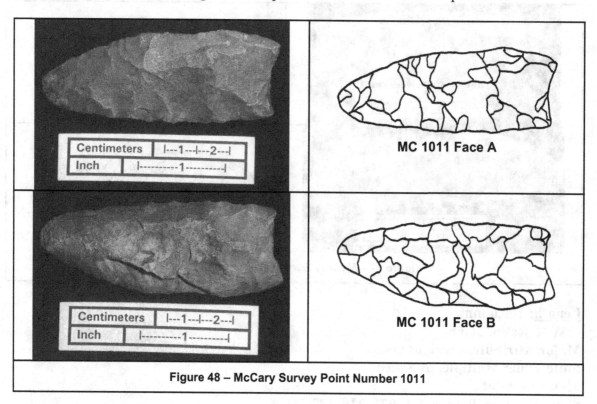

Figure 48 – McCary Survey Point Number 1011

Length: 63.0 mm
L/W*T Ratio: 21.000
Major Attribute: Blade technology
Flute Type: Single, percussion
Material: Coral
Similar Survey Points: MC 635, MC 631
Provenance: Halifax County

Comment:
Southern Virginia has a mixture of southeastern cultures that produced numerous point styles. This point represents the first published evidence of coral usage in Virginia. However, the stone's redness could also indicate jasper. Microscopic comparison confirms coral (Figure 49). As observed on Florida specimens and the Virginia point, both contain black crystals. Crystals are probably feldspar. The need for comparative lithic specimens for each state's archaeological agencies and institutions cannot be overly emphasized. As

suggested in Hranicky (2002), an archaeological lithic thin section library is truly needed in Virginia.

Figure 49 – Close-up Comparisons of artifacts made from Florida Coral.

Figure 50 shows a basal ground paleopoint from Florida that is made from coral. It has a bold overstrike flute on one face. Note the similar shape between MC 1011 and the Florida specimen. Both are simple knives. Perhaps these specimens do not show true fluting, and these scars are simply basal thinning results – the technology difference is ignored (as in Hranicky 2006). See MC 1053, this paper.

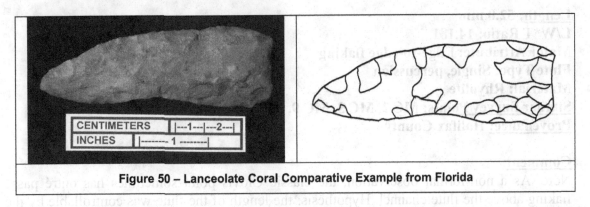

CENTIMETERS |---1---|---2---|
INCHES | -------- 1 -------- |

Figure 50 – Lanceolate Coral Comparative Example from Florida

McCary Survey Point Number 1012

MC 1012 was field recorded and is made from quarried rhyolite that has suffered post-Indian damage to one basal corner. It is heavily patinated; most flake scars are gone. The remaining basal area has moderate grinding. Flute scars are short and shallow. The basic style is a constricting stem which reflects southeastern influences. The blade edges have fine, systematic retouch. The Survey LW*T benchmark is: 13.103; number 1012 is 14.181. Its D/P is .938; flatness. It has several edge-to-edge flake scars. Figure 51 shows point photographs and drawings. Table 2 provides the metrics for this point.

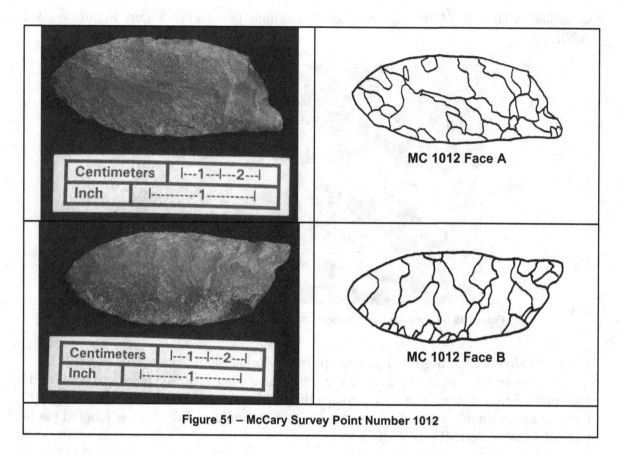

Figure 51 – McCary Survey Point Number 1012

Length: 52.0 mm
L/W*T Ratio: 14.181
Major Attribute: Edge-to-edge flaking
Flute Type: Single, percussion
Material: Rhyolite
Similar Survey Points: MC 2, MC 3, MC 9, MC 318, 934, MC 1046
Provenance: Halifax County

Comment:
Note: As a non-formal observation, the classic Clovis point sometimes has outré passé flaking above the flute channel. Hypothesis: the length of the flute was controllable by the Clovis knapper.

McCary Survey Point Number 1013

MC1013 was field recorded; it appears to be early Dalton (comments by Michael Johnson – Survey Committee) or as suggested here as late Clovis; both are a matter of semantics. It is probably a reworked broken point tip. The point has little fluting, and the basal area is lightly ground. Edge retouch is systematic and was performed for the last time before discarding the point. Parts of the blade show beveling. It is made from high-quality flint which is probably not native to the area. Also, along with the flint, the basal V-shape suggests a Northeast homeland, but distribution is really open archaeologically. The overall flaking quality is fine. The Survey L/W*T benchmark is: 13.103; number 1014 is 7.321. Its D/P is 1.145; flatness but has a slight taper towards the base. Figure 52 shows point photographs and drawings. Table 2 provides the metrics for this point.

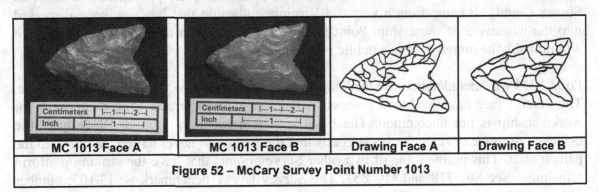

| MC 1013 Face A | MC 1013 Face B | Drawing Face A | Drawing Face B |

Figure 52 – McCary Survey Point Number 1013

Length: 41 mm
L/W*T Ratio: 7.321
Major Attribute: **V-shaped concavity**
Flute Type: **Single, pressure?**
Material: **Flint**
Similar Survey Points: **MC 422, MC 466, MC 874, MC 105**
Provenance: **Halifax County**

Comment:
Fogelman and Lantz (2006) report in the Pennsylvania Survey two V-shaped bases: Lancaster-52 and Huntington-2 paleopoints. Figure 53 shows V-shape point bases from the Debert Paleoindian site in Nova Scotia. There are two V-shaped bases in the Survey. Most importantly, a closely similar point was found during the Thunderbird site excavation (Gardner 1983).

Figure 53 - V-Shaped Bases from the Debert Site, Nova Scotia, Canada (Ellis 2004)

McCary Survey Point Number 1014

MC 1014 was laboratory recorded; it is another wandering point that may have lost its provenance had it not been for Edward Bottoms on the Survey Review Committee. Submitted as Nansemond and with the owner's permission, the provenance is listed as Sussex County. It came from a very old Virginia collection that has now been dispersed into the *whatevers* of ownership. Point is on long-term loan to the Dan River Survey; it will probably be turned over to a public institution.

Point 1014 was included because the knapper was able to get two flutes off the dorsal face. The ventral face has one broad percussion flake scar. Being made from quartzite, poor workmanship is not uncommon. The basal area is moderately ground. Blade has little evidence of usage or retouch; this suggests that the point was never hafted and put into the paleotoolkit. This point is one of two other Survey points that have the striking platform remaining. See MC 718 and MC 857. The Survey LW*T benchmark is: 13.103; number 1015 is 14.360. Its D/P is .673; tapers towards the tip. Figure 54 shows point photographs and drawings. Table 2 provides the metrics for this point.

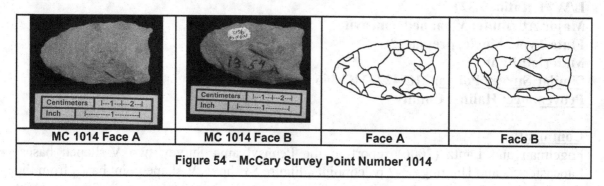

| MC 1014 Face A | MC 1014 Face B | Face A | Face B |

Figure 54 – McCary Survey Point Number 1014

Length: 47.0 mm
L/W*T Ratio: 14.361
Major Attribute: Striking platform
Flute Type: Single, percussion
Material: Quartzite
Similar Survey Points: MC 507
Provenance: Nansemond County

McCary Survey Point Number MC 1015

MC 1015 was field recorded. The point is a classic Clovis point. It is well made with fine lateral retouch. Fluting is pronounced and wide. There are no hinges, and flake scars are well developed. It is made from a black slate which was probably obtained in North Carolina. Basal area grinding is moderate. Blade margins are excurvate and retouched. Flutes are bold, single flutes on both faces (A and B). Both flutes feather on termination. It is a surface find in Buckingham County. Figure 55 shows point photographs and drawings. Table 2 provides the metrics for this point.

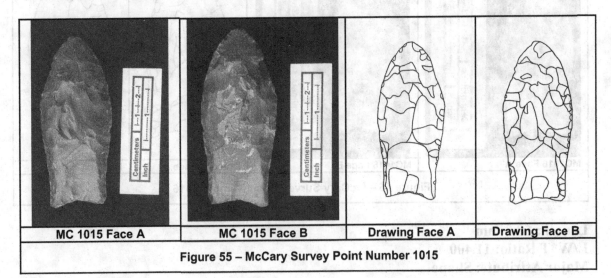

| MC 1015 Face A | MC 1015 Face B | Drawing Face A | Drawing Face B |

Figure 55 – McCary Survey Point Number 1015

Length: 77.0 mm
L/W*T Ratio: 16.267
Major Attribute: Fluting
Flute Type: Single, percussion
Material: Slate
Similar Survey Points: MC 486, MC 510, MC 542, MC 565, MC 685, MC 932
Provenance: Buckingham County

McCary Survey Point Number 1016

MC 1016 was field recorded; it is a classic Clovis point. It has outré passé flaking above the flute and no hinges. It has moderate basal grinding. It was made from blue/grayish chalcedony. Material and point shape are similar to the paleopoints found at the Williamson site in Dinwiddie County. Blade margins are excurvate. Flutes (A1 and B1) are pronounced, and have composite channels. It is a surface find in Buckingham County. For points 1015 and 1016, Hranicky and Painter (1988) attempted to call this style the Williamson point style. From the committee review, Michael Johnson suggests that all Williamson and Thunderbird points have a hint of recurved edges (fishtailing) in the hafting area. He suggests they are a Middle Atlantic area or Virginia Clovis variation rather than a general Clovis form. Figure 56 shows point photographs and drawings. Table 3 provides the metrics for this point.

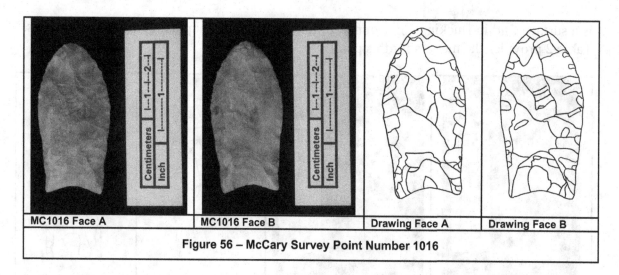

| MC1016 Face A | MC1016 Face B | Drawing Face A | Drawing Face B |

Figure 56 – McCary Survey Point Number 1016

Length: 50.0 mm
L/W*T Ratio: 11.400
Major Attribute: Shape
Flute Type: Single, percussion
Material: Chalcedony
Similar Survey Points: MC 213, MC 58, MC 119, MC 111, MC 337, MC 269, MC 475
Provenance: Buckingham County

Comment:

Figure 57 shows a thin point that was found in proximity with MC 1016. It is made from the same material – chalcedony. This style point is similar to the Cactus Hill point that was recovered by McAvoy (1997). The author has suggested a Paleoindian blade technology for this point, but a pre-Clovis origin is definitely a possibility (Hranicky 2003). The point type is known as the Elys Ford point (as named by Bushnell 1935).

Figure 57 – Chalcedony Blade Point from Buckingham County

McCary Survey Point Number MC 1017

MC 1017 was field recorded; its basal corners are broken (Indian); otherwise, the point is complete. It is made from rhyolite and is light gray. One margin has full lateral retouch. Point has a large flat area on one face suggesting it was made off a large, flat flake. Face A has a pronounced bold flute (A1). Face B has a composite flute (B1n). It was made from a grayish rhyolite. It is narrow suggesting extensive resharpening. Weathering is different on each face, and the blade has a slight twist to it. Basal area grinding is moderate. Blade margins are excurvate and show wear. It is a surface find in Buckingham County. Figure 58 shows point photographs and drawings. Table 3 provides the metrics for this point.

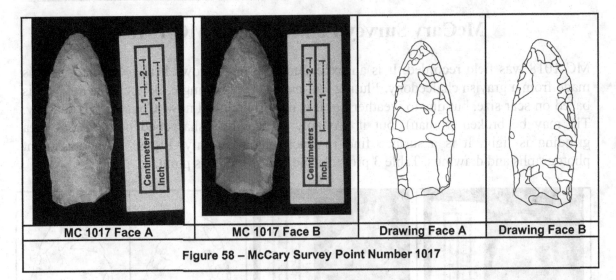

| MC 1017 Face A | MC 1017 Face B | Drawing Face A | Drawing Face B |

Figure 58 – McCary Survey Point Number 1017

<u>Length</u>: **57.0 mm**
L/W*T Ratio: 30.535
Major Attribute: Size
Flute Type: Single, percussion
Material: Rhyolite
<u>Similar Survey Points</u>: **MC 190, MC 227, MC 420, MC 330, MC 337**
<u>Provenance</u>: **Buckingham County**

<u>Comment</u>:
One purpose of the Survey is to have data and information on Virginia paleopoints from which comparisons can be made. MC 1017 and MC 444 show similarities in both morphology and technique. Each point has a knapping signature which identifies the pointmaker's cultural conditions and his "way" to make a paleopoint. For example, both points have large flat spots, but also well-developed and executed thin flake removals. There are numerous possibilities for this type of study on Survey paleopoints. Figure 59 shows a similar example from the Survey.

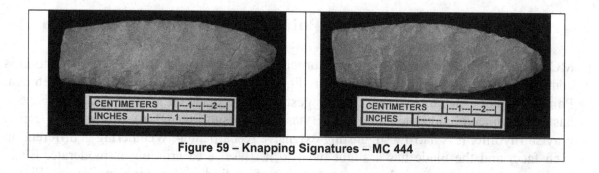

Figure 59 – Knapping Signatures – MC 444

McCary Survey Point Number MC 1018

MC 1018 was field recorded. It is an expended point that shows heavy weathering. It is made from a grayish chalcedony. Fluting (A1 and B1) was a single, bold channel, which is based on scar size, but due to weathering, it is not pronounced now. Concavity is shallow. Tip may be broken (Indian), but it probably is heavily resharpened point. Basal area grinding is light. It is a surface find in Buckingham County. Figure 60 shows point photographs and drawings. Table 3 provides the metrics for this point.

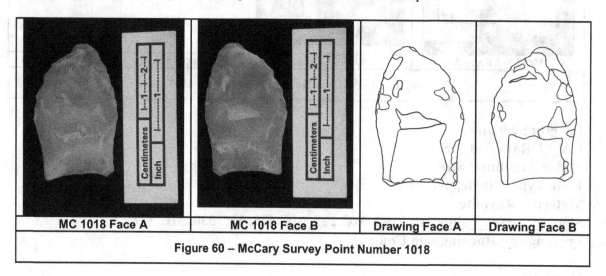

| MC 1018 Face A | MC 1018 Face B | Drawing Face A | Drawing Face B |

Figure 60 – McCary Survey Point Number 1018

Length: 45.0 mm
L/W*T Ratio: 11.250
Major Attribute: Material
Flute Type: Single, percussion
Material: Chalcedony
Similar Survey Points: MC 163, MC 183, MC 230, MC 271, MC 338, MC 469, MC 572,

                         MC 807
Provenance: Buckingham County

McCary Survey Point Number MC 1019

MC 1019 was field recorded. Faces A and B have multiple short flutes (A1, A2, B1, and B2). It is an expended point with a snapped tip. Tip is broken (Indian), but a corner was made into a small burin. Grinding is moderate. Flake scars are well developed and show no hinges. It was made from chalcedony and is a surface find in Buckingham County. Figure 61 shows photographs and drawings. Table 3 provides the metrics for this point.

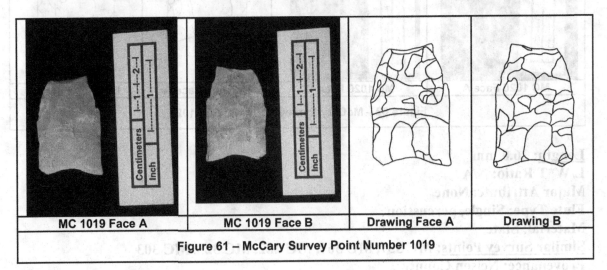

| MC 1019 Face A | MC 1019 Face B | Drawing Face A | Drawing B |

Figure 61 – McCary Survey Point Number 1019

Length: 34.0 mm
L/W*T Ratio: N/A
Major Attribute: None
Flute Type: Multiple, percussion
Material: Chalcedony
Similar Survey Points: MC 1050, MC 806, MC 826
Provenance: Buckingham County

Comment:
Points 1015 to 1019 may suggest a local quarry effort but travel to/from south-central Virginia is suggested. These points may represent an uplands campsite or foraging area (as Gardner 1989). Style and breakage is similar to MC 1050 (this paper).

McCary Survey Point Number MC 1020

MC 1020 was field recorded. It is a heavily patinated, broken (by Indians) point. It is made from a brown/grayish slate. Or, it could be made from a weathered hornfel (from Michael Johnson's review). Basal area grinding is moderate. Cross section is plano-convex suggesting it was made off a large flake. Lateral blade margins appear to be straight to slight excurvate. Flutes (A1 and B1) are wide and bold single channels which are worn by weathering. It has a white streak across its proximal margin. It is a surface find in Nelson County. Figure 62 shows point photographs and drawings. Table 3 provides the metrics for this point.

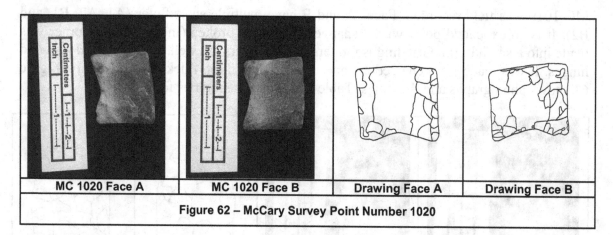

| MC 1020 Face A | MC 1020 Face B | Drawing Face A | Drawing Face B |

Figure 62 – McCary Survey Point Number 1020

Length: 26.0 mm
L/W*T Ratio: N/A
Major Attribute: None
Flute Type: Single, percussion
Material: Slate
Similar Survey Points: MC 357, MC 367, MC 282, MC 325, MC 303
Provenance: Nelson County

McCary Survey Point Number MC 1021

MC 1021 was laboratory recorded and was submitted to the Survey by committee member Charles Bartlett. Point has a small flat area suggesting a flake source in its manufacture. Cross section is classified as plano-convex. It is made from a light gray (7.5 y/5/2) chert (SG 2.503), which is heavily patinated. Basal area has heavy grinding, and point has pointed corners. Flute (A1) hinged out and the reverse face, Flute (B1) feathered out; it is a well-made point. The D/P index (as in Hranicky 2005) is .90, which indicates a base-to-tip taper. It was found on/near the Holston River in Smyth County. Hafting margins are slightly encurvate. Figure 63 shows point photographs and drawings. Table 3 provides the metrics for this point.

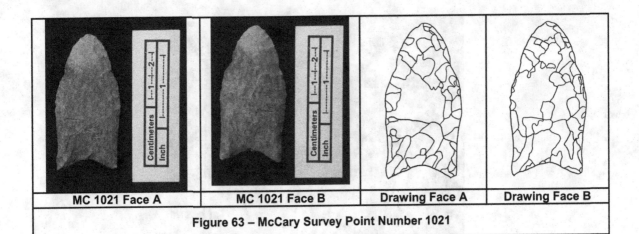

| MC 1021 Face A | MC 1021 Face B | Drawing Face A | Drawing Face B |

Figure 63 – McCary Survey Point Number 1021

Length: 51.0 mm
L/W*T Ratio: 14.280
Major Attribute: Shape
Flute Type: Single, percussion
Material: Chert
Similar Survey Points: MC 25, MC 119, MC 154, MC 304, MC 707, MC 900
Provenance: Smyth County

McCary Survey Point Number MC 1022

MC 1022 was laboratory recorded. It is a blade point (plano cross section) which was confirmed by Dennis Stanford of the Smithsonian (Figure 64). It is made from brown (7.5YR/6/8) quartzite. The blade's medial ridge (Face A) is still present. Each face has a short, single flute/flake (A1 and B1) which hinges out. The bulb scar is not present. The base-to-tip (D/P index) is 0.86, or base-to-tip taper. Basal area has moderate grinding. Corner is broken (Indian); point may have been longer when initially made. It was a surface find on/near the Nottoway River in Dinwiddie County. MC 68 was recorded by McCary at a thickness of 3.5 mm; its drawing resembles MC 1022. Figure 65 shows point photographs and drawings. Table 3 provides the metrics for this point.

Figure 64 – Dennis Stanford of the Smithsonian Examining Survey Point Number MC 1022

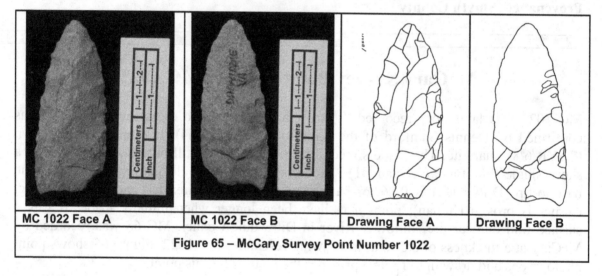

| MC 1022 Face A | MC 1022 Face B | Drawing Face A | Drawing Face B |

Figure 65 – McCary Survey Point Number 1022

<u>Length</u>: 64.0 mm
L/W*T Ratio: 23.040
Major Attribute: Blade technology
Flute Type: Single, percussion/pressure?
Material: Quartzite
<u>Similar Survey Points</u>: MC 68, MC 1045
<u>Provenance</u>: Dinwiddie County

<u>Comment</u>:
The blade point has been identified by the Survey. However, their true nature as a paleopoint needs to be established in an archaeological context. Figure 66 shows another example. It is made from rhyolite and has short basal flutes or thinning flakes. Base

margins are moderately ground. Measurements are: L = 73, W = 24, T = 9 mm. This specimen will not be given a number until more morphological data are collected; it is a type, and perhaps it could be called the Stanford point type?

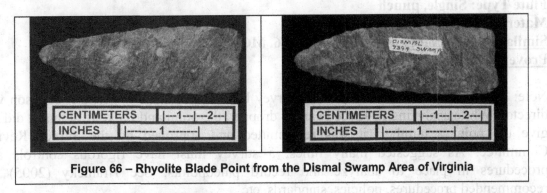

Figure 66 – Rhyolite Blade Point from the Dismal Swamp Area of Virginia

McCary Survey Point Number MC 1023

Point 1023 was laboratory recorded. It is the distal end of a point, which is generally called the Redstone type. It was found by Fred Morgan in the 1950s. Point suffered post-Indian and Indian breakage. It is made of a dark gray (2.5YR/4/1) shale (SG 2.050). One face shows probably 50% full-face fluting (A1). It has fine edge retouch, and cross section is flat. The unfluted distal end's face has the medial ridge remaining. It is a surface find off the middle James River; no provenance remains with the point notes.

This point has edge-to-edge outré passé percussion flaking. The author has suggested this technique has Old World similarities – not suggesting any cross-Atlantic relationships (Hranicky 2005). This point style illustrates why all fluted points are not Clovis points. The point could be classified as a Redstone or Cumberland point (Hranicky 2007). Figure 67 shows point photographs and drawings. Table 3 provides the metrics for this point.

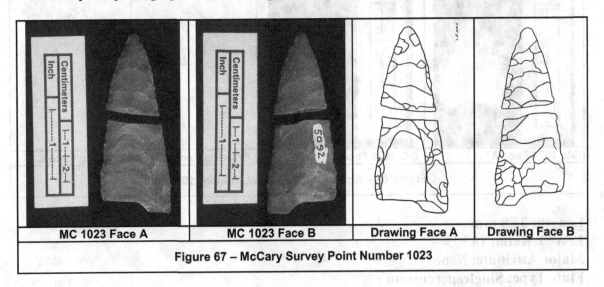

| MC 1023 Face A | MC 1023 Face B | Drawing Face A | Drawing Face B |

Figure 67 – McCary Survey Point Number 1023

179

Length: 59.0 ?
L/W*T Ratio: 14.160
Major Attribute: Fluting
Flute Type: Single, punch
Material: Shale
Similar Survey Points: MC 1040, MC 226, MC 13, MC 158, MC 478
Provenance: Henrico County ?

Note: This point was submitted to the Survey by the author while Michael Johnson was director. While analyzing it, Joyce Pearsall dropped the point and broke it. Johnson did not give the point a number; it was resubmitted and approved by the Survey Review Committee. As suggested many times, a survey must have rigorous controls and procedures in place to analyze and record paleopoints. See Hranicky (2005) for recommended procedures, policies, standards, etc.

McCary Survey Point Number MC 1024

MC 1024 was laboratory recorded. It is an expended small, white (2.5Y/8/1) quartz (SG 2.204) point. Both blade edges are beveled. Flute (A1) hinged out and the reverse face, Flute (B1) feathered out; it is a well-made point. Cross section is bi-convex. Point has rounded corners and probably represents the Late Paleoindian era. It was a surface find on/near the Dan River, Halifax County. Michael Johnson suggests the point certainly has Dalton and Hardaway attributes. It was included because its lateral margin has a flake broken or damaged in hafting. The round corners are also presented on points MC 1025 and 1028 below. Figure 68 shows point photographs and drawings. Table 3 provides the metrics for this point.

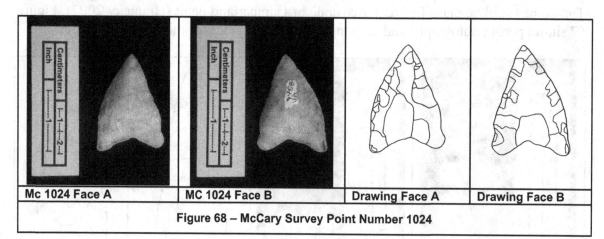

| Mc 1024 Face A | MC 1024 Face B | Drawing Face A | Drawing Face B |

Figure 68 – McCary Survey Point Number 1024

Length: 36.8 mm
L/W*T Ratio: 10.903
Major Attribute: None
Flute Type: Single, percussion

Material: Quartz
Similar Survey Points: MC 607, MC 644, MC 930
Provenance: Halifax County

McCary Survey Point Number MC 1025

MC 1025 was field recorded. It is made from a gray chert point. It is lightly serrated, and cross section is bi-convex. Blade edges are slightly excurvate and are translucent. Basal area grinding is light. Concavity is deep and corners are round. Flutes are difficult to discern and record; they are composite flutes. It was found in the early 1990s near Dublin, Virginia and is assigned to Pulaski County. It is a typical Paleoindian fluted triangle point; it does not appear to have been reworked into its current structure. Figure 69 shows point photographs and drawings. Table 3 provides the metrics for this point.

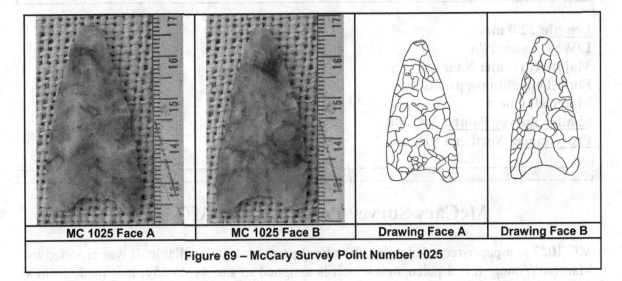

| MC 1025 Face A | MC 1025 Face B | Drawing Face A | Drawing Face B |

Figure 69 – McCary Survey Point Number 1025

Length: 45.0 mm
L/W*T Ratio: 12.272
Major Attribute: Triangle shape
Flute Type: Composite, pressure?
Material: Chert
Similar Survey Points: MC 178, MC 249, MC 607, MC 669
Provenance: Pulaski County, Virginia.

McCary Survey Point Number MC 1026

MC 1026 was laboratory recorded. It is a broken base (snap fracture) which probably shows a hafting break (Indian). Corner breakage may have occurred during manufacture. It is made of a gray (Gley #2/5/5GB) chert (SG 1.760). Cross section is bi-convex, and basal area grinding is light. Flutes (A1 and B1) are bold, single channel, and feathered. It was a 1970s surface find in northern Virginia. Figure 70 shows point photographs and drawings. Table 3 provides the metrics for this point.

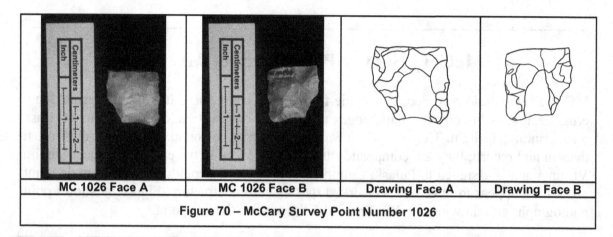

| MC 1026 Face A | MC 1026 Face B | Drawing Face A | Drawing Face B |

Figure 70 – McCary Survey Point Number 1026

Length: 22.0 mm
L/W*T Ratio: N/A
Major Attribute: None
Flute Type: Single, pressure
Material: Chert
Similar Survey Points: MC 400
Provenance: Northern Virginia ?

McCary Survey Point Number MC 1027

MC 1027 is a paper-recorded point; the actual point was not available. It was reported by Manfred Young. It is a paleopoint which is assigned to site 44MY359. It is made from a cream-colored chert. Both faces show flutes, and blade edges are excurvate. Flutes are bold and probably a single channel on both faces. Flute A1 is short due to point breakage; Flute B1 is long and hinged. Point's original length was probably approximately 79.9 mm based on edge curve. The cause of breakage cannot be determined accurately, but a snap break is suggested. It is a surface find on a site in Montgomery County. Figure 71 shows point photographs and drawings. Table 3 provides the metrics for this point.

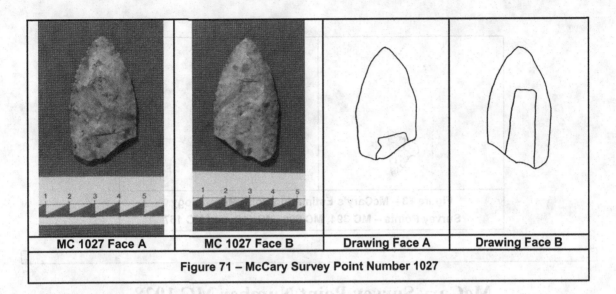

| MC 1027 Face A | MC 1027 Face B | Drawing Face A | Drawing Face B |

Figure 71 – McCary Survey Point Number 1027

Length: 51.0 mm ?
L/W*T Ratio: N/A
Major Attribute: Flaking
Flute Type: Single, punch?
Material: Chert
Similar Survey Points: MC 873, MC 875
Provenance: Montgomery County, Virginia.

Comment:
This method can be used to estimate the point's (approximal fragment A^F) length for broken tips (Figure 72). The A^F is considered the maximum length of the point based on general Clovis symmetry. By using a French curve (drafting tool), the excurvate blade edge is used to estimate the point's maximum base (Hranicky 2008).

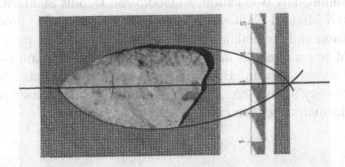

Figure 72 – Approximal Fragment Length Estimate Method (McCary Point Number 1027)

This technique was applied by McCary during his term of recording paleopoints. See Figure 73. The estimate is always subjective and the point's true form will never be known.

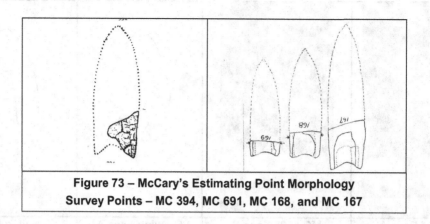

**Figure 73 – McCary's Estimating Point Morphology
Survey Points – MC 394, MC 691, MC 168, and MC 167**

McCary Survey Point Number MC 1028

MC 1028 was laboratory recorded. And, it was reviewed by more archaeologists than any previous point in the Survey. Point was displayed by the current owner's father, C. C. Hatfield, at the 1961 Scientific Exhibit, Medical Society of Virginia, at which he comments in a flyer: *All articles are displayed from Smyth County, Virginia unless otherwise labeled. All objects are authentic finds by the exhibitor or his associates except those marked by a star.* Point and its history were submitted by Charles Bartlett.

It is a gray (Gley 4/N or 5/N) flint (SG 2.360), which appears to be southwestern Virginia flint. Patination is light, but the point has all required attributes, especially basal thinning flakes after fluting. Fluting on Face A is composite fluting (A1n); fluting of Face B is a single channel flute (B1). It is probably a surface find in Smyth County. It has a flat cross section and probably is made by a biface reduction strategy.

The author took the point to the October 2005 Paleo-Conference in Columbia, South Carolina. It was examined by Bob Patton, Al Goodyear, Dennis Stanford, David Anderson, Gary Fogelman, and Michael Collins – all agreed it was a "good" point. Even with this review, Mike Johnson and the author agreed that the point had to pass a ferric oxidation test before it would be accepted (as in Hranicky 2008); it did pass somewhat satisfactorily. From the Survey review, Edward Bottoms suggested it be included in the Survey; his opinion was the Survey's key here. Figure 74 shows point photographs and drawings. Table 3 provides the metrics for this point.

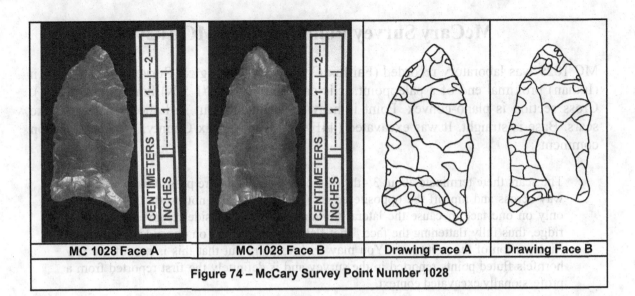

| MC 1028 Face A | MC 1028 Face B | Drawing Face A | Drawing Face B |

Figure 74 – McCary Survey Point Number 1028

<u>Length</u>: 56.0 mm
L/W*T Ratio: 10.266
Major Attribute: Flaking
Flute Type: Composite, pressure
Material: Flint
<u>Similar Survey Points</u>: MC 230, MC 439, MC 475, MC 507, MC 811, MC 736
<u>Provenance</u>: Smyth County, Virginia. ?

<u>Comment</u>:
When first examining the point, Johnson and the author both thought it was a newly-made point. This "newness" could be the result of washing the point with a detergent soap. As such, the final acceptance comes down to the Survey director, but the Survey Review Committee recommended its assignment as Survey point MC 1028. Survey recommends that paleopoints not be washed; however, if needed, only use distilled water.

McCary Survey Point Number MC 1029

MC 1029 was laboratory recorded (Fairfax County Archaeological Survey). It is a broken (Indian) proximal end of a paleopoint. It is dark gray (Gley #1 5/N) hornfel (SG 2.461). Cross section is plano-convex. Point is heavily weathered, but still shows parallel flake scars. Base is straight. It was excavated (44FX2553) in Fairfax County. Michael Johnson comments:

> The scars there terminate about 3/4ths of the way across. Outré passé flakes go all the way across and nip off the opposite edge. These flakes did not do that. It is fluted only on one face, because the lateral thinning on the other side removed the fluting ridge, thus fully flattening the face. That flattening is present on one side of the distal (tip) portion of the point too. You may wish to point out that this is one of the few hornfels fluted points reported in the survey and is definitely the first reported from a professionally excavated context.

Figure 75 shows point photographs and drawings. Table 3 provides the metrics for this point.

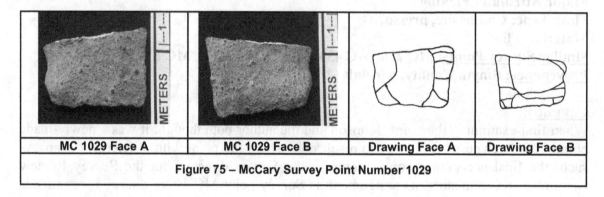

MC 1029 Face A	MC 1029 Face B	Drawing Face A	Drawing Face B

Figure 75 – McCary Survey Point Number 1029

Length: 24.7 mm ?
L/W*T Ratio: N/A
Major Attribute: Material
Flute Type: Single, percussion
Material: Hornfel
Similar Survey Points: ?
Provenance: Fairfax County, Virginia.

Comment:
Figure 76 and Figure 77 show a heavily weathered point tip that was found in association with MC 1028. It was laboratory recorded (Fairfax County Archaeological Survey). It is a broken (Indian) distal end of a paleopoint. It is dark gray (Gley #1 5/N) hornfel (SG 3.415). Cross section is plano-convex. Since it is not fluted, it was not given a survey number. It has bold outré passé flake scars. It was excavated in Fairfax County. Its measurements are L = 37.3, W = 32.0, and T = 7.5. Weight is 8.4 g.

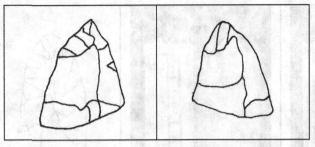

Figure 76 – Point Drawings (Faces A and B)

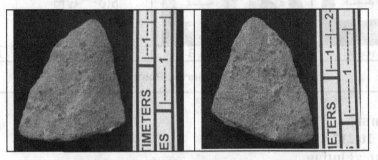

Figure 77 – Point Photographs (Faces A and B)

This point(s) is reported in Johnson (2006) and he defines hornfel as "a thermally metamorphosed (cooked) shale from the Culpeper Basin of central and northern Virginia and southern Maryland."

McCary Survey Point Number MC 1030

MC 1030 was field recorded. It is a well-made medium, tan (10YR 8/4) rhyolite (cobble) point. It has a deep concavity (16.7 x 8.0 mm) and basal area grinding is moderate. Point has three hinged flakes; all other scars are feathered. Cross section is D-shaped with parallel flaking. Flute A1 is broad and is a single channel flute. Flute B1 is a long narrow single channel flute. This well-made point has lower parallel lateral thinning. Other flake scars are outré passé and suggest its Paleoindian nature. The point's maker set up a medial ridge from which he struck off the flute. Flutes on both faces are wide and well formed. After the flutes were taken, basal thinning was performed on both base faces. Point has one attribute that needs noting: shallow waisting. This attribute appears to be Late Paleoindian and may be characteristic of Virginia and North Carolina points in this time period. The D/P index is 1.153, which indicated a thicker blade than base. It was a surface find in Patrick County near/on the Dan River. Figure 78 shows point photographs and drawings. Table 3 provides the metrics for this point.

187

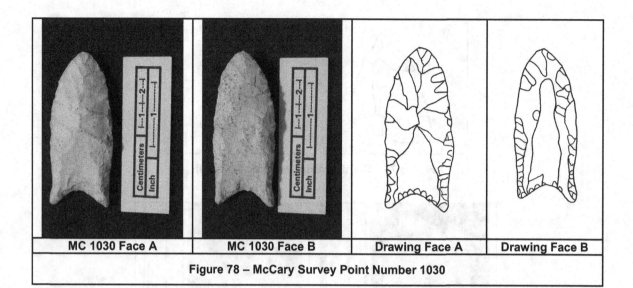

| MC 1030 Face A | MC 1030 Face B | Drawing Face A | Drawing Face B |

Figure 78 – McCary Survey Point Number 1030

Length: 57.0 mm
L/W*T Ratio: 16.217
Major Attribute: Fluting
Flute Type: Single, percussion
Material: Rhyolite
Similar Survey Points: MC 341, MC 553, MC 431, MC 617
Provenance: Patrick County

McCary Survey Point Number MC 1031

MC 1031 was field recorded. It is made from white (Gley 8/N) quartz (Type 1 – brittle). The D/P index is 1.088 which is a relatively flat base-to-tip point; however, it is a thick point. Flake scars and flutes are difficult to discern; however, both faces have wide shallow flutes (A1 and B1). Basal grinding is heavy. It is a thick point due to being made from quartz (see L/W*T ratio). It was a surface find in Patrick County. The point is classified as a Wheeler point (Cambron 1955 and Holland 1970:92). Holland also illustrates the point style as his Patrick indented base type.

This style paleopoint is tentatively named the Chapel Hill type (Hranicky 2006) after a city where an old friend taught archaeology. For type justification, these points are made primarily from white quartz (and some rhyolite), thick (>12 mm), always fluted, cross section is biconvex, have a shallow-to-deep concave base, and are basally ground. Fluting is by percussion flaking. Distribution appears to be southern Virginia and North Carolina. Figure 79 shows point photographs and drawings. Table 3 provides the metrics for this point.

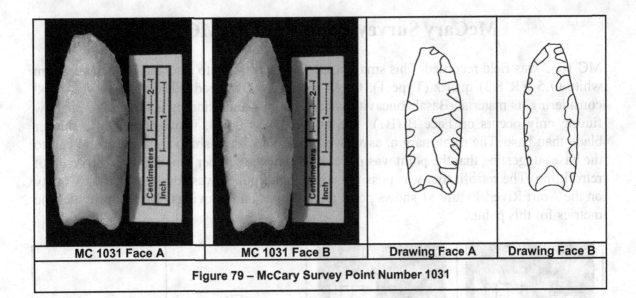

| MC 1031 Face A | MC 1031 Face B | Drawing Face A | Drawing Face B |

Figure 79 – McCary Survey Point Number 1031

Length: 67.98 mm
L/W*T Ratio: 34.283
Major Attribute: Pointed corners
Flute Type: Thinning, percussion
Material: Quartz
Similar Survey Points: MC 138, MC 536, MC 819, MC 890, MC 949
Provenance: Patrick County

Comment:
The model for this point comes from the Williamson site, Dinwiddie County, Virginia. These points have not been identified in Clovis technology. See Figure 80.

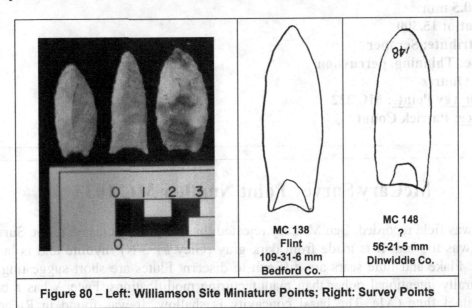

MC 138
Flint
109-31-6 mm
Bedford Co.

MC 148
?
56-21-5 mm
Dinwiddie Co.

Figure 80 – Left: Williamson Site Miniature Points; Right: Survey Points

McCary Survey Point Number MC 1032

MC 1032 was field recorded. This small point was modified into a scraper. It is made from white (7.5 YR 8/3) quartz (Type 1). Cross section is D-shaped. Flaking quality is good considering its material. Basal concavity is very shallow and grinding is moderate. Shallow fluting only occurs on Face B (B1). The D/P index is 0.944, which indicated a thicker blade than base. The right margin, as viewed from Face B, is sharp from the distal end to the base suggesting that the point was never hafted or the scraper function was the result of retrofitting. The retrofit tool was possibly a handheld tool. It was found in Patrick County on the Arart River. Figure 81 shows point photographs and drawings. Table 3 provides the metrics for this point.

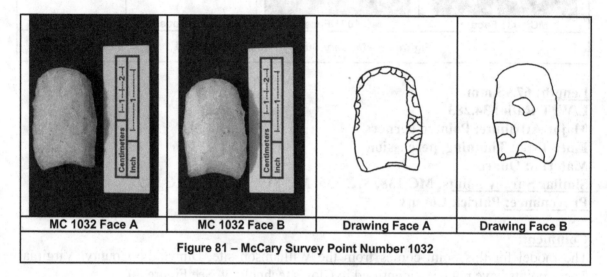

| MC 1032 Face A | MC 1032 Face B | Drawing Face A | Drawing Face B |

Figure 81 – McCary Survey Point Number 1032

Length: 40.5 mm
L/W*T Ratio: 15.300
Major Attribute: Scraper
Flute Type: Thinning, percussion
Material: Quartz
Similar Survey Points: MC 222
Provenance: Patrick County

McCary Survey Point Number MC 1033

MC 1033 was field recorded. Ben McCary rejected this point for inclusion in the Survey – he said it was too big. It is made from dark gray (Gley #1 3/N) rhyolite and is heavily weathered. Flake and flute scars are difficult to discern. Flutes are short suggesting they were culturally intentional rather than manufacturing modifications. Face A has a broad, single channel flute (A1). The basal concavity is shallow. It was found in Richmond on/near the James River. Each face has a different degree of patination.

Flute function/purpose has a lengthy discussion in the literature (see Hranicky 2008) and is noted because the flutes on this point are short. It has a flat profile and moderate basal grinding. It is now the longest point in the Survey and is easily classified as a fine point due to its length. Figure 82 shows point photographs. Table 3 provides the metrics for this point.

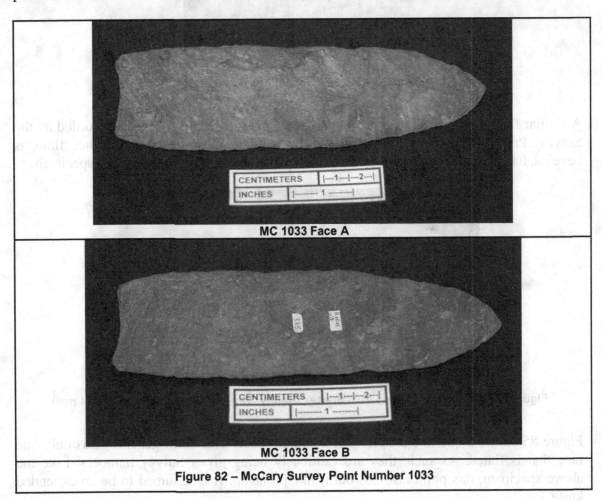

Figure 82 – McCary Survey Point Number 1033

Length: 171.00 mm
L/W*T Ratio: 32.858
Major Attribute: Size
Flute Type: Single, percussion
Material: Rhyolite
Similar Survey Points: MC 1000
Provenance: City of Richmond

Comment:
Figure 83 shows fluting (A1) which was struck by percussion.

Figure 83 – MC 1033 Point Flute (Face A – A1)

A similar fine-grain quartzite point from Sussex County, Virginia has been recorded by the Survey. Presently, no Survey number has been assigned. It has a single face flute, is beveled, has burin tip, was made by high quality flaking. Figure 84 shows this specimen.

Figure 84 – Large Fluted Biface from Sussex County, Virginia (L = 125, W = 44, T = 14 mm)

Figure 85 shows a quartz example with a straight base. This form generally has only one face that is fluted. As such, they are cautiously being given Survey numbers. Like the above specimen, this point also has burin-like point tip. It is assumed to be an expended knife.

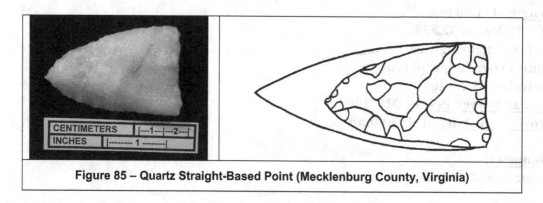

Figure 85 – Quartz Straight-Based Point (Mecklenburg County, Virginia)

McCary Survey Point Number MC 1034

MC 1034 was field recorded. It is an expended small white (7.5 YR 8/3) quartz (SG 2.350). Cross section is bi-convex and has fine flaking. It is a completely expended paleopoint. Face A has a composite flute (A1.1 and A1.2); Face B has a single flute (B1) channel. Basal area grinding is heavy. For its width, it has wide flutes which were probably percussion flaked. It is a surface find from a probable Paleoindian area on the Dan River in Halifax County. The middle Dan River basin has produced numerous points for the Survey; it is worthy of a major archaeological investigation. Six points from this area were donated to the ASV's museum. Figure 86 shows point photographs and drawings. Table 3 provides the metrics for this point.

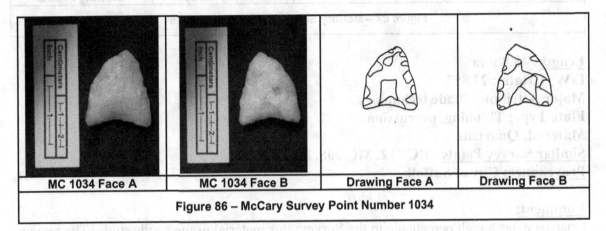

MC 1034 Face A	MC 1034 Face B	Drawing Face A	Drawing Face B

Figure 86 – McCary Survey Point Number 1034

Length: 32.0 mm
L/W*T Ratio: 9.481
Major Attribute: None
Flute Type: Single, percussion
Material: Quartz
Similar Survey Points: MC 315, MC 366, MC 367
Provenance: Halifax County

McCary Survey Point Number MC 1035

MC 1035 was laboratory recorded. It is a medium, brown (10 YR 5/3) fine-grain quartzite (SG 2.707) point. Due to resharpening, blade margins are irregular. Base is shallow and moderately ground. Both faces (A and B) have wide, basal, paper-thin shallow thinning flutes/flakes (A1 and B1). Cross section is plano-convex suggesting it was made off a blade or large flat flake. Flaking quality is poor showing numerous hinges. It is a surface find in the city of Suffolk. The basal concavity grinding treatment is shallow which is argued – it is Paleoindian.. Figure 87 shows point photographs and drawings. Table 3 provides the metrics for this point.

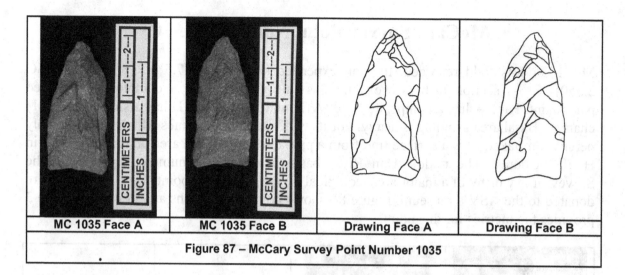

| MC 1035 Face A | MC 1035 Face B | Drawing Face A | Drawing Face B |

Figure 87 – McCary Survey Point Number 1035

Length: 48.8 mm
L/W*T Ratio: 23.857
Major Attribute: Blade technology
Flute Type: Thinning, percussion
Material: Quartzite
Similar Survey Points: MC 212, MC 208, MC 209
Provenance: City of Suffolk

Comment:

Quartizite has a high percentage in the Survey; this material usage needs study. The review committee suggested it was a Woodland knife. However, quartzite and slate blade points do occur in the Paleoindian era. See MC 1022, this paper. The L/W*T ratio for blade (nonexpended) points is > 25.000 to 1.

McCary Survey Point Number MC 1036

MC 1036 was laboratory recorded; it is a small, triangularly-shaped point with a deep concavity. One corner is broken, and the other one is pointed. It is made from white quartz (Gley – chart 1 8/N), and its surface has heavy oxidation. As with many white quartz paleopoints, it is only fluted on one face; however, Face B was struck producing a shallow indention. Flute A1 is shallow and feathers. Face B has stacked basal hinges which were attempts at fluting the point. The overall flaking quality is poor. Cross section is biconvex and tip is broken. Figure 88 shows point photographs and drawings. Table 4 provides the metrics for this point.

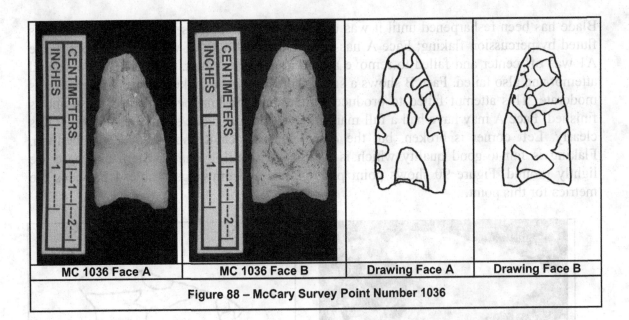

| MC 1036 Face A | MC 1036 Face B | Drawing Face A | Drawing Face B |

Figure 88 – McCary Survey Point Number 1036

Length: 47 mm
L/W*T Ratio: 18.800
Major Attribute: Triangle shape
Flute Type: Single, percussion
Material: Quartz
Similar Survey Points: MC 969, MC 345, MC 688, MC 799, MC 823, MC 328
Provenance: Franklin County.

Comment:
Fluting on quartz points is difficult to record because they are often have shallow flute channels. Figure 89 show MC 1036's flute channel.

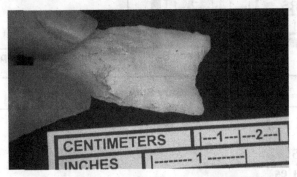

Figure 89 – Flute (A1) Channel on MC 1036

McCary Survey Point Number MC 1037

MC 1037 was laboratory recorded. It is made from a fine-grain, white (5Y 8/1) quartz. The shape is classified as a triangle form; however, its history was probably a lanceolate shape.

Blade has been resharpened until it was considered by its user as being expended. It was fluted by percussion flaking; Face A has two bold fluted both of which hinged out. Flute A1 was off center and failed to remove a high area on the point. Flute A2 was a second attempt and also failed. Face B shows a small flake removal (stacked hinges). Patination is moderate. This attempt failed to produce a flute, and the knapper accepted the point as finished. Face A may have had a full margin bevel, but the blade/stem does not show this clearly. Left corner is broken, but the complete basal cavity shows a deep indention. Flaking is fair-to-good quality which is relative to working quartz. Stem and base are lightly ground. Figure 90 shows point photographs and drawings. Table 4 provides the metrics for this point.

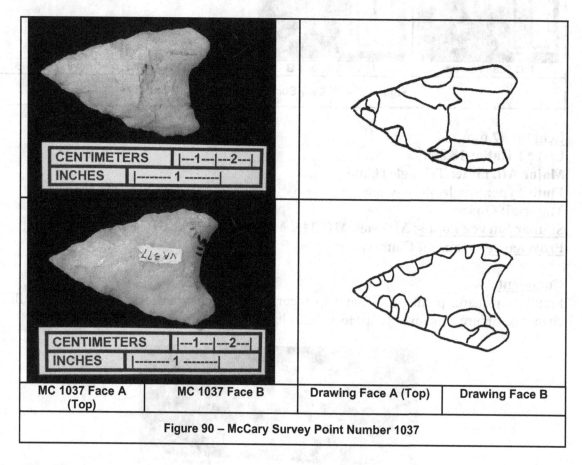

| MC 1037 Face A (Top) | MC 1037 Face B | Drawing Face A (Top) | Drawing Face B |

Figure 90 – McCary Survey Point Number 1037

Length: 50 mm
L/W*T Ratio: 15.625
Major Attribute: Flutes
Flute Type: Multiple, percussion
Material: Quartz
Similar Survey Points: MC 607, MC 625, MC 786
Provenance: Mecklenburg County, Virginia

Comment:
Figure 91 shows both flutes on Face A. They are bold and hinge rather than have a feathering end to them. Hinge and flute have oxidation residue. Expended quartz

196

paleopoints are frequently overlooked by collectors; they are usually classified by professional archaeologists as triangles.

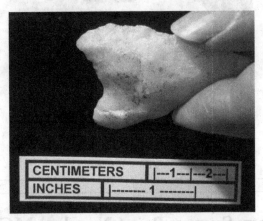

Figure 91 – MC 1037 Showing Flutes A1 and A2

Figure 92 shows possible retrofitting which probably applies to MC 1037. Once a tip is broken, it can be placed back into service as a new point. The tip may or may not have remnant fluting.

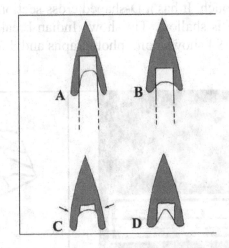

Figure 92 – Possible Retrofitting of a Triangle Paleopoint (After: Ellis 2004)

MC 1037 provides an excellent opportunity to measure it flute depth (Figure 93). On problem in measuring flute depth is the reference spot from which to make the measurement. Usually, it is the highest spot on the point's face. Instruments exist for 1000th of an inch; naturally, they have been replaced by digital equipment. But, not for the Survey. Maximum flute depth for MC 1037 is: 1.680 mm or 0.01076 in. The production energy through quartz to produce the flute is a topic for the next generation of paleopoint archaeologists.

Figure 93 - Measuring Flute Depth

McCary Survey Point Number MC 1038

MC 1038 was laboratory recorded. It is a small point made from chalcedony. It is a gray (Gley - #2 8/5PB). It is fluted (A1) only on one face which may have also been an attempt to remove the stacked hinges. It is truly one of the poorest-made points in the Survey (see MC 1006). Both lateral basal margins are moderately ground or smoothed. Left margin shows tip-to-base edge retouch. It has a D-shaped cross section suggesting it was made off a large flake. Basal cavity is shallow. Tip shows Indian breakage. Material also suggests the Paleoindian era. Figure 94 shows point photographs and drawings. Table 4 provides the metrics for this point.

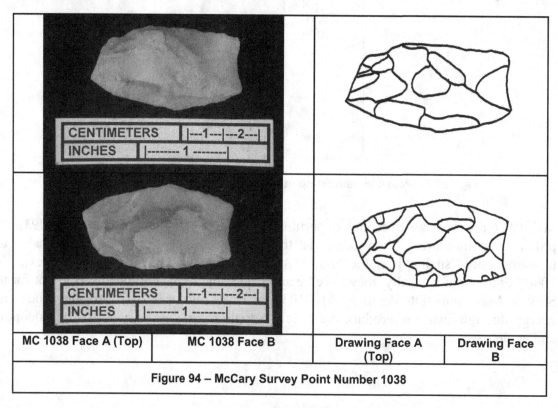

MC 1038 Face A (Top)	MC 1038 Face B	Drawing Face A (Top)	Drawing Face B
Figure 94 – McCary Survey Point Number 1038			

Length: 47 mm
L/W*T Ratio: 18.076
Major Attribute: Stacked hinges
Flute Type: Single, percussion
Material: Chalcedony
<u>Similar Survey Points</u>: MC 175, MC 793
<u>Provenance</u>: Nelson County.

McCary Survey Point Number MC 1039

MC 1039 was field recorded. It is a small, expended point made from a tan quartzite. It is fluted on Face A (Flute A1) with Face B (Flute B1?) being difficult to determine, if it is fluted. It has a biconvex cross section and shows poor quality flaking. It has moderate basal grounding. It is classified a Late Paleoindian as it shows minor waisting or flared corners. Figure 95 shows point photographs and drawings. Table 4 provides the metrics for this point.

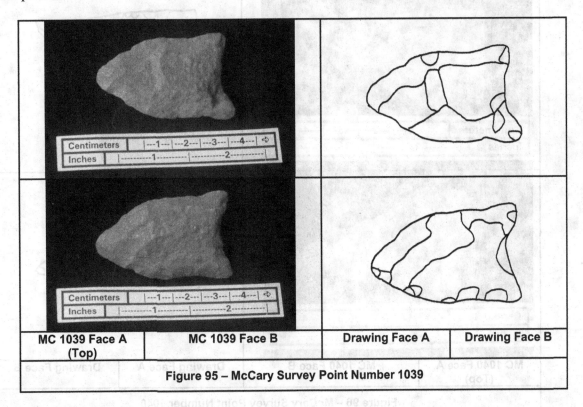

| MC 1039 Face A (Top) | MC 1039 Face B | Drawing Face A | Drawing Face B |

Figure 95 – McCary Survey Point Number 1039

Length: 47 mm
L/W*T Ratio: 29.766
Major Attribute: Flared corners
Flute Type: Single, percussion
Material: Quartzite

McCary Survey Point Number MC 1040

MC 1040 was field recorded and represents one of the greater contributions from the Survey. It was found near a spring on what appears to be a Pleistocene ledge that was covered with Holocene soils. It is a broken point that suggests it was ceremonially broken, perhaps upon the death of its owner. Both faces show only one margin with lateral thinning. The opposite face does not have enough margin to determine thinning, retouch, or resharpening. It has part of a corner flare which identifies it as a Cumberland (Lewis 1954). It is made from a flint which is not found in Virginia. Flute A1 has ripples (ondulations) which suggest that the point did not have full-face fluting. Flute B1 hinged about midpoint with a massive hinge scar. Figure 96 shows point photographs and drawings. Table 4 provides the metrics for this point.

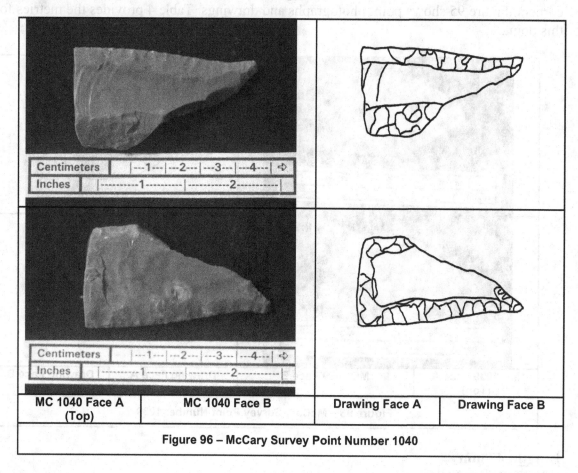

MC 1040 Face A (Top)	MC 1040 Face B	Drawing Face A	Drawing Face B

Figure 96 – McCary Survey Point Number 1040

Length: N/A
L/W*T Ratio: N/A
Major Attribute: Fluting

Flute Type: Single, punch
Material: Flint
Similar Survey Points: MC 226, MC 260, MC 465, MC 158
Provenance: Halifax County, Virginia

Comment:
A possible Cumberland tip was found in Virginia. Since it was not fluted, it was not included in the Survey; however, its metrics were recorded. It has a diamond cross section, but it is questionable because it is made from North Carolina slate. Figure 97 shows this specimen.

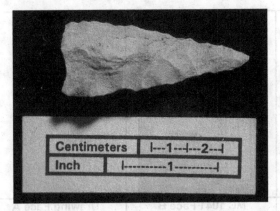

Figure 97 – Possible Distal End of a Cumberland Point from Halifax County, Virginia

As examples of the completed Cumberland point shapes, Figure 98 provides drawings by Floyd Painter. The type is identified as a long narrow point with full-face fluting and flared corners. Full-face fluting often failed in Cumberland technology. Knappers did not create an adequate ridge to carry the fluting energy, or they did not apply enough force to complete the flute.

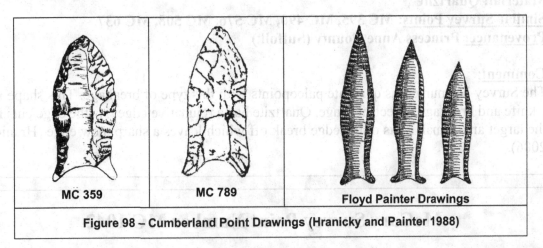

MC 359   MC 789   Floyd Painter Drawings

Figure 98 – Cumberland Point Drawings (Hranicky and Painter 1988)

The Cumberland point is not related to Clovis and may be older by 1000 years (Hranicky 2005). Clovis is a biface reduction technology; Cumberland is a blade reduction technology (Hranicky 2007).

201

McCary Survey Point Number MC 1041

MC 1041 was laboratory recorded. It is a well made broken quartzite (Gray 5Y 6/1) point. Flutes (A1 and B1) are bold, single channel flutes and probably extended past its midblade. It has fine flaking and a biconvex cross section. Breakage is Indian and was a snap break. It was found in the same field as MC 1042. Figure 99 shows point photographs and drawings. Table 4 provides the metrics for this point.

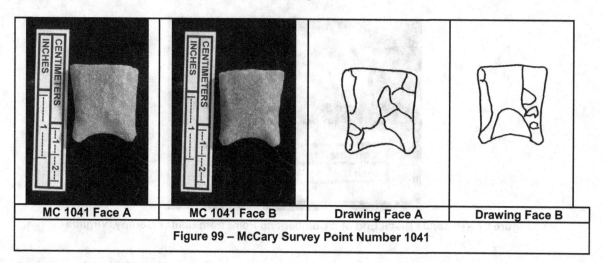

| MC 1041 Face A | MC 1041 Face B | Drawing Face A | Drawing Face B |

Figure 99 – McCary Survey Point Number 1041

Length: x 33 mm
L/W*T Ratio: N/A
Major Attribute: Grinding
Flute Type: Single, percussion
Material: Quartzite
Similar Survey Points: MC 395, MC 490, MC 576, MC 508, MC 637
Provenance: Princess Anne County (Suffolk)

Comment:
The Survey has numerous quartzite paleopoints with this type of breakage. This shape was a knife and breakage reflects it usage. Quartzite has a rejunative edge. As the edge cuts into the target area, small parts of the edge break off which leaves a sharp, new edge (Hranicky 2006).

McCary Survey Point Number MC 1042

MC 1042 was laboratory recorded. It is a small triangularly-shaped point made from white (10Y 8/1) quartzite. It was a surface find in the same field as MC 1041. Base is lightly ground. It has a single face flute (A1). Corners are pointed and turn inward. Tip is broken.

Face B has stacked hinges around a large flat spot. Figure 100 shows point photographs and drawings. Table 4 provides the metrics for this point.

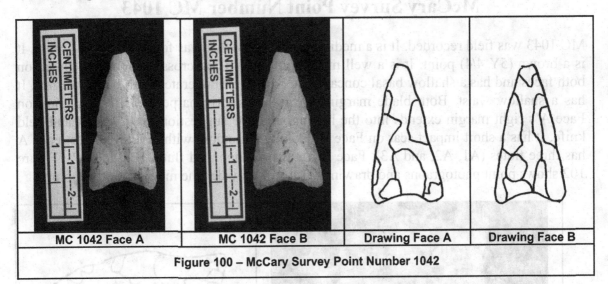

| MC 1042 Face A | MC 1042 Face B | Drawing Face A | Drawing Face B |

Figure 100 – McCary Survey Point Number 1042

Length: x 49 mm
L/W*T Ratio: 16.000
Major Attribute: Triangle shape
Flute Type: Single, percussion
Material: Quartz
Similar Survey Points: MC 969, MC 140, MC 460, MC 559, MC 966
Provenance: Princess Anne County (Suffolk)

Comment:
For some archaeologists, the triangle does not occur in paleopoints, or the Paleoindian Period. Obviously for the Survey, and as recorded by Ben McCary, the triangle paleopoint does occur in Virginia. However, they are not generally fluted as with the lanceolate forms. Basal thinning flakes are usually removed; if not, then it is almost impossible to distinguish them from Woodland Period triangles. Figure 101 is a case where all applies. Note the classic shallow concavity. It has small basal thinning flakes and is not ground. The reader can judge – Woodland or Paleoindian? And, do not forget the controversial Santa Fe triangle paleopoint of Florida (Bullin 1968/75).

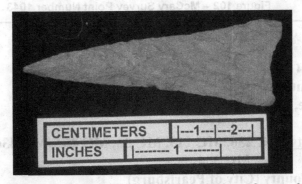

Figure 101 - Slate Triangle Point from Mecklenburg County, Virginia

203

McCary Survey Point Number MC 1043

MC 1043 was field recorded. It is a medium jasper point that was found on a CCC camp. It is a brown (5Y 4/4) point. It is a well made point with a flat cross section. It is fluted on both faces and has a shallow basal concavity. Grinding is moderate on all basal margins. It has a shallow waist. Both blade margins are retouched (resharpened). Resharpening on Face A's right margin extends into the hafting area; the suggestion is: It was a hand-held knife. It has a short impact scar on Face B. Flaking is random with several hinges. Face A has three flutes (A1, A2, and A3). Face B has two pronounced flutes (B1 and B2). Figure 102 shows point photographs and drawings. Table 4 provides the metrics for this point.

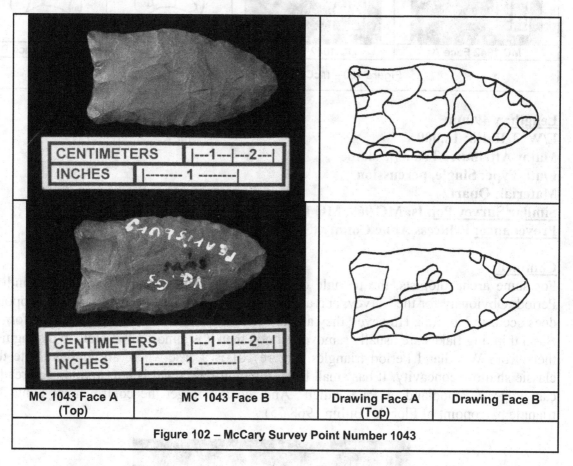

| MC 1043 Face A (Top) | MC 1043 Face B | Drawing Face A (Top) | Drawing Face B |

Figure 102 – McCary Survey Point Number 1043

Length: 52 mm
L/W*T Ratio: 14.274
Major Attribute: Fluting
Flute Type: Multiple, pressure
Material: Jasper
Similar Survey Points: MC 230, MC 119, MC 56, MC 461, MC 436, MC 366, MC 300, MC 304
Provenance: Giles County (City of Pearisburg)

Comment:
Point will be given to Virginia's Department of Historic Resources (DHR). The Survey
encourages paleopoint owners to donate their points to public institutions or agencies.

McCary Survey Point Number MC 1044

MC 1044 was laboratory recorded. It is a broken blade with a flute scar on one face. The
flute hinged. It is a blue/red/gray (10Y 8/1) point showing good flaking. It has a flat cross
section. It has a reference to Virginia site number 44AM20. It was heat treated either by its
maker or a subsequent forest fire. Break appears to be post-Indian. Judging by the blade's
curve, the original length was probably over 100 mm. Figure 103 shows point photographs
and drawings. Table 4 provides the metrics for this point.

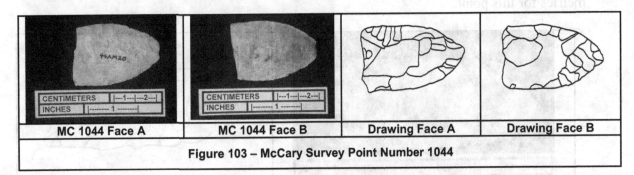

| MC 1044 Face A | MC 1044 Face B | Drawing Face A | Drawing Face B |

Figure 103 – McCary Survey Point Number 1044

Length: x 46 mm
L/W*T Ratio: N/A
Major Attribute: Flaking
Flute Type: Single, percussion
Material: Chalcedony (Cattail Creek, Nottoway County)
Similar Survey Points: MC 928, MC 908, MC 873
Provenance: Amelia County

Comment:
Figure 104 shows the flute.

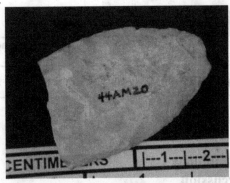

Figure 104 – MC 1044 Close Up Shows Flute Channel

Heat treatment has wide-range, mostly opinionated viewpoints in archaeology. For a serious overview of the topic, see Domanski and Webb (2007).

McCary Survey Point Number MC 1045

MC 1045 was field recorded. It is a large point made off a blade. One face has parts of a medial ridge remaining causing a D-shaped cross section. One corner is broken. Both faces are fluted. Flute A1 is broad and shallow; Flute B is short and shallow. It has a shallow basal concavity. To date, this is the largest jasper blade paleopoint. It is heavily weathered; flake scars are almost gone. It has a pronounced stem area. Point shows heat treatment or subsequent to Indian usage, it was located in a forest fire. This point is similar to MC 1022 (this paper). Figure 105 shows point photographs and drawings. Table 4 provides the metrics for this point.

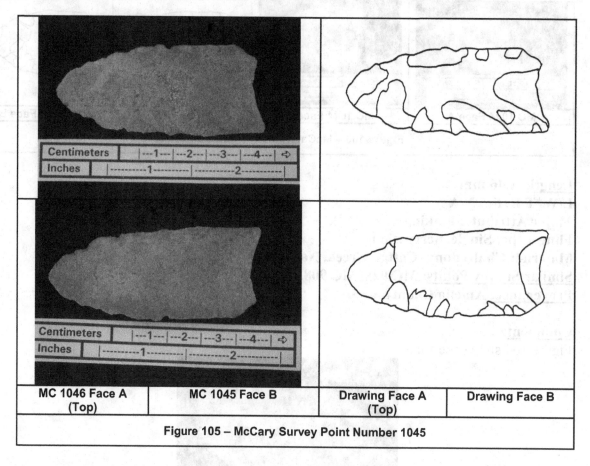

| MC 1046 Face A (Top) | MC 1045 Face B | Drawing Face A (Top) | Drawing Face B |

Figure 105 – McCary Survey Point Number 1045

Length: 55 mm
L/W*T Ratio: 15.000
Major Attribute: Blade technology
Flute Type: Thinning, percussion
Material: Jasper

<u>Similar Survey Points:</u> MC 1022
<u>Provenance:</u> Prince George County

McCary Survey Point Number MC 1046

MC 1046 was laboratory recorded. It is a medium white (5Y 7/3) quartz (Type 1) point. Stem area is broken, but one face has a remaining flute. Flute A1 is shallow, but pronounced. It feathers upon termination, which is difficult in Type 1 quartz. Due to the brittleness of quartz, flaking is poor. Base has light grinding. It is a thick point that has a biconvex cross section. Specimen is above thinness average which is due to the lack of workability of quartz. Figure 106 shows point photographs and drawings. Table 4 provides the metrics for this point.

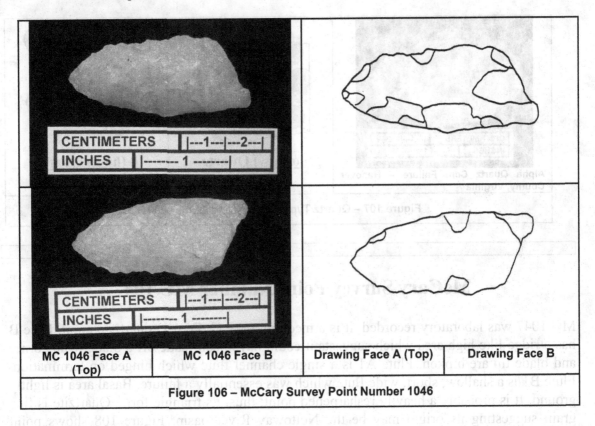

| MC 1046 Face A (Top) | MC 1046 Face B | Drawing Face A (Top) | Drawing Face B |

Figure 106 – McCary Survey Point Number 1046

Length: 53 mm
L/W*T Ratio: 27.652
Major Attribute: Material
Flute Type: Single, percussion
Material: Quartz
<u>Similar Survey Points:</u> MC 871, MC 498, MC 437, MC 421, MC 392
<u>Provenance:</u> City of Suffolk

Comment:

For the Paleoindians, the use of brittle quartz is unusual. However, knappers worked every stone in Virginia into paleopoints, such as greenstone and basalt.

The workability of clear and milky quartz depends on its crystal structure. There are two types: alpha and beta quartz (Figure 107). The beta form was heated during its origin to temperatures above 1300 degrees at 35+ kilobars of pressure. Then it cooled and reformed as alpha quartz; thus, so the theory explains. They are not the same. The alpha (low) quartz has a tendency to be brittle and is practically unworkable. This is true of the pure forms, known as crystal quartz. The alpha quartz oxygen and silicon bonds are "kinked" (bent); whereas, the higher temperature allows bonds to unlink or straighten and produce higher symmetry. This argument is used for heat-treatment of flint and chert. As a consequence for workability, quartz is classified here as Type 1 (alpha) and Type 2 (beta). Type 2 is workable – or usually fine grain.

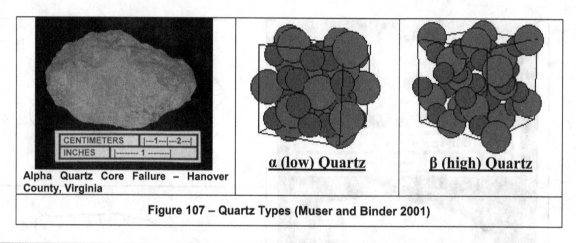

CENTIMETERS |---1---|---2---|
INCHES |------- 1 -------|

Alpha Quartz Core Failure – Hanover County, Virginia

α (low) Quartz   β (high) Quartz

Figure 107 – Quartz Types (Muser and Binder 2001)

McCary Survey Point Number MC 1047

MC 1047 was laboratory recorded. It is a medium, gray (2.5Y 6/1) quartzite point. Face B has a ridge-like high area which suggests it could have been made off a blade. One corner and blade tip are broken. Flute A1 is a single channel flute which hinged on termination. Flute B1 is a shallow, short, wide flute which was essentially a failure. Basal area is lightly ground. It is probably a heavily resharpened point; thus, its triangle form. Quartzite is fine grain suggesting its origin may be the Nottoway River basin. Figure 108 shows point photographs and drawings. Table 4 provides the metrics for this point.

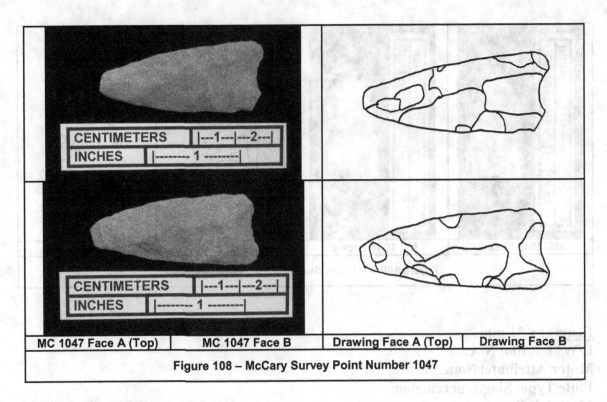

| MC 1047 Face A (Top) | MC 1047 Face B | Drawing Face A (Top) | Drawing Face B |

Figure 108 – McCary Survey Point Number 1047

<u>Length</u>: 48.5 mm
L/W*T Ratio: 18.187
Major Attribute: Triangle form
Flute Type: Single, percussion
Material: Quartzite.
<u>Similar Survey Points</u>: MC 108, MC 1031, MC 152, MC 287
<u>Provenance</u>: City of Suffolk

McCary Survey Point Number MC 1048

MC 1048 was laboratory recorded. It is a small, broken white (Gley #1 8/N) quartz (Type 1) point. Base concavity is chipped. Basal side margins are lightly ground. Both faces are fluted. Face A contains a composite flute (A1.1 and A1.2). Face B has a short, single channel flute (B1). Tip breakage is an Indian snap break. Figure 109 shows point photographs and drawings. Table 4 provides the metrics for this point.

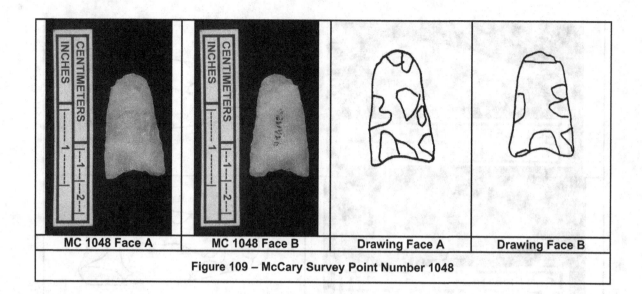

| MC 1048 Face A | MC 1048 Face B | Drawing Face A | Drawing Face B |

Figure 109 – McCary Survey Point Number 1048

Length: x 31 mm
L/W*T Ratio: N/A
Major Attribute: None
Flute Type: Single, percussion
Material: Quartz
Similar Survey Points: MC 226, MC 332, MC 460
Provenance: Franklin County

McCary Survey Point Number MC 1049

MC 1049 is a field recorded point. It is a medium triangularly-shaped point. It is made of fine grain, white (2.5Y 8/1) quartz (Type 2). It is fluted only on Face A. Cross section is biconvex with a moderate concavity. Both faces have short, wide flutes (A1 and B1). Basal margins are lightly ground. It is an expended point. The triangle paleopoint is probably a hand-held knife. The triangle form is the result of point symmetry maintenance (Hranicky and McCary 1995). Figure 110 shows point photographs and drawings. Table 4 provides the metrics for this point.

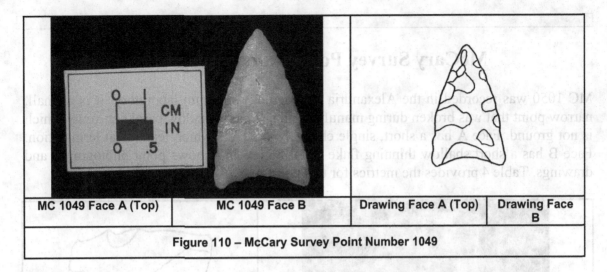

| MC 1049 Face A (Top) | MC 1049 Face B | Drawing Face A (Top) | Drawing Face B |

Figure 110 – McCary Survey Point Number 1049

Length: 52 mm
L/W*T Ratio: 13.000
Major Attribute: Material
Flute Type: Single, percussion
Material: Quartz
Similar Survey Points: N/A
Provenance: Southampton County

Comment:
Figure 111 shows a probable reconstruction. Since quartz produces a sharp cutting edge, the triangle forms a wedge which would make it an ideal spearpoint. Function still remains to be proven. Kraft (1973) refers to these points as "stubby" forms. The expended Clovis point shape has not been truly identified. Hranicky and McCary (1995) maintain that the average length of an expended Clovis point was approximately 50 mm. MC 1049's statistical length is 87.56 mm. Since it is a resharpened point, there can only be a statistical inference to the point's original width.

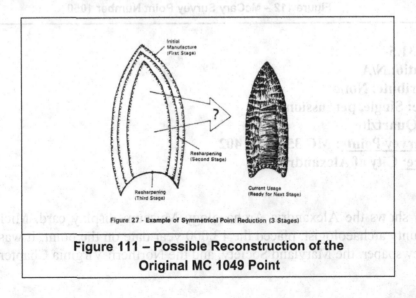

Figure 27 - Example of Symmetrical Point Reduction (3 Stages)

**Figure 111 – Possible Reconstruction of the
Original MC 1049 Point**

211

McCary Survey Point Number MC 1050

MC 1050 was recorded in the Alexandria Archaeology museum laboratory. It is a small, narrow point that was broken during manufacturing. It has a shallow basal concavity which is not ground. Face A has a short, single channel flute (A1) which feathers at termination. Face B has a short shallow thinning flake (B1). Figure 112 shows point photographs and drawings. Table 4 provides the metrics for this point.

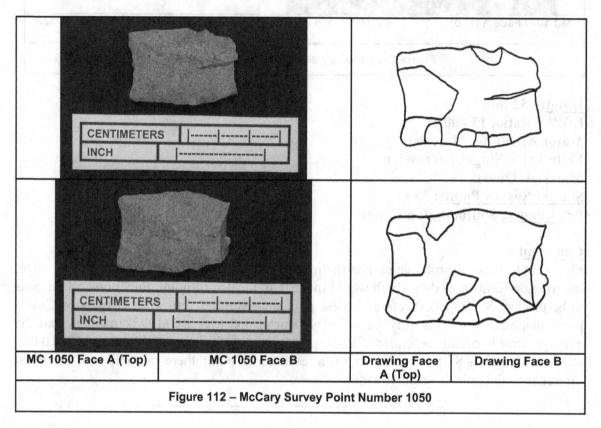

| MC 1050 Face A (Top) | MC 1050 Face B | Drawing Face A (Top) | Drawing Face B |

Figure 112 – McCary Survey Point Number 1050

Length: x 31.5
L/W*T Ratio: N/A
Major Attribute: None
Flute Type: Single, percussion
Material: Quartzite
Similar Survey Points: MC 354, MC 402
Provenance: City of Alexandria

Comment:
Figure 113 shows the Alexandria Archaeology Museum display card. Michael Johnson, Fairfax County archaeologist, placed the 13,000 year date on the point. It was published in the local newspaper, the Maryland Society, and the Northern Virginia Chapter of the ASV.

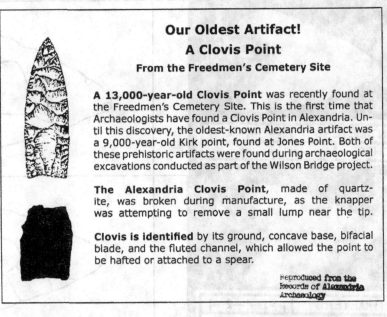

Our Oldest Artifact!

A Clovis Point

From the Freedmen's Cemetery Site

A 13,000-year-old Clovis Point was recently found at the Freedmen's Cemetery Site. This is the first time that Archaeologists have found a Clovis Point in Alexandria. Until this discovery, the oldest-known Alexandria artifact was a 9,000-year-old Kirk point, found at Jones Point. Both of these prehistoric artifacts were found during archaeological excavations conducted as part of the Wilson Bridge project.

The Alexandria Clovis Point, made of quartzite, was broken during manufacture, as the knapper was attempting to remove a small lump near the tip.

Clovis is identified by its ground, concave base, bifacial blade, and the fluted channel, which allowed the point to be hafted or attached to a spear.

Reproduced from the Records of Alexandria Archaeology

Figure 113 – Display Card – Alexandria Archaeology Museum

Using digital, close-up photography, the fracture was cause by a downward force that caused a V-shaped fracture which broke the distal tip off (Figure 114). The striking force was applied on the missing piece which broke free.

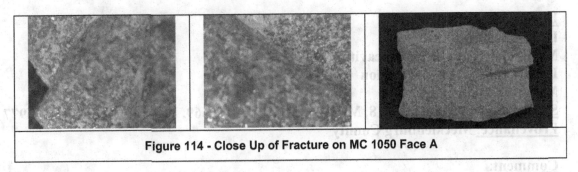

Figure 114 - Close Up of Fracture on MC 1050 Face A

<u>Note</u>: Starting with MC 1050, video are made showing all sides and angles (positions) of the point.

McCary Survey Point Number MC 1051

MC 1051 was field recorded. It is a small triangle white (10YR 8/2) quartz point. Corners are round with a deep concavity. Only one face is fluted. Cross section is biconvex. Base is moderately ground. It is a finely made, but expended point. It was a surface find in the 1980s in Clarksville, Virginia. It has a deep concavity. Flute A1 is bold and hinged at its termination. Face B has composite basal thinning flakes which were not numbered. Figure 115 shows point photographs and drawings. Table 4 provides the metrics for this point.

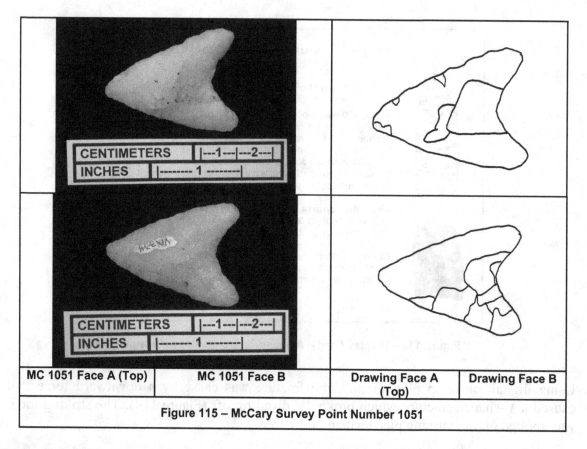

| MC 1051 Face A (Top) | MC 1051 Face B | Drawing Face A (Top) | Drawing Face B |

Figure 115 – McCary Survey Point Number 1051

Length: 42.0 mm
L/W*T Ratio: 13.548
Major Attribute: Deep concavity
Flute Type: Single, percussion
Material: Quartz
Similar Survey Points: MC 8, MC 120, MC 454, MC 669, MC 249, MC 799, MC 977
Provenance: Mecklenburg County

Comment:

The expended triangle paleopoint is difficult to discern from Woodland triangle points. The paleopoint was sometimes resharpened until a small triangular blade remains MC 1051 shows the reduction. Figure 116 shows hypothetical lateral margin reduction for a paleopoint.

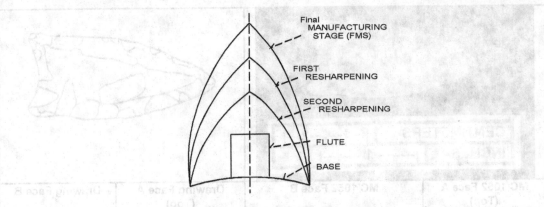

Figure 116 – Lateral Margin Reduction by Resharpening

McCary Survey Point Number MC 1052

MC 1052 was field recorded. This point was recorded in 2002; obviously, a decision was made to include it in the Survey. It is a medium point that has full-face fluting. It has a flat cross section. Basal area is lightly ground. The point is slightly waisted with flared (eared) corners. Face B has a small potlid. Both faces have long flute scars (A1 and B1) which feather at terminations. After fluting, the basal margins were additionally thinned (chipped). Fluting on both faces created beveled edge margins.

This point may be the Huntly type (Miller 1962) which is always fluted, but morphologically, it is suggestive of the transition from Paleoindian to the Archaic Period. For the moment, style distribution is limited to south-central Virginia. Figure 117 shows point photographs and drawings. Table 4 provides the metrics for this point.

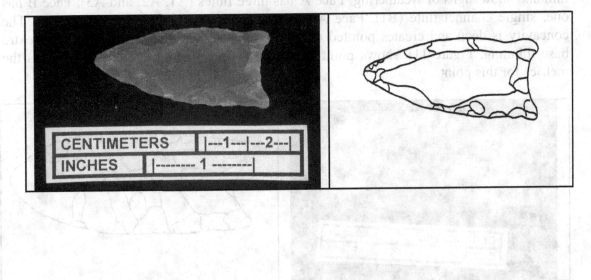

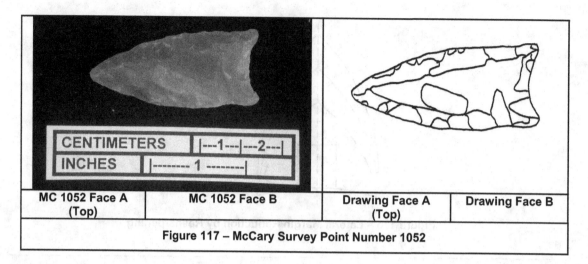

| MC 1052 Face A (Top) | MC 1052 Face B | Drawing Face A (Top) | Drawing Face B |

Figure 117 – McCary Survey Point Number 1052

Length: 47 mm
L/W*T Ratio: 8.400
Major Attribute: Eared
Flute Type: Single, percussion ?
Material: Chalcedony
Similar Survey Points: MC 504, MC 359, MC 369, MC 42
Provenance: Mecklenburg County

McCary Survey Point Number MC 1053

MC 1053 was field recorded. It is a well made slate point. Point has two different degrees of facial weathering. It has a long prehistory with one face being exposed. Flake scars are thin and show signs of weathering. Face A has three flutes (A1, A2, and A3); Face B has one, single channel flute (B1). Face A has two shallow, edge-to-edge flake scars. The concavity is deep and creates pointed corners. The base has microchipping to add extra base thinning. Figure 118 shows point photographs and drawings. Table 4 provides the metrics for this point.

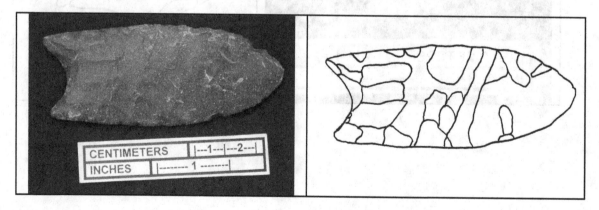

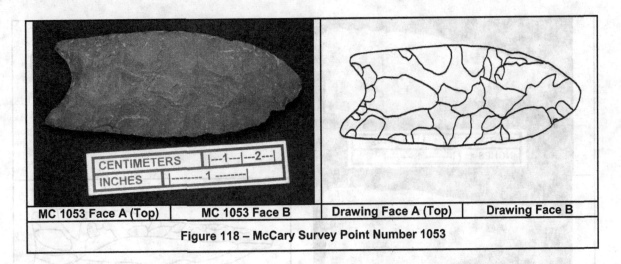

| MC 1053 Face A (Top) | MC 1053 Face B | Drawing Face A (Top) | Drawing Face B |

Figure 118 – McCary Survey Point Number 1053

Length: 85.5
L/W*T Ratio: 17.100
Major Attribute: Flaking
Flute Type: Multiple, pressure
Material: Slate
Similar Survey Points: MC 14, MC 161, MC 293, MC 289, MC 822, MC 375, MC 422, MC 555
Provenance: Lunenburg County

Comment:
Face up – face down patination is observable on Survey point. The difference is apparent (mostly obvious) when the point is examined under ultraviolet light. UV light is also used by the Survey to determine if the point has any modern chipping.

McCary Survey Point Number MC 1054

MC 1054 was field recorded. It is made from a tan chert (10YR 8/2) which is not found in Virginia. It has beveled blade edges and a straight base. Cross section is flat, and it is a thin point. Face A has two flutes (A1.1 and A2); and Flute A1.2 is an overstrike. Face B has one long flute (B1). Basal margins are lightly ground. Patination is moderate. Face A has a large flat spot and fine, parallel edge retouch. Face B relies on the central flute channel for setup of the beveled edge. Spots are bee's wax used to hold the point in its display case. Blade has a slight twist. Base has small chipping flakes. Figure 119 shows point photographs and drawings. Table 4 provides the metrics for this point.

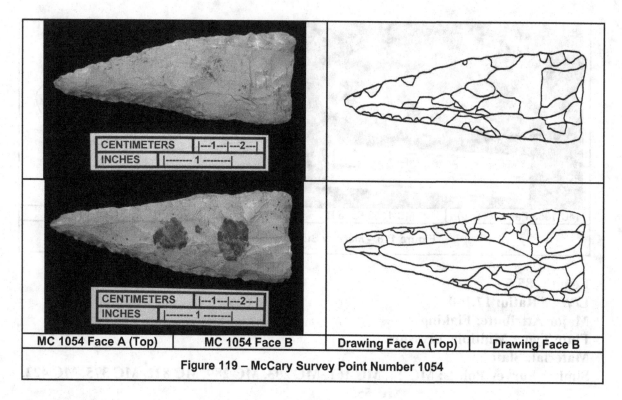

| MC 1054 Face A (Top) | MC 1054 Face B | Drawing Face A (Top) | Drawing Face B |

Figure 119 – McCary Survey Point Number 1054

<u>Length:</u> 91
<u>L/W*T Ratio:</u> 22.100
<u>Major Attribute:</u> **Edge retouch**
<u>Flute Type:</u> **Composite, percussion**
<u>Material:</u> **Chert**
<u>Similar Survey Points:</u> **MC 635**
<u>Provenance:</u> **Mecklenburg County**

<u>Comment</u>:
The straight-base paleopoint has been reported. However, the blade has a slight curve to them suggesting that they could have formed a lanceolate point. This point is often called the Stanfield after the Stanfield-Worley rockshelter in Alabama (DeJarnette, Kurjack, and Cambron 1962). They suggest it is a transition point dating around 10,000 year ago. Kraft (1973) also found these at the Plange paleosite in New Jersey. Figure 120 shows another non-Virginia flint specimen with basal fluting or thinning. Note its composition when compared to MC 1001. Southeastern tools and materials are found on Virginia's south-central river fall lines.

Figure 120 - Flint Paleoknife from Halifax County, Virginia

McCary Survey Point Number MC 1055

MC 1055 was field recorded. It is a dark gray/brown (10YR 4/1). It is probably a retrofitted distal end of a broken paleopoint. However, fluting was added. Base is ragged and not ground. Edge has parallel retouch. Corners are slightly rounded, and concavity is shallow. Flute A1 is original; Flute B1 was probably added during the retrofitting. Face B has a high spot which is the result of gluing the point to a board. No other reworking occurs. See MC 572. Figure 121 shows point photographs and drawings. Table 4 provides the metrics for this point.

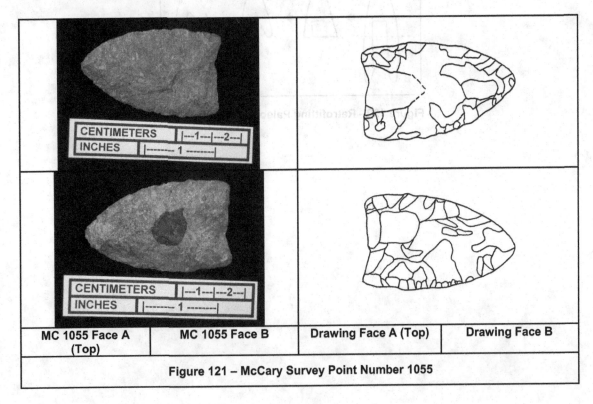

MC 1055 Face A (Top)	MC 1055 Face B	Drawing Face A (Top)	Drawing Face B

Figure 121 – McCary Survey Point Number 1055

219

Length: x 53 mm
L/W*T Ratio: N/A
Major Attribute: Flaking
Flute Type: Single, percussion
Material: Flint
Similar Survey Points: MC 572, MC 407, MC 682
Provenance: Mecklenburg County

Comment:
MC 1055 is an excellent example of what a collector should not do: glue points to boards. The black spot on the point will never come off (Hranicky 1989b).

MC 1055 may have been an attempt to retrofit a broken point tip into a useable point. Figure 122 shows retrofitting examples.

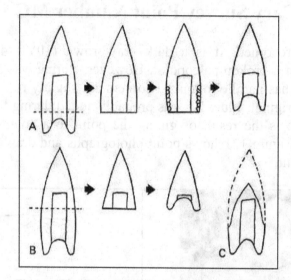

Figure 122 - Retrofitting Paleopoints (Ellis 2004)

Survey References

Ahler, Stanley A. and Phil R. Geile
(2000) Why Flute? Folsom Design and Adaptation. Journal of Archaeological Science, Vol. 27, No. 9, pp. 799-820.

Anderson, David G. and Michael K. Faught
(2000) Paleoindian Artifact Distribution: Evidence and Implications. Antiquity, Vol. 74, pp. 507-513.
(1998) The Distribution of Fluted Paleoindian Projetile Points, Update 1998/ Archaeology of Eastern North America, Vol. 26, pp.163-187.

Anderson, David G. and Michael J. O'Brian
(1998) Missouri Paleo-Indian Projectile Point Recording Project: A Call for Data. Missouri Archaeology Society Quarterly, Vol. 15, No. 3, pp. 4-9.

Andrefsky, William, Jr. (ed)
(2001) Lithic Debitage – Context, Form, and Meaning. The University of Utah Press, Salt Lake City, UT.

Brennan, Louis A.
(1982) A Complilation of Fluted Points of Eastern North America by Count and Distribution. Archaeology of Eastern North America, Vol. 10, pp. 27-46.

Bullin, Ripley P.
(1975) A Guide to the Identification of Florida Projectile Points. Kendall Books, Gainesville, FL.
(1968) A Guide to the Identification of Florida Projectile Points. Florida State Museum, University of Florida, Gainesville, FL.

Bushnell, D. I., Jr.
(1935) The Manahoac Tribes in Virginia, 1608. Smithsonian Miscellaneous Collections, No. 94(8), Washington, DC.

Callahan Errett
(1979) The Basics of Biface Knapping in the Eastern Fluted Point Tradition – A Manual for Flintknappers and Lithic Analysis. Archaeology of Eastern North America, Vol. 7, No. 1, pp. 1-179.

Cambron, James W.
(1955) The Wheeler Point. Newsletter. Oklahoma Anthropological Society, Vol. IV, No. 4.

Carroll, Thad L.
(1986) The Gualden Clovis Point. Chesopiean, Vol. 24, No. 1, pp. pp. 10-11.

Carter, Brinner, James S. Dunbar, and David G. Anderson
(1998) Paleoindian Projectile Point Recording Project: A Call for Data. Florida Anthropologist, Vol 51, pp. 37-44.

Carter, Loy C.
(1986) The Loy Carter Point. Chesopiean, Vol. 24, No. 2, pp. 8-9.

Coe, Joffry L.
(1964) The Formative Cultures of the Carolina Piedmont. Transactions of the American Philosophical Society, New Series, Vol. 54, Part 5, Philadelphia, PA.

Collins, Michael B.
(1999) Clovis Blade Technology. University of Texas Press, Austin, TX.

Crabtree, Don E.
(1972) An Introduction to Flintknapping. Occasioal Papers of the Idaho /museum, No. 28, Pocatello, ID.

DeJarnette, David L., Edward Kurjack, and James W. Cambron
(1962) Stanfield-Worley Bluff Shelter Excavation. Journal of Alabama Archaeology, Vol. III, Nos 1&2.

Deller, D. Brian and C. J. Ellis
(1984) Crowfield: A Preliminary Report on a Probable Paleo-Indian Cremation in Southwestern Ontario. Archaeology of Eastern North America, Vol. 11, pp. 98-108.

Dent, Richard J.
(1995) Chesapeake Prehistory – Old Traditions, New Directions. Plenum Press, New York, NY.

Domanski, Marian and John Webb
(2007) A Review of Heat Treatment Research. Lithic Technology, Vol, 32, No. 2, pp. 15194.

Eggloff, Keith T. and Joseph M. McAvoy
(1998) A Tribute to Ben C. McCary. ASV Quarterly Bulletin, Vol. 53, No. 4, pp. 138-148.

Ellis, Christopher
(2004) Understanding "Clovis" Fluted Point Variability in the Northeast: A Perspective from the Debert Site, Nova Scotia. Canadian Journal of Archaeology, Vol. 28, pp.205-253.

Fogelman, Gary L. and Stanley W, Lantz
(2006) The Pennsylvania Fluted Point Survey. Fogelman Publishing Company, Turbotville, PA.

Gagliano, S. M. and Hiram F. Gregory
(1965) A Preliminary Survey of the Paleo-Indian Points from Louisiana. Louisiana Studies, Vol. 4, No. 1.

Gardner, William M.
(1989) An Examination of Cultural Change in the Late Pleistocene and Early Holocene (circa 9200 to 68 BC). In: Paleoindian Research in Virginia: A Synthesis, eds. M. Wittkofski and T. Reinhart, ASV Special Publication No. 19.
(1983) Stop Me If You've Heard This One Before: The Flint Run Paleoindian Complex Revisited. Archaeology of Eastern North America, Vol. 11, pp. 49-64.
(1974) The Flint Run Complex: Pattern and Process during the Paleoindian to Early Archaic – A Preliminary Report 1971-73 Seasons. Occasional Publication No. 1, Catholic University, Washington, DC.

Goodwin, Asthely J. H.
(1960) Chemical Alteration (Patination) of Stone. South African Anthropological Bulletin, T. 15, No. 59, pp. 67-76.

Holland, C. G.
(1970) An Archeological Survey of Southwest Virginia. Smithsonian Contributions to Anthropology, No. 12, Washington, DC.

Hranicky, Wm Jack
(2008) Recording Clovis Points. To be published.
(2007) North American Projectile Points. AuthorHouse, Bloomington, IN.
(2006) Experimental Archaeology: A Method for the Study of Prehistoric Technology. AuthorHouse, Bloomington, IN.
(2006) Fluting – Mechanics or Culture? Paper given at Society for American Archaeology's Annual Meeting, San Juan, Puerto Rico.
(2006) McCary Fluted Point Survey: Points 1015 to 1035 – A Continuing Study of Virginia Paleoindian Technology. ASV Quarterly Bulletin, Vol. 61, No. 3, pp. 119-136.
(2005) All Prehistoric Technology Flows from the Southeast. Paper: Society for American Archaeology Annual Meeting, Salt Lake, UT.
(2005) Florida's Santa Fe River – A Gateway to the New World. Paper: Eastern States Archeological Federation Annual Meeting, Williamsburg, VA.
(2005) A Microblade Core from the Williamson Site, Dinwiddie County, Virginia. Archaeology of Eastern North America, Vol. 33, pp. 51-56.
(2005) A Model for a Paleoindian Fluted Point Survey. AuthorHouse, Bloomington, IN.
(2005) McCary Fluted Point Survey®: Points 1009 to 1014 – A Continuing Study of Virginia Paleoindian Technology. ASV Quarterly Bulletin, Vol., No., pp. 15-31.
(2004) McCary Fluted Point Survey®: Points 1000 to 1008 – A Continuing Study of Virginia Paleoindian Technology. ASV Quarterly Bulletin, Vol. 59, No. 1, pp. 25-52.
(2004) An Encyclopedia of Concepts and Terminology in American Lithic Technology. AuthorHouse, Bloomington, IN.
(2003) Prehistoric Projectile Points Found along the Atlantic Coastal Plain. Universal Publishers, FL.
(2003) Excessive Artifact Size – Ceremonial Exceptions in Class Size. Paper presented at the Annual Meetings of the Archaeological Society of Virginia (Williamsburg, Virginia) and Eastern States Archeological Federation (Mt Laurel, New Jersey).
(2002) Lithic Technology in the Middle Potomac River Valley of Maryland and Virginia. Kluwer Academic/Plenum Publisher, New York, NY.
(2001) Projectile Point Typology for the Commonwealth of Virginia. Virginia Academic Press, Alexandria, VA.
(1996a) McCary Fluted Point Survey. ASV Quarterly Bulletin, Vol. 51, No. 3, p. 94.
(1996b) Arrowheads, Antiques, Relics, and Junque. ASV Quarterly Bulletin, Vol. 51, No. 3, pp. 118-138.
(1996c) Probably the Oldest Published Clovis Point in Virginia. ASV Quarterly Bulletin, Vol. 51, No. 4, pp. 177.
(1989a) The McCary Survey of Virginia Fluted Points: An Example of Collector Involvement in Virginia Archeology. ASV Quarterly Bulletin, Vol. 44, No. 1, pp. 20-24.
(1989b) Do's and Don't's of Collecting and Displaying Projectile Points. Ohio Archaeologist, Vol. 39, No. 2, pp. 31-32.
(1987) The Classic Clovis Point: Can It Be Defined? Chesopiean, Vol. 25, No. 1, pp. 18-28.
(1984) Virginia Paleoindians: A Perspective on Origins. Chesopiean, Vol. 22, No. 4, pp. 15-19.

Hranicky, Wm Jack and Ben C. McCary
(1995) Clovis Technology in Virginia. ASV Special Publication Number 32.

Hranicky, Wm Jack and Floyd Painter
(1988) Projectile Point Types in Virginia and Neighboring Areas. Special Publication No. 16, Archeological Society of Virginia.

Hranicky, Wm Jack and Gary L. Fogelman
(1994) To be supplied.

Johnson, Michael F.
(2006) Lee Road #2 (44FX2553): A Multi-Component Paleoindian Through Potomac Creek, Hornfels Quarry Base Camp. ASV Quarterly Bulletin, Vol. 61, No 1, pp. 1-37.
(2003) Comments from his review of this Survey report.
(1993) Dissecting Clovis Point No 325 from 45DO423 in East Wenatchee, Washington. ASV Quarterly Bulletin, Vol. 48, No. 2, pp. 64-72.
(1989) The Lithic Technology and Material Culture of the First Virginians: An Eastern Clovis Perspective. In: Paleoindian Research in Virginia: A Synthesis, eds. J. Wittkofski and T. Reinhart, ASV Special Publication Number 19.

Johnson, Michael F. and Joyce E. Pearsall
(1999) The Dr. Ben C. McCary Virginia Fluted Point Survey: Numbers 975-999. ASV Quarterly Bulletin, Vol. 54, No. 1, pp. 36-53.

Kraft, Herbert C.
(1973) The Plenge Site: A Paleoindian Occupation Site in New Jersey. Archaeology of Eastern North America, Vol. 1, No. 1, pp. 56-117.

Lewis, T. M. N.
(1954) The Cumberland Point. Bulletin, Oklahoma Anthropological Society.

Lowery, Darrin
(1989) The Paw Paw Cove Paleoindian Site Complex, Talbot County, Maryland. Archaeology of Eastern North America, Vol. 17, pp. 143-164.

McAvoy, Joseph M.
(2003) The Williamson Clovis Site, 44DW1, Dinwiddie County, Virginia: An Analysis of Research Potential in Threatened Areas. Research Report Series No. 13, Virginia Department of Historic Resources, Richmond, VA.

McCary, Ben C.
(1982) An Uncommon Paleo-Indian Artifact. ASV Quarterly Bulletin, Vol. 37, No. 4, pp. 210-211.
(1951) A Workshop Site of Early Man, Dinwiddie County, Virginia. American Antiquity, Vol. 17, pp. 9-17.
(1947) Folsom Survey. ASV Quarterly Bulletin, Vol. 2, No. 1.

McCary, Ben C. and Glenn R. Bittner
(1978) The Paleo-Indian Component of the Mitchell Plantation Site, Sussex County, Virginia. ASV Quarterly Bulletin, Vol. 34, No. 1, pp. 33-42.

McGahey, Samuel O.
(2000) Mississippi Projectile Point Guide. Mississippi Department of Archives and History, Jackson, MS.

Mayer-Oakes, William J.
(1955) Prehistory of the Upper Ohio Valley. Annals of Carnegie Museum, Pittsburgh, PA.

Merry, Charles W.
(1988) Paleo-Indian Finds in Maryland. Chesopiean, Vol 26, Nos 3&4, p. 37.

Miller, Carl F.
(1962) Archaeology of the John H. Kerr Reservior Basin, Roanoke River Virginia – North Carolina, No. 25, River Basin Surveys Papers, Bureau of American Ethnology, Smithsonian Institution, Washington, DC.

Morrow, Toby and Juliet Morrow
(1994) A Preliminary Survey of Iowa Fluted Points. Current Research in the Pleistocene, Vol. 11, pp. 47-48.

Muser, M. H. and K. Binder
(2001) Molecular Dynamics Study of the Alpha-Beta Transition in Quartz: Elastic Properties, Finite Size Effects, and Hysteresis in the Local Structure. Physics and Chemistry of Minerals, Vol. 28, Pt. 10, pp. 746-755.

Painter, Floyd
(1963) The Alamance Point. Chesopiean, Vol. 1, No. 2, p. 6.

Plew, Mark G., James C. Woods, and Max G. Pavesic
(1985) Stone Tool Analysis – Essays in Honor of Don C. Crabtree. University of New Mexico Press, Albuquerque, NM.

Purdy, B.
(1974) Investigations concerning the thermal alteration of silica minerals. Tebiwa 17:37-66.
Rottlander, R.
(1975) Formation of Patina on Flint. Archaeometry 17:106-110.

Robertson, Arthur
(1947) The Folsom Culture in Southside Virginia. ASV Quarterly Bulletin, Vol. 10, No. 2.

Whittaker, John C.
(1994) Flintknapping – Making and Understanding Stone Tools. University of Texas Press, Austin, TX.

Wilkison, Elizabeth M.
(1986) A Complex of Paleo-Indian Quarry-Workshop and Habitation Sites in the Flint Run Area of the Shenandoah Valley of Virginia. Chesopiean, Vol. 24, No. 3, pp. 2-36.
(1966) Paleo-Indian Components of the Flint Run Jasper Quarry Site, 44-WC-1. Chesopiean, Vol. 4, No. 1.
(1965) Discovery of an Indian Jasper Quarry in N.W. Virginia. Anthropological Journal of Canada, Vol. 3, No. 1.

McCary Survey Point Data

The following tables contain data for the paleopoints described in this publication.

Table 1 – McCary Point Summary

Table 1a – Survey Fluted Point Data

Point Number	Length	Width	Thickness	Material	Color	Flute #1 (Max)	Flute #2 (Max)	Shape	Condition	Site	Location
1000	136.0	36.5	9.5	Quartzite	Tan	24.0 x 20.0	26.0 x 17.0	Lanceolate	Complete	Surface	Beines Farm
1001	37.9	23.7	7.5	Slate	Gray	31.5	23.5	Lanceolate	Expended	Site	N/A
1002	30.0	20.0	5.0	Flint	Black	21.0 x 12.0	17.0 x 12.0	Triangle	Complete	Surface	Nansemond River
1003	96.0	33.8	8.2	Rhyolite *	Tanish	20.0 x 15.0	31.0 x 16.0	Lanceolate	Complete	Surface	Lake Gaston
1004	35.9	26.0	5.0	Flint	4/10G	19.5	20.0	Lanceolate	Expended	Surface	Dan River
1005	109	38.0	6.5	Flint	Tan	31.0 x 15.0	48.0 x 20.0	Lanceolate	Complete	Surface	?
1006	43.0	26.0	11.0	Rhyolite	Gray	18.0 x 16.0	18.9 x 15.5	Lanceolate	Broken	Surface	N/A
1007	23.5 B	27.0	7.0	Flint	Black	16.0 x 12.0	14.0 x 18.0	?	Broken	Surface	
1008	95.3	35.2	9.0	Chert	Dk gray	44.8 x 13.6	None	Lanceolate	Complete	Surface	Potomac River

*Metavolcanic (silicified volcanic tuff)

Table 1b – Survey Fluted Point Data (Continued)

Point Number	Concavity	Lateral Thinning	Weight	Cross Section	Grinding	Serrations Beveling	Quality	Discovery Date	County	Owner
1000	32.0 x 2.5	Lateral	X	Bi-convex	Moderate	None	Fine	1960s ?	Dinwiddie	Formerly: Ben McCary
1001	X	Yes	7.0 grams	Flat	Light	None	Poor	7-19-1994	Rockbridge	W&L University
1002	14.0 x 3.0	Yes	3.0 grams	Bi-convex	Moderate	None	Fine	8/22/2000	Suffolk	George Helmintoller
1003	17.5 x 4.5	Yeas	34.5 grams	Bi-convex	Heavy	None	Fine	February 2003	Brunswick	Glenn Richardson
1004	15.0 x 3.5	Yes	X	Flat	Light	Yes	Fine	April 2000	Mecklenburg	Janice Hornick
1005	22.0 x 8.0	Yes	21.0 grams	Bi-convex	Heavy	None	Fine	1970s	Mecklenburg	Stephen Lavagnino
1006	19.5 x 5.1	?	14.0 grams	Bi-convex	Moderate	None	Poor	1980s	Smyth	Anonymous
1007	4.0 H	?	6.0 grams	Bi-convex	Moderate	?	?	1960s	Halifax	Samuel F. Brookes
1008	9.3 x 1.2	Yes	27.5	Bi-convex	Light	None	Fine	1980s	PG-MD	Mark Kelly

Table 2 – McCary Point Summary

Table 2a – Survey Fluted Point Data

Point Number	Length	Width	Thickness	Material	Color	Flute #1 (Max)	Flute #2 (Max)	Shape	Condition	Site	Location
1009	48.0	29.9	7.3	Rhyolite	2.5Y 7/6	16.0	8.0	Lanceolate	Complete	No	S. Virginia
1010	100.0	30.0	11.0	Flint	2.5Y 6/2	15 x 13	19	Lanceolate	Complete	No	--
1011	63.0	24.0	8.0	Coral	10R 4/8	14.5 x 11	14.0	Lanceolate	Complete	No	South Boston
1012	52.0	22.0	6.0	Rhyolite	5YR 2.5/1	9.5		Lanceolate	Broken	No	Not known
1013	41.0	28.0	5.0	Flint	2.5YR 3/3	15x7	9x8	Triangle	Complete	No	Dan River
1014	41.0	28.0	5.0	Flint	2.5YR 3/3	15 x 7	9 x 8	Triangle	Complete	No	Dan River
1015	47.0	36.0	11.0	Quartzite	2.5Y 6/2			Lanceolate	Complete	No	Stoney Creek

Table 2b – Survey Fluted Point Data (Continued)

Point Number	Concavity	Lateral Thinning	Weight	Cross Section	Grinding	Serrations Beveling	Quality	Discovery Date	County	Owner
1009	18.5 x 8	No	X	Biconvex	Moderate	No	Fine		S. Virginia*	Gary Fogelman
1010	4.5 x 2.0	No	39 g	Biconvex	Light	No	Good	1970s	Augusta	Jack Hranicky
1011		No	14 g	Biconvex	Moderate	No	Fine	1960s	Halifax	Sam Brookes
1012		Yes	8.5 g	Biconvex	Light	No	Fine	1960s	Halifax	Cliff Jackson
1013	19 x 8	No	6 g	Biconvex	Moderate	Yes	Fine	June 1999	Halifax	Dan River Survey
1014		No	13 g	Biconvex	Light	No	Poor	1980s	Sussex	Anonymous

Table 15   County is known, but confirmation being requested from a previous owner.

Table 3 – McCary Point Data Summary

Table 3a – Survey Fluted Point Data

Point Number	Length	Width	Thickness	Material	Color	Flute #1 (Max)	Flute #2 (Max)	Shape	Condition	Site	Location *
1015	77.0	35.5	7.5	Slate	Black	15.5	17.0	Lanceolate	Complete	N/A	
1016	50.0	25.0	5.7	Chalcedony	Blue/gray	10.0	12.0	Lanceolate	Complete	N/A	
1017	57.0	14.0	7.5	Rhyolite	Lt Gray	21.0	15.0	Lanceolate	Complete	N/A	
1018	45.0	30.0	7.5	Chalcedony	Gray	22.0	13.0	Lanceolate	Expended	N/A	
1019	34.0	23.0	7.0	Chalcedony	Grayish	16.0	19.0	?	Broken	N/A	
1020	26.0	29.0	7.0	Slate	Gray/tan			?	Broken	N/A	
1021	51.0	26.0	7.0	Chert	Gray	17.5	12.0	Lanceolate	Complete	N/A	
1022	64.0	25.0	9.0	Quartzite	Brown	10.0	13.0	Blade	Complete	N/A	
1023	59.0	25.0	6.0	Shale	Dk gray	X	X	Lanceolate	Broken	N/A	
1024	36.8	27.0	8.0	Quartz	White	9.0	8.0	Triangle	Complete	None	
1025	45.0	22.0	6.0	Chert	Gray	19.0	X	Triangular	Complete	N/A	
1026	22.0	21.5	7.2	Chert	Gray	11.0	14.0	?	Broken	None	
1027	51.0	28.0	8.0	Chert	Cream	30.0	9.0	Lanceolate	Broken	Site	
1028	56.0	30.0	5.5	Fling	Gray	20.o	9.0	Lanceolate	Complete	N/A	
1029	24.7	33.6	5.3	Hornfeld	Dk gray			Lanceolate	Broken	Site	
1030	57.2	26.1	7.4	Rhyolite	Tan	26.3	31.6	Lanceolate	Complete	N/A	
1031	67.8	26.5	13.4	Quartz	White	17.9	12.3	Lanceolate	Complete	N/A	
1032	40.5	27.0	10.2	Quartz	White	16.9	13.6	Scraper	Complete	N/A	
1033	171.0	51.0	9.8	Rhyolite	Dk gray			Lanceolate	Complete	N/A	
1034	32.0	27.0	8.0	Quartz	White	10	8	Triangle	Complete	N/A	
1035	48.8	22.5	11	Quartzite	Brown	12		Blade	Complete	N/A	

Table 15   See Survey records, (available upon request by qualified scholars)

Table 3b – Survey Fluted Point Data (Continued)

Point Number	Concavity	Lateral Thinning	Weight	Cross Section	Grinding	Serrations Beveling	Quality	Discovery Date	County	Owner
1015		Yes		Bi-convex	Moderate	No	Fine	1950s	Buckingham	R. Garland
1016		Yes		Bi-convex	Moderate	No	Fine	1965	Buckingham	R. Garland
1017		Yes		Flat	Moderate	No	Good	6-2000	Buckingham	R. Garland
1018		Yes		Bi-Convex	Light	No	Good	1967	Buckingham	R. Garland
1019		No		Bi-Convex	Moderate	No	Good	1987?	Buckingham	R. Garland
1020				Plano-Conv	Moderate	No	Fine	9-1997	Nelson	J. Wooten
1021	4x19 mm	?	11 g	Plano-Conv	Moderate	No	Fine	?	Smyth	D. Kegley
1022	?	No	15 g	Plano	Moderate	No	Fine		Dinwiddie	P. Porcelli
1023	X	Minor	9.0 g	Plano	?	No	Fine	1950s	?	J. Hranicky
1024	4.2x27 mm	?	7.0 g	Bi-Convex	Moderate	Beveled	Fine	11-1999	Halifax	J. Hranicky
1025	5x22 mm	No		Bi-convex	Light	No	Fine	1990s	Pulaski	D. Harman
1026	X	?	4.0 g	Bi-Convex	Light	?	?	1970s	No Va	S. Silsby
1027	X	No		Flat		No	Fine	7-1985	Montgomery	E. Turner
1028	4.5x21 mm	Yes	9.1 g	Flat	Light	No	Fine	Unknown	Smyth (?)	
1029	X	No	6.0	Plano		No		2004	Fairfax	Fairfax County
1030	8x16.7	Yes	12 g	D-shaped	Moderate	No	Fine	1-2005	Patrick	J. Saunders
1031	3x12 mm	?	26 g	Bi-Convex	Heavy	No	Good	2000	Patrick	J. Saunders
1032	1x16 mm	No	13 g	D-shaped	Moderate	No	Good	2000	Patrick	J. Saunders
1033	2.5x21 mm	?	108 g	Flat	Moderate	No	Fine		Richmond City	J. Goldberg
1034	3x23 mm	?	7.0 g	Bi-Convex	Heavy	No	Fine	10-2003	Halifax	J. Maus
1035	1.6x11 mm	No	9.53 g	Plano-Conv	Moderate	No	Fine	2-2004	Suffolk City	G. Helmintoller

Table 4 – McCary Point Data Summary

Table 4a – Survey Fluted Point Data

Point Number	Length	Width	Thickness	Material	Color	Flute #1 (Max)	Flute #2 (Max)	Shape	Condition	Site	Location *
1036	47	25	10	Quartz	White	15x11		Triangle	Complete	No	
1037	50	32	10	Quartz	White	15x11	6.5x11	Triangle	Complete	No	
1038	47	26	10	Chalcedony	Gray	15x7.5		Lanceolate	Damaged	No	
1039	47	30	19	Quartzite	Tan	30x17		Lanceolate	Complete	No	
1040				Flint	Gray				Broken	No	
1041		27	8	Quartzite	Gray				Broken	No	
1042	49	24.5	8	Quartz	White	21x10		Triangle	Complete	No	
1043	52	25.5	7	Jasper	Brown	12x12	12x11	Lanceolate	Complete	No	
1044	46	32	9	Chalcedony	Blue	17x9			Broken	No	
1045	55	22	6	Jasper	Brown	17x10	17x8	Lanceolate	Complete	No	
1046	53	23	12	Quartz	White			Lanceolate	Broken	No	
1047	48.5	20	7.5	Quartzite	Gray	15x9,5	10x5	Triangule	Complete	No	
1048	31	29	8	Quartz	White	12x9	12x7	Lanceolate	Broken	No	
1049	52	32	8	Quartz	White	18x13		Triangle	Complete	No	Meherrin R. Freedman's Cemetery
1050	31.5	22	7	Quartzite	Tan	12x10	15.1x11	Lanceolate	Broken	No	
1051	42	31	10	Quartz	White	13x10		Triangle	Complete	No	Clarksville
1052	47	20	4	Chalcedony	Gray	44x16	43x12	Lanceolate	Complete	No	
1053	85.5	35	7	Slate	Dk Brn			Laceolate	Complete	No	
1054	91	35	8.5	Chert	Gray/Tan	17x14	20x13	Lanceolate	Complete	No	
1055	53	32	8	Flint	Dk Gray/Brb	15x10	19x11	?	?	No	

Table 4b – Survey Fluted Point Data (Continued)

Point Number	Concavity	Lateral Thinning	Weight	Cross Section	Grinding	Serrations Beveling	Quality	Discovery Date	County	Owner
1036	14x3	No	9.9	Biconvex	Light	No	Poor	?	Franklin	F. Amos
1037	18x5	No	12	Flat	Light	No	Good	1970s	Mecklenburg	Anonymous
1038		No	12	D-shaped	Moderate	No	Poor		Nelson	H. Clements
1039	15x4	No	15	Biconvex	Moderate	No	Good	1995	Nansemond	B. Wendell
1040				D-shaped		No	Fine	2006s	Halifax	T. Hoskins
1041		No	10	Biconvex	Heavy		Fine	1950s	Princ Anne	Anonymous
1042	20x3.5	No	8	D-shaped	Light	No	Fair	1950s	Princ Anne	Anonymous
1043	18.5x2	Yes	11	Flat	Moderate	No	Fine	1970s	Giles	S. Trail
1044		Minor	15	Flat		No	Good		Amelia	T. Barnard
1045		None	8	D-shaped	Light	No	Fine		Prince Georg	R. Bunce
1046		No	14	Biconvex	Light	No	Poor	1950s	Suffolk	Anonymous
1047		No	8	Biconvex	Light	No	Fair	1950s	Prin Anne	Anonymous
1048		No	3	Biconvex	Light	No	Good		Franklin	A. Conners
1049	23x4	No	13	Biconvex	Light	No	Fine	1970s	Southampton	Anonymous
1050		No	7	Biconvex	Light	No	Poor	2007	Alexandria City	City
1051	22x9	Yes	8	Biconvex	Light	No	Fine	1980s	Mecklenburg	J. Hranicky
1052		No		Flat	Light	Yes	Fine		Mecklenburg	J. Meyer
1053				Flat	Moderate	No	Fine		Lunenburg	J. Goldberg
1054	None	No		Flat	Light	Yes	Fine	1960s ?	Mecklenburg	MacCullum More
1055		No	16	Biconvex	Light	No	Fine	1990s ?	Mecklenburg	J. Maus

Part Five – Appendices and References

📖 Clovis [Lanceolate] Point -

first reported by Howard (1935) and as described in Wormington (1957), it was named after the city in New Mexico. Numerous Clovis points have been found in the study area (Hranicky 1984 and 1987; and Hranicky and McCary 1996). There is a predominant usage of jasper, which comes either from Warren and Culpeper Counties, Virginia, Point of Rocks, Maryland, or numerous outcrops in Pennsylvania. The Potomac River valley points tend not to have the pronounced indentation along the lateral base as do specimens occurring further north. This is probably due to northeastern  influences, namely Debert, Shoop, Bull Brook, and Vail sites. For southern Virginia, the point dominance is located in Dinwiddie County. The major material is the Cattail Creek chalcedony. Obviously, other materials were used. Type is manufactured with bifacial antler percussion flaking with pressure flaking to finalize the point. Pressure flaking is used to resharpen a point. Virginia materials are flint, chert, jasper, quartzite, rhyolite, and quartz. It is a macrotypic point. For Virginia, it is found in all regions. Expention length; 49 mm (Hranicky and McCary 1996); general L/W*T ratio: 12.92 (Hranicky and McCary 1996). *Basic Description*: Lanceolate; it is a small-to-large lanceolate point with a fluting that is usually short-to-long in length. Base is concave. Grinding is found on the base and lower lateral sides. Lateral sides are parallel to excurvate. Type dates 9500 to 9000 BC and is found all over the U.S. According to Wormington (1957), the Clovis point is:

Fluted lanceolate points with parallel or slightly convex sides and concave bases. They range in length from one and a half to five inches but are usually some three inches or more in length and fairly heavy. The flutes sometimes extend almost the full length of the point but usually they extend no more than half way from the base to the tip. Normally, one face will have a longer flute than the other. The fluting was generally produced by the removal of multiple flakes. In most instances the edges of the basal portion show evidence of smoothing by grinding. Certain fluted points found in the eastern United States resemble the Clovis type, but they have a constriction at the base which produces a fish-tailed effect. These have sometimes been called Ohio points or Cumberland points. Many of these tend to be somewhat narrower relative to their length than other fluted points. The earliest published Clovis (see drawing b) point in Virginia is Holmes (1897).

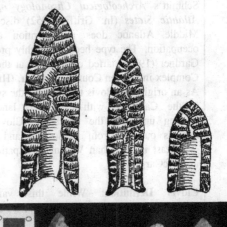

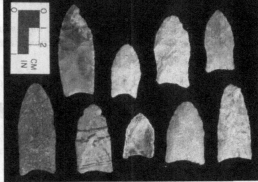

Above: Williamson Site, Dinwiddie County, Virginia

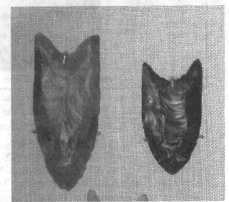

Display Points

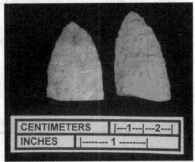

Clovis point tips, Mecklenburg County, Virginia

Modality: Its primary functions are a knife and spearpoint. **Comments**: The Clovis point is essentially a recent addition to the Virginia point catalog, as Schmitt's *Archeological Chronology of the Middle Atlantic States* (In: Griffin 1952) discussion of the Middle Atlantic does not mention a Paleoindian occupation. The type becomes highly prominent when Gardner (1974) started excavations at the Thunderbird Complex in Warren County, Virginia. (Hranicky 1995). As an origin for Clovis technology, the suggestion here is the Carolinas with pre-Clovis lanceolate forms coming up from the Southeast. Clovis technology spreads outward from its sources and as such, the Northeast is later than Virginia occupations (Hranicky and McCary 1996).

Clovis Definition: While this varies in the archaeological literature, Clovis is defined here as:

A Clovis point is a lanceolate implement that was made using a biface reduction strategy. Its manufacture determines the type.

Note: This definition is not always used in this publication.

Clovis tip, Amelia County, Virginia

Rhyolite Point MC 1033. It is one of the largest paleopoints found in the eastern U.S.

There were times in Virginia where paleopopulations existed and then left the state leaving the state with no people. Other technological groups then moved into Virginia. **User Lifeways**: Large bands with hunter/gatherer strategies. **User Ecology**: Occupied all environments during a preboreal climate. Major attributes: Fluting and basal grinding. **Type Validity**: Traditional. **Comparative Types**: Cumberland (Lewis 1954), Folsom (Figgins 1927), Debert (McDonald 1968), and Ross County (Prufer 1963).

Reference: Howard, Edgar B. (1935) *Evidence of Early Man in North America*. Museum Journal, Vol. 24, pp. 2-3, University of Pennsylvania Museum.

Clovis point continued.

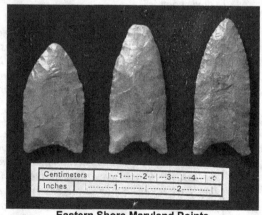
Eastern Shore Maryland Points

238

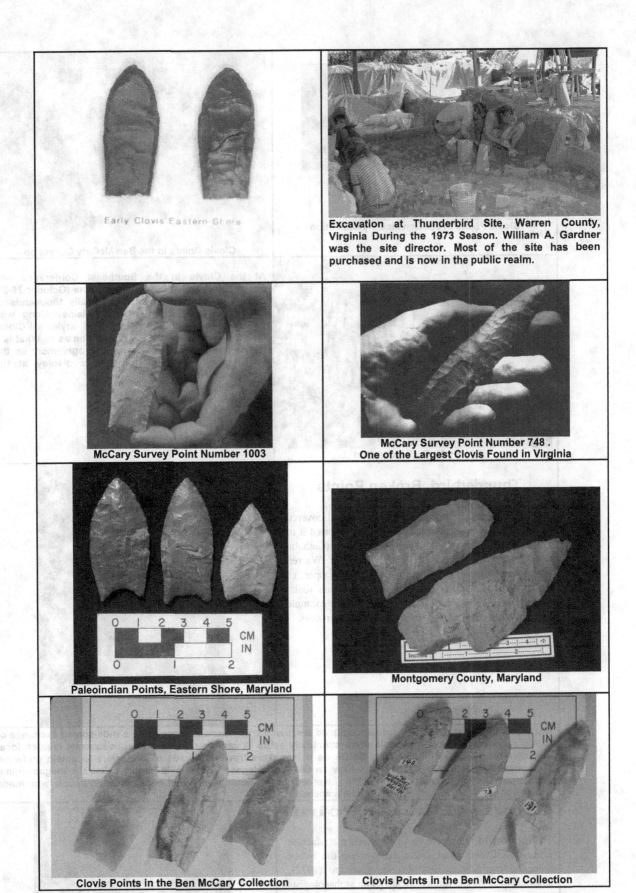

Early Clovis Eastern Store

Excavation at Thunderbird Site, Warren County, Virginia During the 1973 Season. William A. Gardner was the site director. Most of the site has been purchased and is now in the public realm.

McCary Survey Point Number 1003

McCary Survey Point Number 748 .
One of the Largest Clovis Found in Virginia

Paleoindian Points, Eastern Shore, Maryland

Montgomery County, Maryland

Clovis Points in the Ben McCary Collection

Clovis Points in the Ben McCary Collection

239

Clovis Points in the Ben McCary Collection

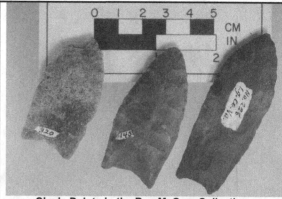

Clovis Points in the Ben McCary Collection

Rodney M. Peck Collection

At the Clovis in the Southeast Conference and Exhibition in Columbia South Carolina (October 26-29, 2005), the displays contained literally thousands of Clovis points – from Texas to Maine. Along with papers and exhibits, variety and style in Clovis technology was apparent – discussion as to What is a Clovis point? Was lively, with little agreement on the basic type. Left photograph is a display at the conference.

Thunderbird, Broken Points

The Thunderbird site in Warren County was discovered by Elizabeth Wilkinson in the 1960s. She reported it to archaeologists, one of whom was Bill Gardner (Catholic University, Washington, DC). This area of Warren County has massive outcrops of high-quality jasper, of which the Paleoindians quarried and made into tools, namely the Clovis point. These specimens are example of points that failed during the manufacturing process.

Did Clovis people spread over large unoccupied areas of North America or was there a wide-spread exchange of Clovis technology? Did Clovis colonizers eventually settle in various regions and subsequently created local variations of the Clovis point? Why did Clovis pointmakers travel hundreds of kilometers to obtain preferred lithic materials? Is Clovis biface technology an Old World legacy? Did Clovis people cause the megamammal extinction? Did the Clovis point originate (invented) in the Southeast? What became of the people who made Clovis points? Who were the Clovis people's ancestors?

Clovis (Blade) Point

The majority of references to Clovis point manufacture assume all Clovis points were made using the biface reduction method and described by Crabtree (1972), Callahan (1979), and others. While some archaeologists

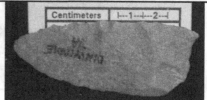

will concede large flake reduction for making a Clovis point, few will accept the blade manufacture as a way to produce a Clovis point.

Right: Both faces of MC 1022 which is a Clovis made off a quartzite blade.

Reference: Hranicky, Wm Jack and Michael F. Johnson (2006) *Recording Clovis Points – Techniques, Examples, and Methods*. To be published.

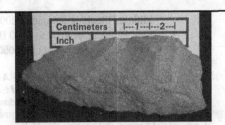

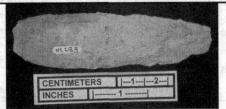

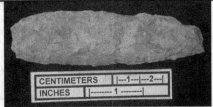

Clovis blade, Guilford County, North Carolina, heavily patinated slate, no flute on ventral face; distal tip is broken. >>>

<<< Dorsal face, fluted, L = 93?, W = 26, T = 9 mm, flute 28 mm, lower margins are ground, see Chapel Hill type.

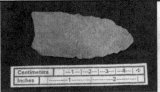

Face A (MC 1036)

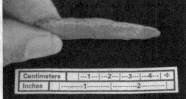

Side View (MC 1036)

Flat Face (Mc 1036)

Clovis Caches

Numerous biface caches has been assigned to the Paleoindian with inferences that they are Clovis. However, the cache general morphologies rearely point directly to Clovis. A recent cache discovery by Thomas Hoskins have bifaces that indicate that the cache is definitely Clovis. The 25-piece cache is poorly made and shows attempts at fluting. See Hoskins Clovis Cache.

Rhyolite Cache, Caswell County, North Carolina

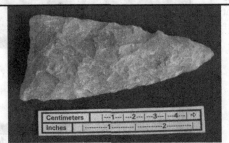

Rhyolite Cache, Caswell County, North Carolina

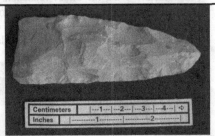

Rhyolite Cache, Caswell County, North Carolina

Clovis Dates

Gardner (1989) provides the basic chronology for Clovis in Virginia, which are:

- Post-9500 BC but before 8000 BC with a duration of 900 years

Clovis Date Averages on the High Plains (From: Jablonski 2002)	
Site	Date Range
Lehner, AZ	10,950 +/- 40 yr BP
Blackwater Draw, NM	11,300 +/- 240 yr BP
Murray Springs, AZ	10,880 +/- 50 yr BP

241

- Middle Paleoindian around 9200 BC
- Late Paleoindian 9100 to 8100 BC
- Early Archaic starts around 8000 BC.

References: Gardner, William A. (1989) *An Explanation of Change in the Late Pleistocene and Early Holocene (Circa 9200 to 6800 BC)*. In: Paleoindian Research in Virginia – A Synthesis, M. Wittkofski and T. Reinhart, eds., ASV Special Publication No. 19.

Dates: 11,050 to 10,800 RCYBP or 9,050 to 8,800 BC. This date assignment is based on the work of Michael R. Waters and Thomas Stanford as reported in Largent (2007).

Largent, Floyd (2007) *Clovis Dethroned*. Mammoth Trumpet, Vol. 22, No. 3, pp. 1-3 and 20.

Dent, CO	10,750 +/- 40 yr BP	
Domebo, OK	10,944 +/- 59 yr BP	
Lange-Ferguson, SD	11,000 +/- 160 yr BP	
Anzick, MT	10,831 +/- 56 yr BP	
Colby, WY	10,960 +/- 120 yr BP	
More Clovis Dates (From: Stuiver and Reimer 1993)		
Paleo Crossing, OH	12150 +/- 75 yr BP	
Big Eddy, MO	11900 +/- 80 yr BP	
Aubrey, TX	11570 +/- 7P	
Vail. ME	11120 +/- 180 yr BP	
Whipple, NH	11050 +/- 300 yr BP	
Shawnee-Minisink, PA	10940 +/- 90 yr BP	
Cactus Hill, VA	10920 +/- 250 BP	
Debert, NS	10590 +/- 50 yr BP	
Templeton, CT	10190 +/- 300 yr BP	

Clovis –First Technology

With no apparent technological ancestry, Clovis may have been invented by a single individual who was a highly skilled flintknaper. For the time of Clovis, blademaking was present in the New World which provided a "toolmaking focus" of high quality stone tools. Any individual can, over a life time, make several thousand Clovis points. Based on numbers, the first Clovis technician lived in the Southeast. He taught others how to make the points and from what were humble beginnings, launched a technology that would spread throughout the Americas.

Reference: Hranicky, Wm Jack (2004) *An Encyclopedia of Concepts and Terminology in American Lithic Technology*. AuthorHouse, Bloomington, IN.

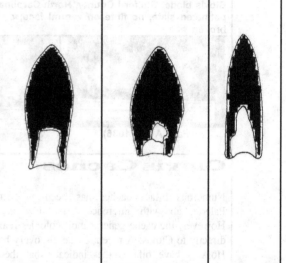

Clovis Off A Flake

Most archaeologists assume that all Clovis points were manufacture using the biface reduction technique. The Clovis off a flake is shown below and in the right photograph. The contex is still remains on once corner indication the the point was made off a flake.

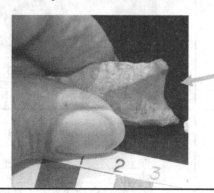

Paleoindian Points, Eastern Shore, Maryland

Clovis Preform

Based on the Williamson site in Dinwiddie County and the Thunderbird site in Warren County, the Clovis preform has a consistent shape and size. It was manufactured off a large flake. However, the classic biface reduction (as in Callahan 1978) was also practiced. Additionally, blades were used to produce the Clovis point. The flake form has rounded basal corners. The tradition perform is a heart-shaped that has lateral and basal thinning. The tip shows the basic point angle. Parallel-side performs also occur.

References: Collins, Michael B. (1999) *Clovis Blade Technology*. University of Texas Press, Austin, TX.

Callahan, Errett (1979) *The Basics of Biface Knapping in the Eastern Fluted Point Tradition – A Manual for Flintknappers and Lithic Analysis*. Archaeology of Eastern North America, Vol. 7, No. 1, pp. 1-179.

 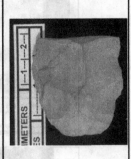

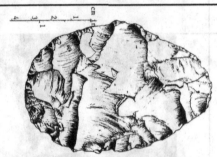

Clovis Preform – Callahan (1979)

Quartzite, Halifax County, Virginia, L = 93, W = 60, T = 19 mm

Clovis (Triangle)

In respect to McCary (1947), who first suggested this shape for paleopoints, this category is included. This point is probably the result of resharpening, or quite possibly – most specimens are mistyped Woodland Period points. Basal thinning is not an absolute requirement for Clovis points.

Reference: McCary, Ben C. (1947) *A Survey and Study of Folsom-Like Points Found in Virginia, Nos. 1-131*. Quarterly Bulletin, Archeological Society of Virginia, Vol. 2, No. 1.

North Carolina Text >>>>

This point (left) is made from fine-grain quartzite, has a small flute, all lower margins are ground, and has edge-to-edge flake scars. Most archaeologists would not call it a Paleoindian specimens, but where does it belong in the prehistory classification schema used by archaeologists?

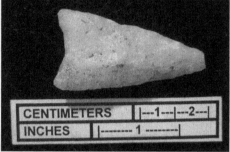

MC1042 – Suffolk, Virginia

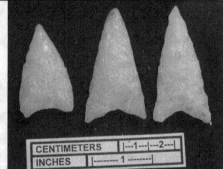

Quartz Triangle Forms – Mecklenburg County, Virginia
Is the left point Paleoindian or Woodland?

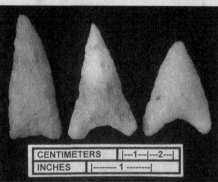

Quartz Forms – Halifax County, Virginia

Clovis – Deep-Base Points

The deep-base Clovis point is probably a Late Paleoindian point that is related closer to Dalton than Clovis. The form occurs unfluted, but some specimens have short flutes.

Fluted
South Carolina
Pointed corners may represent the Santa Fe point type.

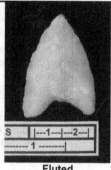

Fluted
North Carolina

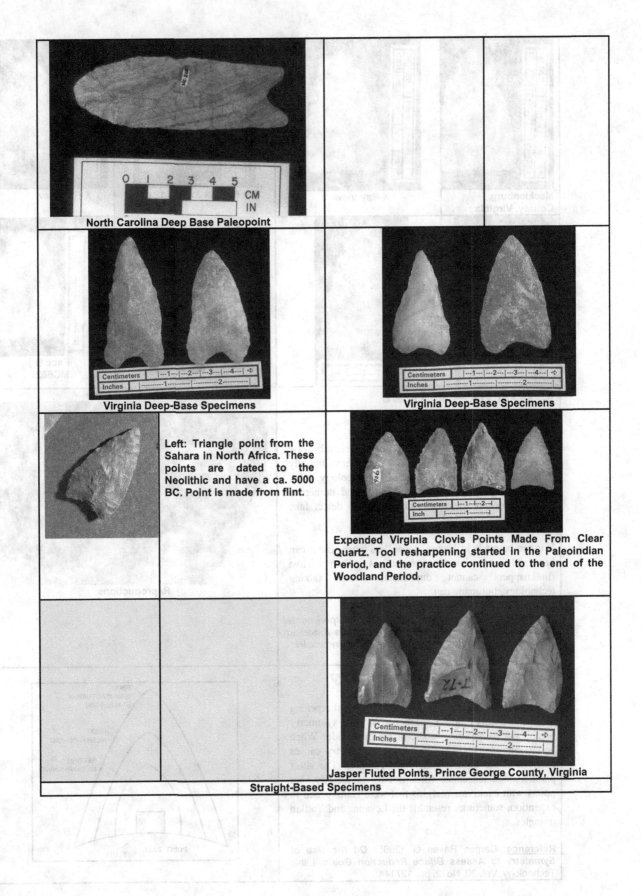

North Carolina Deep Base Paleopoint

Virginia Deep-Base Specimens

Virginia Deep-Base Specimens

Left: Triangle point from the Sahara in North Africa. These points are dated to the Neolithic and have a ca. 5000 BC. Point is made from flint.

Expended Virginia Clovis Points Made From Clear Quartz. Tool resharpening started in the Paleoindian Period, and the practice continued to the end of the Woodland Period.

Jasper Fluted Points, Prince George County, Virginia

Straight-Based Specimens

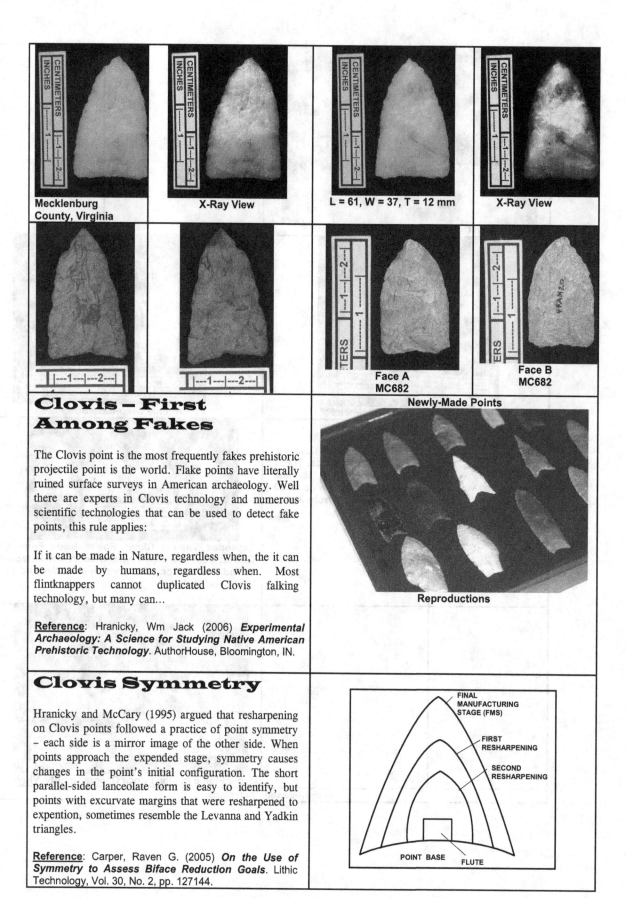

Mecklenburg County, Virginia	X-Ray View	L = 61, W = 37, T = 12 mm	X-Ray View
		Face A MC682	Face B MC682

Clovis – First Among Fakes

The Clovis point is the most frequently fakes prehistoric projectile point is the world. Flake points have literally ruined surface surveys in American archaeology. Well there are experts in Clovis technology and numerous scientific technologies that can be used to detect fake points, this rule applies:

If it can be made in Nature, regardless when, the it can be made by humans, regardless when. Most flintknappers cannot duplicated Clovis falking technology, but many can...

Reference: Hranicky, Wm Jack (2006) *Experimental Archaeology: A Science for Studying Native American Prehistoric Technology*. AuthorHouse, Bloomington, IN.

Newly-Made Points

Reproductions

Clovis Symmetry

Hranicky and McCary (1995) argued that resharpening on Clovis points followed a practice of point symmetry – each side is a mirror image of the other side. When points approach the expended stage, symmetry causes changes in the point's initial configuration. The short parallel-sided lanceolate form is easy to identify, but points with excurvate margins that were resharpened to expention, sometimes resemble the Levanna and Yadkin triangles.

Reference: Carper, Raven G. (2005) *On the Use of Symmetry to Assess Biface Reduction Goals*. Lithic Technology, Vol. 30, No. 2, pp. 127144.

FINAL MANUFACTURING STAGE (FMS)

FIRST RESHARPENING

SECOND RESHARPENING

POINT BASE   FLUTE

246

Clovis Variety

One only has to read the literature to discover that many archaeologists see over 300 varieties of Clovis. As Hranicky and Johnson (2006) suggest: there is Clovis and there is not Clovis. Additionally, the 1000+ points in the McCary survey provide a wide-range of styles. Two other types are part of the array and are used:

- Redstone
- Ross County
- And, Clovis.

__Reference__: Morrow, Juliet E. and Cristobal Gnecco (2006) ***Paleoindian Archaeology – A Hemisphere Perspective***. Press of the University of Florida, Gainesville, FL.

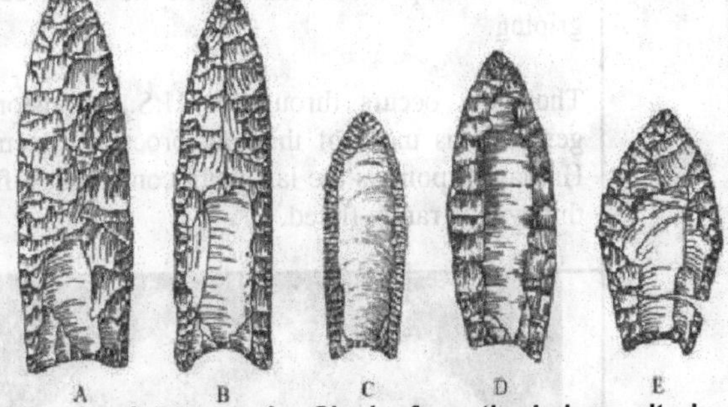
A
B
C
D
E

Fluted point types, A . Clovis, from the Lehner site in Arizona. B. Gainey type from the Butler site in Michigan. C. Folsom from Marion County, Iowa. D. Barnes Fluted from the Thedford site in Ontario. E. Crowfield type from the Crowfield site in Ontario, Canada. (all from Morrow 1996 except the Barnes point that was redrawn from Ellis and Deller 1990).

Clovis [Unfluted] Point -

probably attributed to Cambron and Hulse (1989). It is a Clovis point that has its major attribute missing. This fails as standard typology. Unfluted points are occasionally included in the McCary Fluted Point Survey, but most are excluded. By definition, a Clovis point cannot be unfluted; but, certainly, early Paleoindian points that would eventually become Clovis were unfluted.

__Reference__: Cambron, James W. and David C. Hulse (1989 version) ***Handbook of Alabama Archaeology, Part 1 – Point Types***. Alabama Archaeological Society, Huntsville, AL.

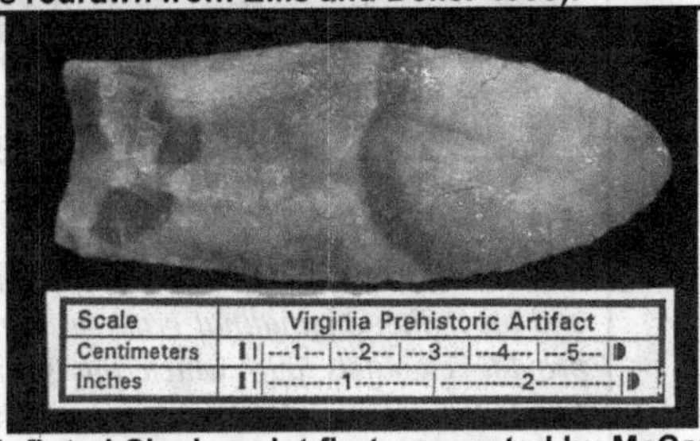
Scale
Virginia Prehistoric Artifact
Centimeters
Inches

Note: Unfluted Clovis point first suggested by McCary as Survey Point Number 18.

Point to right: Flint, Mecklenburg County, Virginia, L = 52, W = 32, T = 7 mm.

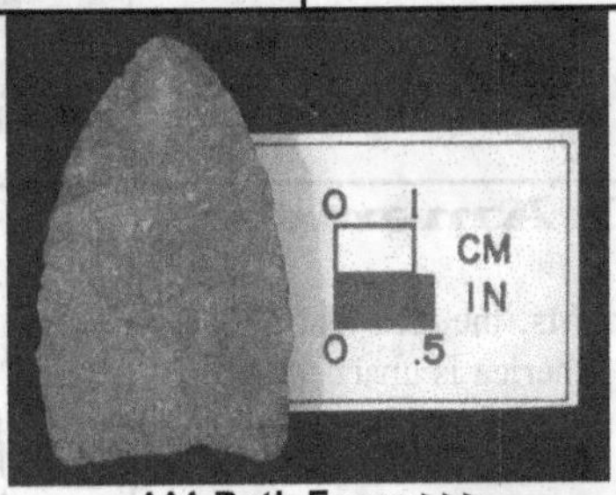
0 1
CM
IN
0 .5

^^^ Both Faces >>>

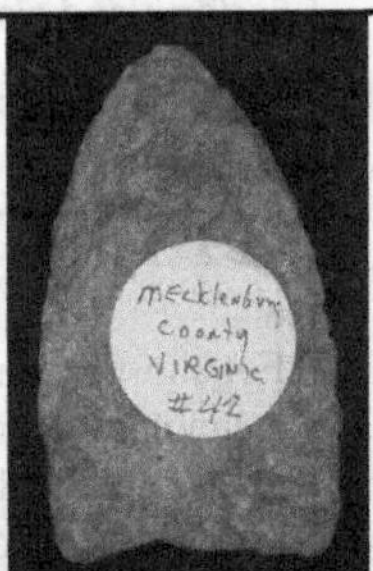
Mecklenburg
County
VIRGINIA
#42

Clovis Fluting

As from all the archaeological theories concerning the purpose or function of fluting, few studies have argued for the origin of the flute. As suggested many times, the author contents that fluting is a process the originated in Old World blademaking. The flute is a natural procedure in working stone. The basic principle is sending flaking energy down the center aires (ridge) of a blade. The ridge acts as a wave guide.

As for flute purpose, it is generally considered a part of the chassis (hafting) mounting for the point. However, fluted blades that are not in the form of a projectile point suggest a hand-held function, probably as a butchering

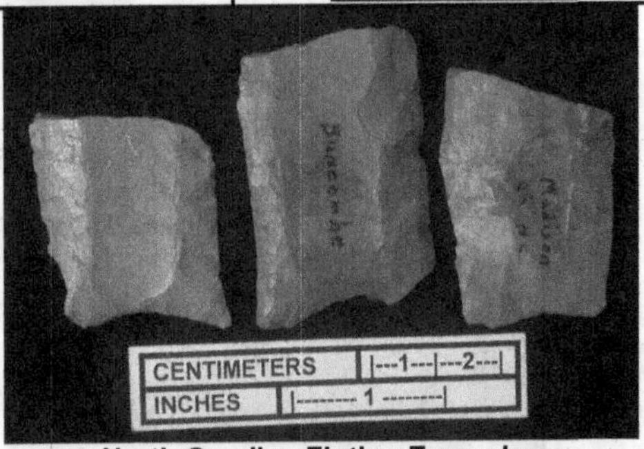
CENTIMETERS
INCHES

North Carolina Fluting Examples

Experimentally, the flute can be removed using a punch, free-hand striking with a flaker, using an anvil, vice-grips, and probably methods that remain to be

knife. The butchering process is – quite simply – messy and tools slip in the hand. The flute served in better griping.

The flute occurs throughout U.S. prehistory, but it generally is more of thinning process. Essentially, the Hardaway point is the last point containing a flute. And, this type is rarely fluted.

discovered. The basic method suggested here is using a deer flaker to remove the flute. For discussion on fluting, see Callahan (1979) and Whittaker (1994).

MIDDLE PALEOLITHIC PERIOD (MOUSTERIAN):
80,000 – 40,000 years ago
Fontmaure, West Central France

Georgia – Paleoindian

Waldorf (1987) in regards to fluting:

First of all, the reason for fluting was to thin and taper the longitudinal cross-section of the base and provide channels into which the split shaft could be fitted, thus when glued and lashed, the haft would be quite stable. The Indian may have been aware of not one, but several ways to achieve this end, because some Clovis points have single flutes on one face and multiples on the other. With such flexibility of technique he would be able to overcome variability in both ⬚*erform and raw material.*

Fluting Examples in Jasper, Prince George County, Virginia

Clovis – South America

For most American archaeologists, the idea that Clovis technology is found in South America is unacceptable – least wise, the argument that Clovis technology originated in South America.

<u>Reference</u>: Lavallee, Daniele (1995/2000 English Translation) *The First South Americans – The Peopling of a Continent from the Earliest Evidence to High Culture*. Translated: Paul Bahn, University of Utah Press, Salt Lake, UT.

South American Point Comparisons: 1 – USA, 2, 3 – Fluted SA points, 4, 5 – El Inga, 6, 7 – Piura, and 8,9 –

Clovis – There is Clovis – Then There Is Not Clovis

Virginia Clovis technology organization is complicated and poorly understood. Current thinking, based on two quarry sites (Williamson and Thunderbird), does not completely match surface finds in southern Virginia and North Carolina. This photograph and the McCary Survey show a tremendous range of structure, and probably function, for Virginia Paleopoints. Quarry sites skew the lithic material usage; but at the same time, it shows large tool format – knife function. Resharpened/expended points by their form do not provide the initialization manufacture. The only commonality among Paleoindian points is the lanceolate form. Basal grinding and fluting is not a necessary attribute set to define Clovis.

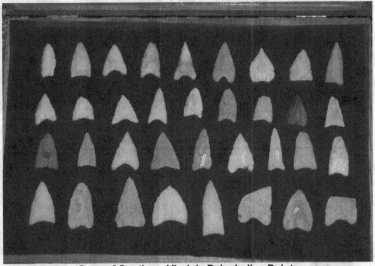

Case of Southern Virginia Paleoindian Points

Clovis – How Many?

Hranicky and McCary (1995) estimated the number of fluted points that were made and used in Virginia. Depending on the recovered specimens being a percentage of the total count, they argued:

Recovered Point Count	Total Est
1%	95,000
5 %	47,500
10%	9,500
15 %	7,125
20 %	4,750
25 %	2,375

Clovis Display at the 50th Anniversary (October 1990) of the Archaeological Society of Virginia. Organized by Jack Hranicky, display contained over 500 Virginia Paleopoints

Appendix B - Clovis Points Williamson Site, Dinwiddie County, Virginia

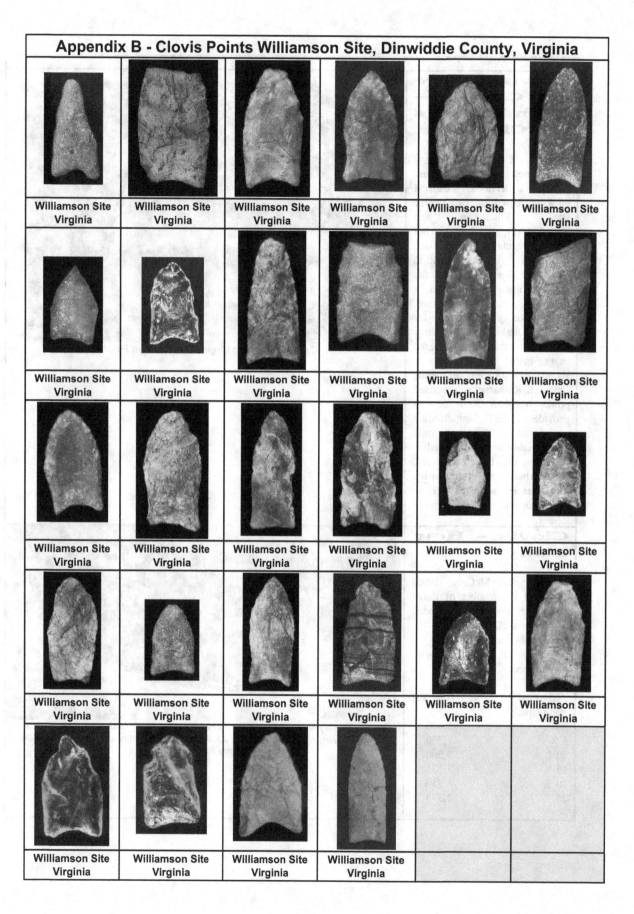

Williamson Site Virginia	Williamson Site Virginia	Williamson Site Virginia	Williamson Site Virginia	Williamson Site Virginia	Williamson Site Virginia
Williamson Site Virginia	Williamson Site Virginia	Williamson Site Virginia	Williamson Site Virginia	Williamson Site Virginia	Williamson Site Virginia
Williamson Site Virginia	Williamson Site Virginia	Williamson Site Virginia	Williamson Site Virginia	Williamson Site Virginia	Williamson Site Virginia
Williamson Site Virginia	Williamson Site Virginia	Williamson Site Virginia	Williamson Site Virginia	Williamson Site Virginia	Williamson Site Virginia
Williamson Site Virginia	Williamson Site Virginia	Williamson Site Virginia	Williamson Site Virginia		

Various Clovis Paleoindian American Points

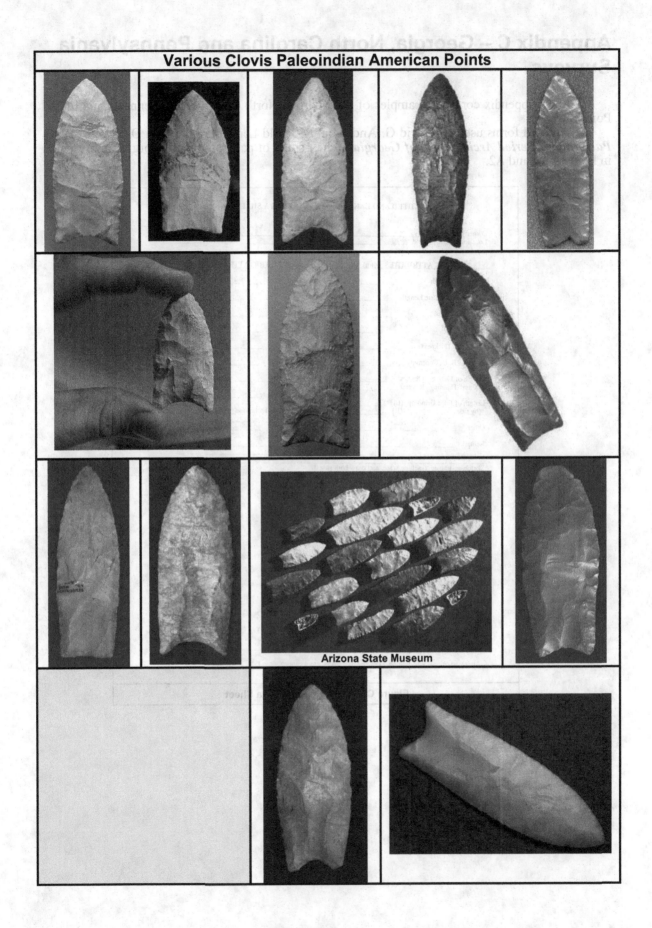

Arizona State Museum

Appendix C – Georgia, North Carolina and Pennsylvania Surveys

This appendix contains examples of the Georgia, North Carolina, and Pennsylvania Fluted Point Surveys.

Record forms used by David G. Anderson, R. Jerald Ledbetter, and Lisa O'Steen's (1990) *Paleoindian Period Archaeology of Georgia* in their study of paleopoints of Georgia are presented in Figures A1 and A2.

FLUTED AND LANCEOLATE POINT DATA SHEET

Owner Name_____ Type Name_____ Specimen No._____
Location of Site of Find_____ Negative No._____

METRIC ATTRIBUTES (mm)	NON-METRIC ATTRIBUTES
Maximum Length	Raw Material
Estimated Complete Length	Color
Maximum Width	Patination
Basal Width	Edge Shape
Maximum Thickness	Edge Retouch
Depth of Basal Concavity	Facial Retouch
Length of Fluting: Obverse or Basal Thinning Reverse	Basal Grinding
	Fluting Technique
Length of Edge Grinding: (L) (by side) (R)	Manufacturing Technique
Other	Reworking

Remarks:_____

Sketch or tracing (include scale, and draw both sides):

Recorder_____ Date_____

(Attach additional information, sketches, site maps, etc. as appropriate.)

Figure C1 – Georgia Point Data Sheet

252

GEORGIA PALEOINDIAN RECORDATION PROJECT
ATTRIBUTE KEY

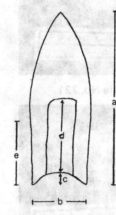

METRIC ATTRIBUTES

a. Maximum Length (mm)

b. Basal Width (mm)

c. Depth of Basal Concavity (mm)

d. Length of Fluting or Basal Thinning (mm)

e. Length of Edge Grinding (mm)

Record Maximum Width and Maximum Thickness at greatest point (mm).

If broken, estimate probable intact length, if possible (mm).

NON-METRIC ATTRIBUTES

Raw Material: Describe as best as possible, naming the probable source area or quarry if this is known.

Color: General color; give Munsell Color Chart values if at all possible.

Patination: Note presence or absence of patination/weathering layer.

Edge Shape: Describe shape of lateral margins (i.e., straight, excurvate, etc).

Edge Retouch: Describe treatment of margins of the biface (i.e., fine pressure retouch, crude, etc).

Facial Retouch: Describe flaking of interior facial area of biface (i.e., broad percussion scars, fine pressure retouch, etc).

Basal Grinding: Note presence or absence of basal grinding.

Fluting Technique: Note special manufacturing characteristics if evident.

Reworking: Note presence of evidence for reworking or reuse (i.e., burinated, re-sharpened, reworked into a scraper, etc).

Remarks: Note any other pertinent information about the artifact or its discovery.

Figure C2 – Georgia Survey Attribute Key

253

North Carolina Fluted Point Survey by Rodney M. Peck

NC Survey Example No. 721

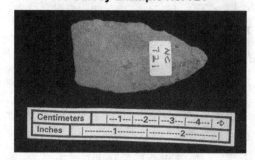

   The North Carolina Fluted Point Survey was started in 1977 by the author and is an ongoing survey of Clovis, Cumberland, Folsom or their generalized forms that is published by the Piedmont Archaeological Society of North and South Carolina, Inc. To date (March, 2007) their have been 810 Fluted points recorded. The data of these points is outstanding and is partially shared in the attached tables. Fluted-like points not included in the North Carolina Fluted Survey are Quad, Alamance, Haw River, Dalton, Hardaways and their generalized forms. If these were included, the total would surpass 4,000 in count.

   The history of recordings of Fluted Points from North Carolina is by itself very interesting. The first North Carolina Fluted Point recorded was that by H. M. Wormington in her book *"Ancient Man in North America"* printed in May, 1939. Virginia archaeologist, Dr. Ben C. McCary of Williamsburg, Virginia recorded 65 Fluted Points from North Carolina in 1948 in the Archaeological Society of Virginia publication *"the Quarterly Bulletin"* which was collected by the late A.D. Capehart. In the late 1960's and early 1970's Mr. Edward Bottoms of Portsmouth, Virginia recorded in *"the Chesopiean"* several surveys that included fluted points, Alamance points, Haw River points, and Hardaway points from North Carolina. A selection of Fluted Points from Granville County, North Carolina was published in the *"Ohio Archaeologist"*, Vol.10, No.1, January 1960 that was in the A.D. Capehart collection. A brief survey of 83 North Carolina fluted points was published by Mr. Phil Perkinson of Norlinda, North Carolina in *"Southern Indian Studies"*, Vol.XXIII, Oct.,1971 and Vol.XXV, October, 1973. Over the years, several individual points have also been pictured or recorded in various archaeological journals.

   Most all examples recorded to date have their bases and basal sides ground smooth; however, a few specimens do not have any basal smoothing at all. Also, most all of the fluted projectile points recorded support Floyd Painter's "Cattail Creek Fluting Tradition"-the generally thinning of performs and blanks of fluted projectile points from the rough stages through the finish stages by fluting. The majority of the Clovis-like points can be separated into three rather distinct shapes of forms: (1) convex-sided points or those whose sides diverge from the base to within approximately one-half to two-thirds of the distance to the tip; (2) straight or parallel-sided points or those points whose sides are parallel; (3) concave-convex sided points or those which become slightly or decidedly concave just above the base, and concave at or near the middle of the blade. Other forms, like the well known varieties such as Ross County, Debert (deep concave base), Redstone and Cumberland have all been recorded. The straight sided points are the most common found (405 points or 50%) and the Redstone variety is the most scarce (6 points or only 1%). See *Fluted Type Bar and Pie Charts*.

The average size fluted point from North Carolina is between 25mm to 60mm in length and is classified as "small". This makes up of 558 points or 68.9% of fluted points recorded to date. Miniature points, or those less than 25mm in length is the most scarce, only 4 has been recorded (about 0.5%), see *Fluted Point Size Bar and Pie Charts*. The lithic material in mainly that from the famous Carolina Slate Belt, to classified each type would be very difficult, so we use "shale" to include all the different silicified shale, rhyolite, shale flint, etc...including those that are green, black, dark green, brownish, and the like. This Shale material count is 452 fluted points or 55.8%. The rest of the lithic material are quartz, white quartz, clear or crystal quartz, jasper, chalcedony, flint, Oolithic quartzite, and other material like petrified wood, agate, etc. The scarcest material is Oolithic Quartzite which is from a source in Bertie County, North Carolina. Only 3 fluted points of this Oolithic material has been recorded, or 0.4%.

During the assembly of the North Carolina Fluted Point Survey, the highest assembly of fluted points came from Granville County, North Carolina. There are a total of four Fluted Point Sites recorded (Clovis-like): the Pasquotank Site in Pasquotank County, the Baucom Site in Union County, the Oshnock Site in Harnet County, and the Siloam Site in Surry, County, with the Oshnock Site being the largest, producing 33 Clovis-like points.

A few of the fluted points recorded have been utilized as knives, scrapers, spoke shaves and even drills, but these are very few in number. The data provided here has been obtained from various archaeologists, collectors, printed reports, etc. No one claims to have complete information, for many, many more fluted points must exists in private collections that have not, for some various reasons, been recorded. The total number of 810, is certainly impressive, and will most likely be larger once this paper goes to print. While we may never know for sure where the fluted point originated, we do know that the geographical configuration of landscape, river basins, and lithic out-crops played an important part in the migration of Early Man.

Pennsylvania Fluted Point Survey

The following text was published in *The Pennsylvania Fluted Point Survey* by Gary L. Fogelman and Stanley W. Lantz. It represents the basics on any fluted point recording activity and amplies numerous factors discussed in the publication.

Evaluation Process

It's best to go over the various reasoning and deductive processes involved in pint evaluation. There are several methods to the process. One thing is the history of the point. Where and when and by whom was it found? An authentic piece often has a history that can be followed and verified. Or, it has been in the archaeological record for a long time. This fact in itself is no guarantee of authenticity, however. A questionable piece, on the other hand, often has a trail that dead ends and leads to nowhere and no one, or it may lead to or have come through the hands of individuals with a history of playing with facts.

Next, what is the point made of? With fluted points one has to have an open mind, as these points are often made of the finest and prettiest materials that could be obtained. Flint sometimes, not often, travels 200-400 miles during Paleo times. Still, when Edwards Plateau or Alibates Chert from Texas, or Florida Agatized Coral shows up, it's time for caution. An illustration is a point that presumably originated in Butler County, rumored from a dam breast in a State Park. The point is made of Crowley Ridge Chert, which is from Arkansas. I had it to a Midwestern show where it was definitely identified, and I witnessed other points made of it.

It's most likely that this piece has at some point in the past lost its provenience, and ended up in a collection where the collector just added it in with his local material. However, the judgment can't be 100% certain. Point Lycoming-4, with a strong provenience, is very much the same material. And, point Butler-5, of a material curiously noted as "moonstone," closely resembles Arkansas Novaculite, also from Arkansas. Thus, the possibility exists of such long distance transport of 1600 miles or better, but it's quite rare if it occurs. And, these cherts may be some rare mimics, but at any rate a point like the one from Butler County was relegated to eh miscellaneous categories.

A piece is next viewed as to how it fits specifications for its type. Is it correct in width, length, thickness and form? Is it perfect and pristine, or has it been re-sharpened or show breakage or use? Is there a noticeable patina? These considerations are factored in because of the monetary value of fluted points. This is the main reason fluted points are newly made and marketed. The finer and prettier the piece, the higher the value. It wouldn't be worth it to produce broken bases or scruffy, used up points.

There is a second reason for introducing false points or information into the archaeological record. It is to pave the way for like material in the future. Yet a third reason is a collector wanting to add more importance to himself or his collection by representing everything in the collection as personally found.

There are certainly flintknappers of modern times who can replicate fluted points that are technically correct, and methods have been devised to add an apparent patina. There will always be those who seek to defraud with artifacts and information. An attempt has been made to negate such efforts in this survey by scrutinizing the points on many fronts, and weeding out those that seemed suspicious in any way.

Another litmus test is how the point has been received by the collecting community. Many points have come to us from old-time collections, and many of those have been used in previous publications. Sometimes deception isn't immediately recognized, but eventually realization dawns, or additional information comes forth. These then become part of the learning and educational process and people with more of these experiences, the collectors, therefore have more knowledge. A point that has longevity in the collector community is quite likely authentic.

We feel our knowledge and caution has reduced the likelihood of the introduction of any recently made points. If any have crept in, they are of a nature that they fall within the specifications of fluted pints for the state, and thus would not skew any analysis anyway except in numbers. I don't believe that our methods allowed any in, but if so, surely not enough to be a factor in the number of fluted points occurring in the state.

We have tried to negate the effect of points that may be genuine but geographically misplaced. In other words, points that may have originated elsewhere than Pennsylvania. Many points have little concrete information. Some have passed through several collections, and early on there was not the emphasis on record keeping as to whose collection or where certain points originated. Another reason for confusion is that many collectors like variety and obtain artifacts from other areas. Buying and trading occurs. Sometimes this foreign material is mixed with the local selection. In these cases, we used common sense and acquired and accumulated knowledge to judge the point. In most cases, we erred on the side of caution and relegated many points to the Miscellaneous categories, but accepted those that we felt were clearly ancient and fell within the parameters of the general field of points for the supposed area first, and secondly on a statewide level.

In this way, by comparisons, by visual examination, by seeking the knowledge of others and one's own experiences, a piece will eventually be accepted, or not. Many collectors are now aware of how information is valuable in giving a point both background and reliability, which translates eventually to monetary value.

Appendix D – Williamson Points at the College of William and Mary

These points were purchased from the Williamson family and given to the College of William and Mary. These photographs were taken by Ben C. McCary just prior to John Williamson's turning over the collection to College of William and Mary in Williamsburg, Virginia..

Short History: As boys, John and Josh Williamson searched for Civil War relics on their parent's farm in Dinwiddie County, Virginia. However, it was John Adkins, a collector, who made the Williamsons aware of the Indian artifacts that were to become known as Clovis points. Some of the early investigators on the site were John C. Smith, Rev. J. R. McAllister, and Judge Charles E. Gilliam. Soon afterwards, Ben McCary visited the site and its Paleoindian significance was in Virginia's history books. In 1951, McCary published the site in American Antiquity.

References:

McCary, Ben C. (1951) A Workshop Site of Early Man in Dinwiddie County, Virginia. American Antiquity, Vol. 17, No. 1.

Peck, Rodney M. (2004) America's Largest Paleo-Indian Workshop Site, Dinwiddie County, Virginia: The Williamson Site. Peck's Place, Kannapolis, NC.

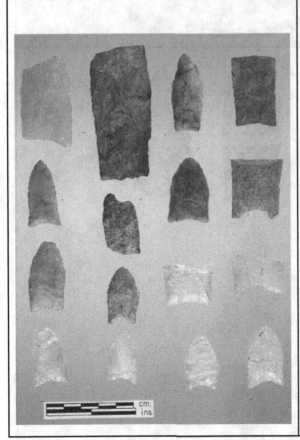

Appendix E – Database Design

Table E1 provides the basic construct for a survey database. If the database principles, discussed previously, are used, then three relational tables should be used. See Fortier (1997)

Table E1 - Point Database (Complex)				
Name	**Type**	**Size**	**Contents**	**Units/Value**
SPECIMEN	Number (Long)	4	Specimen Number	
ARTIFACT	VARCHAR	10	Artifact Number	
ARTIFACT_TYPE	Number (Integer)	2	Lithic Type	0 = Not Recorded, 1 = Uniface, 2 = Biface, 3 = Projectile Point, 4 = Drill, 5 = Utilized Flake, 6 = Scraper, 7 = Spokeshave, 8 = Knife
LITHIC_SHAPE	Number (Integer)	2	Lithic Shape	0 = Indeterminate, 1 = Lanceolate, 2 = Triangular, 3 = Pentagonal, 4 = Ovate, 5 = Discoidal, 6 = Square, 7 = Rectangle
STEM_CHARACTERISTICS	Number (Integer)	2	Stem Characteristics	0 = Indeterminate, 2 = Tapering, 3 = Parallel Sided, 4 = Expanding, 5 = Wide, 6 = Bifurcate, 7 = Side Notched, 8 = Corner Notched, 9 - Not Applicable
BASE_SHAPE	Number (Integer)	2	Base Shape	0 = Indeterminate, 1 = Pointed, 2 = Convex, 3 - Straight, 4 = Concave, 9 = Not Applicable
TANG_SHAPE	Number (Integer)	2	Tang Shape	0 = Indeterminate, 1 = Rounded, 2 = Lateral, 3 = Oblique, 4 = Pointed, 5 = Hanging, 9 = Not Applicable
NOTCHES	Number (Integer)	2	Notches	0 = Indeterminate, 1 = Midsection, 2 = Side, 3 = Corner, 4 = Base, 9 = Not Applicable
NOTCH_DEPTH	Number (Single)	4	Notch Depth	millimeter
SERRATED	Number (Integer)	2	Serrated	0 = Not Recorded, 1 = Heavy Serrated, 2 = Medium Serrated, 3 = Lightly Serrated, 4 = Retouched, 9 = Not Applicable
WEAR_TYPE	Number (Integer)	2	Edge Wear	0 = Indeterminate, 1 = Nibbling, 2 = Polish, 3 = Both Edges and Point, 4 = Hammering, 9 = Undocumented
WEAR_LOCATION	Number (Integer)	2	Wear Location	0 = Indeterminate, 1 = One Edge, 2 = Two Edges, 3 = Both Edges and Point, 9 = Undocumented
WEAR_SIDE	Number (Integer)	2	Wear Sides	0 = Indeterminate, 1 = One Surface, 2 = Two Surfaces, 9 = Undocumented
DRILL_ROTATION	Number (Integer)	2	Drill Rotation	0 = Indeterminate, 1 = Clockwise, 2 = Counterclockwise, 9 = Not Applicable

Table E1 - Point Database (Complex)				
MATERIAL	Number (Integer)	2	Material	0 = Not Recorded, 1 = Quartzite, 2 = Argillite, 3 = Diabase, 4 = Hematite/Ochre/Limonite, 5 = Rhyolite, 6 = Gneiss, 7 = Slate/Shale, 8 = Greenstone, 9 = Schist, 10 = Metavolcanic, 11 = Chalcedony, 12 = Basalt, 13 = Quartz, 14 = Obsidian, 15 = Limestone, 16 = Diorite, 17 = Granite, 18 = Tuff, 19 = Metallic, 20 = Serpentine, 21 = Malachite, 22 = Vesicular Basalt, 23 = Cryptocrystalline Silicate, 24 = Caliche, 25 = Manganese, 26 = Calcite Crystal, 27 = Gypsum, 28 = Galena, 29 = Fossil, 30 = Epidote, 33 = Chert, 34 = Conglomerate, 35 = Jasper, 37 = Sandstone, 38 = Steatite, 39 = Amethyst, 40 = Azurite, 41 = Turquoise, 42 = Asbestos, 43 = Plagioclase Crystal, 44 = Barite Crystal, 45 = Bornite, 46 = Copper, 47 = Mica, 48 = Glass, 49 = Iron, 50 = Undocumented
LENGTH	Number (Single)	4	Length	millimeter
WIDTH	Number (Single)	4	Width	millimeter
THICKNESS	Number (Single)	4	Thickness	millimeter
WEIGHT	Number (Single)	4	Weight	gram
SPECIFIC GRAVITY	Number (Single)	4	SG	
LITHIC_COMPLETENESS	Number (Integer)	2	Completeness	0 = Incomplete, 1 = Complete
CATALOG	Number (Integer)	2	Count	
COMMENT	VARCHAR	100	Text	Words

General Survey References

Adams, William Y.
(1991) Archaeological Typology and Practical Reality. Cambridge University, Cambridge, England.
(1988) Archaeological Classification: Theory versus Practice. *Antiquity,* 61: 40-56

Addington, Lucile R.
(1986) Lithic Illustrations: Drawing Flaked Stone Artifacts for Publication. Prehistoric Archaeology and Ecology Series, University of Chicago Press, Chicago, IL.

Agoston, G. A.
(1979) Color Theory and its Application in Art and Design. Springer-Verlag Publishers, Berlin, Germany.

Anderson, David G.
(2006) Pleistocene Human Occupation of the Southeastern United States: Research Directions for the Early 21st Century. In Paleoamerican Origins: Beyond Clovis, edited by Robson Bonnichsen, Bradley T. Lepper, Dennis Stanford, and Michael R. Waters, pp. 29-43. Texas A&M University Press, College Station, TX.
(2005) Website: The Paleoindian Database of the Americas (http://pidba.tennessee.edu/).
(1990) The Paleoindian Colonization of Eastern North America: a View from the Southeastern United States, in K.B. Tankersley & B.L. Isaac (ed.), Early Paleoindian Economies of Eastern North America: 163-216. Greenwich (CT): JAI Press. Research in Economic Anthropology Supplement 5.
(1990) A North American Paleoindian Projectile Point Database. Current Research in the Pleistocene, Vol. 7, pp.67–69.

Anderson, David G., R. Jerald Ledbetter, and Lisa O'Steen (1990) Paleoindian Period Archaeology of Georgia. Georgia Archaeological Research Design Paper No. 6, University of Georgia, Athen, GA.

Anderson, D.G. & Michael .K. Faught
(2000) Paleoindian Artifact Distributions: Evidence and Implications. Antiquity, Vol. 74, pp.507-513.

(1998) The Distribution of Fluted Paleoindian Projectile Points: Update 1998, Archaeology of Eastern North America 26: 163-87.

Anderson, D.G. & J.C. Gillam
(2000) Paleoindian Colonization of the Americas: Implications from an Examination of Physiography, Demography, and Artifact Distribution. American Antiquity 65(1): 43-66.

Anderson, David G., and Glen T. Hanson
(1988) Early Archaic Settlement in the Southeastern United States: A Case Study from the Savannah River. American Antiquity, Vol. 53, pp. 262-286.

Anderson, David G., and Michael J. O'Brien
(1998) Missouri Paleo-Indian Projectile Point Recording Project: A Call for Data. Missouri Archaeological Society Quarterly, Vol. 15, No. 3, pp. 4–9.

Anderson, David G., D. Shane Miller, Stephen J. Yerka, and Michael K. Faught
(2005) Paleoindian Database of the Americas: 2005 Status Report. Current Research in the Pleistocene, Vol. 22, pp. 91-92.

Andrefsky, William, Jr.
(2001) Lithic Debitage – Context, Form, Meaning (editor). University of Utah Press, UT.
(1998) Lithics - Macroscopic Approaches to Analysis. Cambridge University Press, New York, NY.
(1997) Thoughts on Stone Tool Shape and Infrared Function. Journal of Middle Atlantic Archaeology, Vol. 13, pp. 125-44.
(1994) Raw Material Availability and the Organization of Technology. American Antiquity, Vol. 59, pp. 21-34.

Alten, Helen
(1997) Materials for Labeling Collections in Marking Collection Objects: Beyond Fingernail Polish II. American Association for Museums, Annual Meeting, Atlanta, GA.

Bacon, William S.
(1977) Projectile Point Typology: The Basic Base. Archaeology of Eastern North America, Vol. 5, pp. 107-122.

Bailey, C. M.
(1999) Simplified Geologic Map of Virginia. College of William and Mary, Williamsburg, VA.

Bedford, Tim and Roger Cooke
(2001) Probabilistic Risk Analysis. Cambridge University Press, Cambridge, England.

Bell, Robert E.
(1958) Guide to the Identification of Certain American Indian Projectile Points. Special Bulletin No. 1, Oklahoma Anthropological Society.

Bennett, James R.
(2003) Relics & Fakes – Identifying Reproductions & Altered Ancient American Artifacts. Homestead Publishing Company, Polk, OH.

Benthall, Joseph L. and Ben C. McCary
(1973) The Williamson Site: A New Approach. Archaeology of Eastern North America, Vol. 1, pp. 127-132.

Bladock, H. M.
(1972) Social Statistics. McGraw-Hill, Inc., New York, NY.

Blanton, Dennis B. and Donald W. Linebaught
(1996) Archaeological Assessment of Sites 44PY43, 44 PY43, and 44PY152 at Leesville Lake, Pittsylvania County, Virginia. Research Report Series No. 7, Virginia Department of Historic Resources, Richmond, VA,

Boldurian, Anthony T. and John C. Cotter
(1999) Clovis Revisited – New Perspectives on Paleoindian Adaptations from Blackwater Draw, New Mexico. University Museum, University of Pennsylvania, PA.

Bonnichsen, R.A. & K.L. Turnmire (ed.)
(1999) Ice age peoples of North America environments, origins, and adaptations of the first Americans. Corvallis (OR): Center for the Study of the First Americans.

Bordaz, Jacques
(1970) Tools of the Old and New Stone Age. The American Museum of Natural History, Natural History Press, Garden City, NY.

Bottoms, Edward
(1988) The Paleoindian Component of the Bennet Site. Chesopiean, Vol. 26, pp. 21-29.
(1985) Additional Paleoindian Artifacts from the Dime Site, Suffolk, Virginia. Chesopiean, Vol. 23, pp. 28-32.
(1974) The Paleoindian Component of the Dime Site, County of Nansemond. Chesopiean, Vol 12, pp. 88-106.
(1972) The Paleoindian Component of the Richmond Site, Chesterfield County, Virginia: A Summary Report. Chesopiean, Vol. 10, pp. 115-135.

Boyd, C. Clifford, Jr.
(2003) Paleoindian Research in Virginia and Beyond. ASV Quarterly Bulletin, Vol. 58, No. 2, pp. 58-93.

Bradley, Bruce A.
(1991) Lithic Technology. In: Prehistoric Hunters of the High Plains, 2nd ed., G. Frison, pp. 369-396. Academic Press, New York, NY.
(1975) Lithic Reduction Sequences: A Glossary and Discussion. In: Lithic Technology - Making and Using Stone Tools, ed. E. Swanson. Aldine Press, Chicago, IL.
(1974) A Technique of Drawing Flaked Stone. Lithic Technology, Vol. III, No. 3, p. 53.

Brennan, Louis A.
(1982) A Compilation of Fluted Points of Eastern North America by Count and Distribution: An AENA Project. Archaeology of Eastern North America, Vol. 10, pp. 27-46.
(1975) Artifacts of Prehistoric America. Stackpole Books, Harrisburg, PA.

Broderick, Michael
(1988) Residue Analysis of Foxie Otter Site Chipped Stone. In: The Foxie Otter Site by Christopher C. Hanks, Anthropological Papers, Museum of Anthropology, University of Michigan, Ann Arbor, MI.

Brown, Allen (Autographed)
(1943) Indian Relic and Their Values. Lightner Publishing Co., Chicago, IL.

Broyles, Bettye
(1971) The St Albans Site, Kanawha County, West Virginia. West Virginia Geological Survey, Report of Archaeological Investigations, Morgantown, WV.
(1966) Preliminary Report: The St Albans Site (46 Ka 27), Kanawha County, West Virginia. West Virginia Archeologist, No. 19, pp. 1-43.

Bullen, Ripley P.
(1968/revised1975) A Guide to the Identification of Florida Projectile Points. Kendall Books, Gainesville, FL.
(1962) Suwannee Points in the Simpson Collection. Florida Anthropologist, Vol. 15, No. 3, pp. 83-88.

Bushnell, David I.
(1940) Evidence of Early Indian Occupation Near the Peaks of Otter, Bedford County, Virginia. Smithsonian Miscellaneous Publication, Vol. 99, No.15, Washington, DC.

Byers, D. S. and F. Johnson
(1940) Two Sites on Martha's Vineyard. Papers of R.S. Peabody Foundation for Archaeology, Vol. 1, pp. 1-104.

Callahan, Errett
(1982) Indian Technology: An Introductory Guide to Making Stone Tools, Pottery, Baskets, and Much More. Thunderbird Museum and Archaeological Park, Front Royal, VA.
(1979) The Basics of Biface Knapping in the Eastern Fluted Point Tradition - A Manual for Flintknappers and Lithic Analysis. Archaeology of Eastern North America, Vol. 7, No. 1, pp. 1-179.

Carr, Kurt W.
(1975) The Fifty Site: A Flint Run Paleoindian Complex Processing Station. M.A. Thesis, Department of Anthropology, Catholic University of America, Washington, DC.
(1974) The Fifty Site: A Stratified Early Archaic Processing Station. In: The Flint Run Paleoindian Complex: A Preliminary Report 1971-73 Seasons. Ed. W. Gardnes, Occasional Publication, No. 1, Archaeology Laboratory, Catholic University of America, Washington, DC.

Carr, Philip J.
(1994) The Organization of Technology: Impact and Potential. In: The Organization of North American Prehistoric Chipped Stone Tool Technologies, edited by Philip J. Carr. Archaeological Series 7, International Monographs in Prehistory, Ann Arbor, MI.

Carroll, Mary S. (ed)
(2002) Delivering Archaeological Information Electronically. Society for American Archaeology, Washington, DC.

Carter, Loy C.
(1989) The Loy Carter Clovis Point. Chesopiean, Vol. 24, No. 2, pp. 8-9.

Charles, Tommy and James L. Michie
(1992) South Carolina Paleo Point Database. In: Paleoindian and Early Archaic Research in the Lower Southeast: A South Carolina Perspective, ed. D. Anderson, et al., pp. 381-389, Council of South Carolina Professional Archaeologists.

Carter, Brinnen, James S. Dunbar, and David G. Anderson
(1998) Paleoindian Projectile Point Recording Project: A Call for Data. The Florida Anthropologist, Vol. 51, pp. 37–44.

Charles, Tommy
(1981) Dwindling Resources: An Overture to the Future of South Carolina's Archaeological Resources. South Carolina Institute of Archaeology and Anthropology, University of South Carolina, The Notebook, Vol.13, pp.1-85.
(1983) Thoughts and Records from the Survey of Private Collections of Prehistoric Artifacts throughout South Carolina: A Second Report. South Carolina Institute of Archaeology and Anthropology, University of South Carolina, The Notebook, Vol.15, pp.1-37.
(1986) The Fifth Phase of the Collectors Survey. South Carolina Institute of Archaeology and Anthropology, University of South Carolina, The Notebook, Vol. 18, pp. 1-27.

Childs, S. Terry (ed)
(2004) Our Collective Responsibility: The Ethics and Practice of Archaeological Collections Stewardship. SAA Press, Washington, DC.

Coe, Joffre L. (autographed)
(1964) The Formative Cultures of the Carolina Piedmont. Transactions of the American Philosophical Society, New Series, Vol. 54, Part 5, Philadelphia, PA.

Collins, Michael B.
(1999) Clovis Blade Technology. University of Texas Press, Austin, TX.

Collins, Michael B. and Jason M. Fenwick
(1974) Heat Treating of Chert: Methods of Interpretation and Their Application. Plains Anthropologist 19(64):134-144.

Craib, Donald
(2003) The Conservancy Acquires Its First Site in Virginia. American Archaeology, Vol. 7, No. 3, p. 44.

Crabtree, Don E.
(1972) An Introduction to Flintworking. Occasional Papers of the Idaho State Museum, No. 28, Pocatello, ID.

Curry, M., M. J. O'Brian, and M. K. Timble
(1985) Classification of Pointed, Hafted Bifaces. Missouri Archaeologist, Vol. 46, pp. 77-189.

Custer, Jay F.
(1984) An Analysis of Fluted Points and Paleo-Indian Site Locations from the Delmarva Peninsula. Bulletin, Archaeological Society of Delaware, Vol. 16, pp. 1-26.

Custer, J. F., J. Ilgenfritz, and K. Doms
(1988) Application of Blood Residue Analysis Techniques in the Middle Atlantic Region. Journal of Middle Atlantic Archaeology 4:99-104.

Dent, Joseph
(1995) Chesapeake Prehistory, Old Traditions, New Directions. Plenum Press, New York, NY.

Dincauze, D.F.
(1993) Fluted points in the eastern forests, in O. Soffer & N.D. Praslov (ed.), From Kostenki to Clovis: Upper Paleolithic Paleo-Indian Adaptations: 279-92. Plenum Press, New York, NY.

Doran, J. and F. Hudson
(1975) Mathematics and Computers in Archaeology. Edinburgh University Press, Edinburgh.

DeJarnette, David L., Edward Kurjack, and James W. Cambron
(1962) Stanfield-Worley Bluff Shelter Excavations. Journal of Alabama Archaeology, Vol. VIII, Nos. 1 and 2.

DeRegnaucount, Tony and Jeff Georgiady
(1998) Prehistoric Chert Types of the Midwest. Occasional Monographs Series of the Upper Miami Valley, Archaeological Research Museum, No. 7, Arcanum, OH.

Dongoske, Kurt, Mark Alenderfer, and Karen Doehner
(2000) Working Together: Native American and Archaeologist. Society for American Archaeology, Washington, DC.

Dougherty, Edward R. and Charles Robert Giardina
(1988) Mathematical Methods for Artificial Intelligence and Autonomous Systems. Prentice Hall, New York, NY.

Ebert, James L.
(2004) Distributional Archaeology. University of Utah Press, Salt Lake, UT.

Ellis, H. Holmes
(1957) Flint-Working of the American Indians: An Experimental Study. Ohio Historical Society, Columbus, OH.

Faught, Michael K., David G. Anderson, and Anne Gisiger
(1994) North American Paleoindian Database—An Update. Current Research in the Pleistocene, Vol. 11, pp. 32–35.

Fiedel, Stuart J.
(2004) The Kennewick Follies: New Theories about the Peopling of the Americas. Journal of Anthropological Research, Vol. 60, No. 1, pp. 75-110.

Fitting, James E.
(1965) A Quantitative Examination of Virginia Fluted Points. American Antiquity, Vol. 30, No. 4, pp. 484-491.

Fogelman, Gary
(2004) Pennsylvania Chert. Fogelman Publishing Co., Turbotville, PA.

Fogelman, Gary L. and Stanly W. Lantz
(2006) The Pennsylvania Fluted Point Survey. Fogelman Publishing Co., Turbotville, PA.

Fortier, Paul J.
(1997) Database Systems Handbook. McGraw-Hill Publishers, New York, NY.

Fortiner, Virginia J.
(1967-1971 version) Science-Hobby Book of Archaeology. Lerner Publications Company, Minneapolis, MN.

Frison, George
(1986) Mammoth Hunting and Butchering from a Perspective of African Elephant Culling. In: G. Frsion and L. Tood, eds., The Colby Mammoth Site: Taphonomy and Archaeology of a Clovis Kill in Northern Wyoming, pp. 115-34, University of New Mexico Press, Albuquerque, NM.

Funk, Robert E.
(1983) Some Observations on Paleo-Indian Studies in the East. Archaeology of Eastern North America, Vol. 11, pp. 18-19.

Gardner, William A.
(1989) An Examination of Cultural Change in the Late Pleistocene and Early Holocene (circa 9200 to 6800 BC) In: Paleoindian Research in Virginia – A Synthesis. ASV Special Publication No. 19.
(1974) The Flint Run Complex: A Preliminary Report 1971-73 Seasons. Occasional Publication No. 1, Catholic University, Washington, DC.

Gardner, William M., and Robert A. Verry
(1979) Typology and Chronology of Fluted Points from the Flint Run Area. Pennsylvania Archaeologist 49(1-2):13-46.

Goddard, E. N., R. K. de Ford, O. N. Rove, J. T. Singewald, and R. M. Overbeck
(1951) Rock Color Chart. Geological Society of America, Denver, Colorado.

Goodwin, Asthely J. H.
(1960) Chemical Alteration (Patination) of Stone. South African Anthropological Bulletin, T. 15, No. 59, pp. 67-76.

Garrad, C.
(1971) Ontario Fluted Point Survey. Ontario Archaeology, Vol. 16, pp. 3-18.

Griffiths, Nick and Anne Jenner
(2002 version) Drawing Archaeological Finds - A Handbook. Henry Ling, Limited, Dorset Press, Dorchester, UK.

Goldsmith, Timothy H.
(2006) What Birds See. Scientific American, Vol. 295, No. 1, pp. 68-75.

Goodyear, Albert C.
(1982) The Chronological Position of the Dalton Horizon in the Southeastern United States. American Antiquity, Vol. 47, pp. 382-395.
(1979) A Hypothesis Of The Use Of Cryptocrystalline Raw Material Among Paleo-Indian Groups Of North America. Research manuscript series No. 156. Institute of Archaeology and Anthropology, University of South Carolina. Columbia.
(1974) The Brand Site, A Techno-Functional Study of a Dalton Site in Northeast Arkansas. Arkansas Archeological Survey Research Series 7.

Grace, Roger
(1989) Interpreting the Function of Stone Tools, BAR International Series 474, Oxford, UK.

Gramly, Richard M.
(1993) The Richey Clovis Cache: Earliest American Along the Columbia River. Persimmon Press, Buffalo New York.
(1992) Prehistoric Lithic Industry at Dover, Tennessee. Persimmon Press Monographs in Archaeology, Buffalo, NY.
(1990) Guide to the Paleo-Indian Artifacts of North America. Persimmon Press Monographs in Archaeology, Buffalo, NY.
(1988a) The Adkins Site: A Paleoindian Habitation and Associated Stone Structure. Persimmon Press, Buffalo, NY.
(1988b) Discoveries at the Lamb Site, Genesee County, New York 1986-7. Ohio Archaeologist, Vol. 38, No. 1, pp. 4-10.
(1984) Kill Sites, Killing Ground and Fluted Points at the Vail Site. Archaeology of Eastern North America, Vol. 11, pp. 110-121.
(1982) The Vail Site: A Paleoindian Encampment in Maine. Buffalo Society of Natural Sciences, Vol. 30.

Hall, Christopher T. and Mary Lou Larson (eds.)
(2004) Aggregate Analysis in Chipped Stone. University of Utah Press, Salt Lake, UT.

Hardy, Bruce L., Marvin Kay, Anthony E. Marks, and Katherine Monigal
(2001) Stone Tool Function at the Paleolithic Sites of Starosele and Buram Kaya III, Crima: Behavioral and Implications. Proceeding of the National Academy of Science, Vol. 98, No. 19.

Hardy, G. H. and E. M. Wright
(1979) An Introduction to the Theory of Numbers. Clarendon Press, Oxford University Press, New York, NY.

Hawk, P. B., B. L. Osen, and W. H. Summerson
(1947) Physiological Chemistry. Blackston Company, Toronto, Canada.

Haynes, C. Vance
(1972) Stratigraphic Investigation at the Williamson Site, Dinwiddie County, Virginia. Chesopiean, Vol. 10, pp. 107-114.

Haynes, Gary
(2002) The Early Settlement of America. Cambridge University Press, Cambridge, UK.
(1983) Fluted Points in the East and West. Archaeology of Eastern North America, Vol. 11, pp. 24-27.

Hill, Phillip J.
(2002) An Excavation of Cores Surface Collected from the Williamson Site (44DW1): A Paleoindian Quarry-Related Site Located in Southeastern Virginia. North American Archaeologist, Vol. 23, No. 1, pp. 1-16.

Holland, John D.
(2003) A Guide to Pennsylvania Lithic Types. Journal of Middle Atlantic Archaeology, Vol. 19, pp. 129-150.

Hothem, Lar
(2005) Paleo-Indian Artifacts. Collector Books, Paducah, KY.
(2001) Indian Relic from the Catalogs of Old-Time Dealers. Hothem House Books, Lancaster, OH.

Howard, Calvin D.
(1995) Projectile Point and Hafting Design Review. North American Archaeologist, Vol. 16, No. 4, pp. 291-301.
(1990) The Clovis Point: Characteristics and Type Description. Plains Anthropologist 35(129):255-262.

Howard, Edgar B.
(1935) Evidence of Early Man in North America. The Museum Journal, Vol. 24, pp. 2-3, University of Pennsylvania Museum.

Hranicky, Wm Jack
(2006) Paleofluting: Mechanics or Culture? Paper: Society for American Archaeology, Annual Meeting, San Juan, PR.
(2006) Experimental Archaeology. AuthorHouse, Bloomington, IN.
(2005) McCary Fluted Point Survey – Points 1009 to 1014: A Continuing Study of Virginia Paleoindian Technology. ASV Quarterly Bulletin, Vol. 60, No. 1, pp. 15-31.
(2005) A Model for a Paleoindian Fluted Point Survey. Authorhouse. Bloomington, IN.
(2004) Encyclopedia of Concepts and Terminology in American Prehistoric Lithic Technology. AuthorHouse, Bloomington, IN.
(2004) McCary Fluted Point Survey: Points 1000 to 1012 – A Continuing Study of Virginia Paleoindian Technology. ASV Quarterly Bulletin, Vol. 59, No. 1, pp. 25-52.
(2003) Prehistoric Projectile Points Found Along the Atlantic Coastal Plain. Universal Publishers, FL.
(2002) Lithic Technology in the Middle Potomac River Valley of Maryland and Virginia. Kluwer Academic/Plenum Publishers, New York, NY.
(1989) Do's and Don't's of Collecting and Displaying Projectile Points. Ohio Archaeologist, Vol. 39, No. 2, pp. 31-32.
(1989) The Do's and Don't's of Collecting and Displaying Projectile Points. Ohio Archaeologist, Vol. 39, No. 2, pp.31-32.

(1989) The Classic Clovis Point: Can it be defined: Chesopiean, Vol. 25, No. 1, pp. 18-27.

(1989) The McCary Survey of Virginia of Virginia Fluted Points: An Example of Collector Involvement in Virginia Archeology. ASV Quarterly Bulletin, Vol. 44, No. 1, pp. 20-34.

(1987) The Classic Clovis Point - Can It Be Defined? Chesopiean, Vol. 25, No. 1, pp. 18-28, Norfolk, VA.

(1985) Defining Prehistoric Indian Art. ASV Quarterly Bulletin, Vol. 40, Nos. 3&4, pp. 112-122.

(1976) Origins for the Fish-Tailed Fluting Tradition of South America. Chesopiean, Vol. 14, Nos. 1-2, pp. 19-25.

Hranicky, Wm Jack and Ben C. McCary
(1995) Clovis Technology in Virginia. ASV Special Publication Number 31.

Hranicky, Wm Jack and Floyd Painter
(1989) A Guide to the Identification of Virginia Projectile Points. ASV Special Publication Number 17.

Huckell, Bruce B. and J. David Kilby
(2004) Readings in Late Pleistocene North America and Early Paleoindians: Selections from American Antiquity. SAA Press, Washington, DC.

Hull, Edward
(1872) A Treatise on the Building and Ornamental Stones of Great Britain and Foreign Countries. MacMillan and Co., London, UK.

Hutchings, Wallace K.
(1997) The Paleoindian Fluted Point: Dart or Spear Armateur? The Identification of Paleoindian Delivery Technology Through the Analysis of Lithic Fracture Velocity. Ph.D. Dissertation, Simon Fraser University.

Jackson, Lawrence J.
(1998) The Sandy Ridge and Halstead Paleo-Indian Sites. Memoirs, Museum of Anthropology, University of Michigan, No. 32, Ann Arbor. MI.

Jennings, Jesse D.
(1989) Prehistory of North America, 3rd ed. Mayfield Publishing Co., Mountain View, CA.

Johnson, Michael F.
(1997) Additional Research at Cactus Hill: Preliminary Description of Northern Virginia – ASV's 1993 and 1995 Excavations. In: McAvoy, Archaeological Investigations of Site 44SX202, Cactus Hill, Sussex County, Virginia. Research Report Series No. 8, Virginia Department of Historic Resources, Richmond, VA.

(1995) Dissecting Clovis Point No. 325 from 45DO432 East Wenatchee, Washington. ASV Quarterly Bulletin, Vol. 50, No. 1, pp. 32-40.

(1993) Dissecting Clovis Point No. 325 from 45DO432 in East Wenatchee, Washington. ASV Quarterly Bulletin, Vol. 48, No. 2, pp. 64-72.

(1992) An Analogy Between Eastern Paleoindian and Historic Caribou Hunters: A Broad Perspective from Virginia. In Paleoindian and Early Archaic Period Research in the Lower Southeast: A South Carolina Perspective, edited by David G. Anderson, Kenneth E. Sassaman, and Christopher Judge, pp. 182-202. Council of South Carolina Professional Archeologists, Columbia.

(1989) Paleoindian Chronology for Virginia. In: Paleoindian Research in Virginia – A Synthesis, eds: J. Wittkofski and T. Reinhart, ASV Special Publication No. 19.

Johnson, Michael F. and Joyce E. Pearsall
(1991a) The Dr. Ben C. McCary Fluted Point Survey: Nos. 846-867. Quarterly Bulletin of the Archeological Society of Virginia 46:55-69.

(1991b) The Dr. Ben C. McCary Fluted Point Survey: Nos. 868-890. Quarterly Bulletin of the Archeological Society of Virginia 46:145-162.

Justice, Noel D.
(1987) Stone Age Spear Points of the Midcontinental and Eastern United States. Indiana University Press, Bloomington.

Kantardzic, Mehmed
(2003) Data Mining – Concepts, Models, Methods, and Algorithms. Wiley-Interscience, New York, NY.

Kay, Marvin
(1996) Microwear Analysis of Some Clovis Experimental Chipped Stone Tools. In: G. Odell, ed., Stone Tools: Theoretical Insights into Human Prehistory, pp. 315-44, Plenum Press, New York, NY.

(1986) Projectile Point Use Infrered from Microwear of Kimmwick Clovis Points. Paper, SAA Meeting, New Orleans, LA.

Keeley, Lawrence H.
(1982) Hafting and Retooling: Effects on the Archaeological Record. American Antiquity 47:798-809.

(1980) Experimental Determination of Stone Tool Uses. The University of Chicago Press, Chicago, IL.

(1977) The Function of Paleolithic Flint Tools. Scientific American, Vol. 237, No. 4, pp. 108-126.

Kintigh, Keith (ed.)
(2006) The Promise and Challenge of Archaeological Data Integration. American Antiquity, Vol. 71, No. 3, pp. 567-578.

Kiser, Robert Taft
(2006) Arrowhead 101.Virginia Living, pp. 166-171.

Kooyman, Brian P.
(2001) Understanding Stone Tools and Archaeological Sites. University of New Mexico Press, Albuquerque, NM.

Kraft, Herbert C.
(1973) The Plenge Site: A Paleoindian Occupation Site in New Jersey. Archaeology of Eastern North America, Vol. 1, pp. 56-117.

(1970) The Miller Field Site, Warren Count, N.J. Seaton Hall University Press, Orange, NJ.

Krech, Shepard III, and Barbara A, Hill (eds)
(1999) Collecting America, 1870 – 1960. Smithsonian Institution Press, Washington, DC.

Krieger, Alex D.
(1944) The Typological Concept. American Antiquity, Vol. 9, pp. 271-288.

Krzanowski, W. J.
(1988) Principles of Multivariate Analysis. Clarendon Press, Oxford.

Lange, Ian M.
(2002) Ice Age Mammals of North America. Mountain Press Publishing Co., Missoula, MT.

Lantz, Stanley W.
(1984) Distribution of Paleo-Indian Projectile Points and Tools from Western Pennsylvania: Implications for

Regional Differences. Archaeology of Eastern North America 12:210-230.

Lattanzi, Gregory D.
(1999) Cultural Resource Management and the Internet: A Touch of "Gray". SAA Bulletin, Vol. 17, No. 4, pp. 30-33.

Lenzen, Victor F.
(1938) Procedures of Empirical Science. Vol. 1, No. 5, International Encyclopedia of Unified Science, University of Chicago Press, Chicago, IL.

Lindsey, J. K.
(1995) Introductory Statistics: A Modeling Approach. Clarendon Press, Oxford.

Lock, Gary
(2004) Using Computers in Archaeology. Routledge, New York, NY.

Loy, T. H. and B. L. Hardy
(1992) Blood Residue Analysis of 90,000-Year-Old Stone Tools from Tabun Cave, Israel. Antiquity, Vol. 66, No. 250, pp..24–35.

Loy, Thomas and E. James Dixon
(1998) Blood Residues on Fluted Points from Eastern Alaska. American Antiquity, Vol. 63, No. 1, pp. 21-46.

Luchterland, Kubet
1970 Early Archaic Projectile Points and Hunting Pattern in the Lower Illinois Valley. Illinois Archaeological Survey, Monograph No. 2, Illinois State Museum, Springfield, IL.

Luedtke, Barbara
(1992) An Archaeologist's Guide to Chert and Flint. University of California Press, Los Angeles, CA.
(1979) The Identification of Sources of Chert Artifacts. American Antiquity 44(4):744-756.
(1978) Chert Sources and Trace-Element Analysis. American Antiquity 43(3):413-423.

MacCord, Howard A. and Wm Jack Hranicky
(1979) A Basic Guide to Virginia Prehistoric Projectile Points. Special Publication Number 6, Archeological Society of Virginia.

MacDonald, George F.
(1968) Debert - A Paleo-Indian Site in Central Nova Scotia. National Museums of Canada, Ottawa.

McGimsey, III, Charles R.
(1972) Public Archaeology. Seminar Press, New York, NY.

McCary, Ben C.
(1984/1991) Survey of Virginia Fluted Points. Archeological Society of Virginia Special Publication 12. (Revised).
(1983) The Paleo-Indian in Virginia. ASV Quarterly Bulletin, Vol. 38, No. 1, pp. 43-70.
(1975) The Williamson Paleoindian Site. Chesopiean, Vol. 13, pp. 48-131.
(1961) Cores from the Williamson Site. ASV Quarterly Bulletin, Vol. 16, No. 1, pp. 7-9.
(1961) Three Uncommon Artifacts from the Potts Site. ASV Quarterly Bulletin, Vol. 15, No. 3, pp. 27-31.
(1951) A Workshop Site of Early Man in Dinwiddie County, Virginia. American Antiquity, Vol. 17, pp. 9-17.

McCary, Ben C., and Glen R. Brittner
(1979) The Paleoindian Component of the Mitchell Plantation Site, Sussex County, Virginia. ASV Quarterly Bulletin, Vol.34, pp. 33-42.
(1978) Excavations at the Williamson Site, Dinwiddie County, Virginia. ASV Quarterly Bulletin, Vol. 33, pp. 45-60.

McCary, B. C., J. C. Smith, and C. E. Gilliam
(1949) A Folsom Workshop Site on the Williamson Farm, Dinwiddie County, Virginia. ASV Quarterly Bulletin, Vol. 4, No. 2, pp. 2-9.

McNett, Charles W., Jr.
(1985a) Artifact Morphology and Chronology at the Shawnee Minisink Site. In: Shawnee Minisink, Academic Press, Orlando, FL.
(1985b) Shawnee Minisink, Academic Press, Orlando, FL.

McAvoy, Joseph M.
(1997) Archaeological Investigations of Site 44SX202, Cactus Hill, Sussex County, Virginia. Research Report Series No. 8, Department of Historic Resources, Richmond, VA.
(1988) A Paleoindian Site Discovered in Greenville County. Paper presented at the 1988 ASV Annual Meeting, Hampton, VA.
(1979) The Point-of-Rocks Paleoindian Site. ASV Quarterly Bulletin, Vol. 34, pp. 93-111.
(1974) A Probable Paleoindian Site in Hanover County, Virginia. ASV Quarterly Bulletin, Vol. 29, pp. 59-62.
(1968) A Descriptive Study of Tools and Projectile Points of Two Early Hunter Camp Sites on the Atlantic Coastal Plain. Chesopiean, Vol. 3, pp. 146-150.

Martingell, H. and A. Saville
(1988) The Illustration of Lithic Artifacts; A Guide to Drawing Stone Tools for Specialist Reports. The Lithic Studies Society, Occasional Paper 5 and Association of Archaeological Illustrators and Surveyors, Technical Paper 9.

Maschner, Herbert D. G. and Christopher Chippindale
(2005) Handbook of Archaeological Methods. AltaMira Press, Walnut Creek, CA.

Mason, Ronald J.
(1958) Fluted Point Measurements. American Antiquity 23(3):311-312.

Meir, R. and V. Maiorov
(1999) On the Optimality of Incremental Neural Network Algorithms. In: Kerans, M.S., Solla, S.A., and Cohn, D.A. (eds.), Advances in Neural Information Processing Systems 11, Cambridge, MA: MIT Press, pp. 295-301.

Meltzer, David J.
(1997) Monte Verde and the Pleistocene Peopling of the Americas. Science, 276:754-5.
(1989) The Texas Clovis Fluted Point Survey: An Update and Request for Assistance. Newsletter of the Texas Archeological Society 33(1):18.
(1995) The Texas Clovis Fluted Point Survey-1995. Current Research in the Pleistocene 12:34-35.

Montel-White, Anta
(1997) The Paleoindians of the North American Midcontinent. Musee Departemental de Prehistorire de Solutre.

Morrow, Juliet E.
(1996) The Organization of Clovis. Lithic Technology in the Confluence Region of the Mississippi, Illinois, and Missouri Rivers. PhD. Dissertation, Washington University, St. Louis. Univ. Microfilms, Ann Arbor.

Morrow, Juliet E. and Toby A. Morrow
(1999) Geographic Variation in Fluted Projectile Points: A Hemisphere Perspective. American Antiquity, Vol. 64, No. 2, pp. 215-230.

Morrow, Toby, A., and Juliet E. Morrow
(1994) Preliminary Fluted Point Survey in Iowa. Current Research in the Pleistocene 11:47-48.

Most, Gregory P. J.
(2002) Manual for Classifying and Cataloguing Slides. National Gallery of Art, Washington, DC

Munyer, Marianna
(1997) How to Mark Objects in Museum Collections, Pts One and Two. Illinois Association of Museums, Springfield, IL.

Neumann, Thomas W. and Robert M. Sanford
(2001) Practicing Archaeology. AltaMira Press, Walnut Creek, CA.

Niven, Ivan, Herbert S. Zuckerman, and Hugh L. Montgomery
(1991) An introduction to the Theory of Numbers. John Wiley & Sons, Inc., New York, NY.

Orton, Clive
(2000) Sampling in Archaeology. Cambridge University Press, New York, NY

Pagoulatos, Peter
(2004) Paleoindian Site Location in New Jersey. Archaeology of Eastern North America, Vol. 32, pp.123-149.

Painter, Floyd
(1987) Lithic Projectile Points: Mislocation or Rejection is the Crux of the Question. Chesopiean, Vol. 25, No. 2, pp 2-8.
(1986) Pointed Weapons of Wood, Bone, and Ivory: Survival Tools of Early Man in North America. Central States Archaeological Journal 33(2):62-76.
(1984) A Search for the Origins of Paleo-Indian Projectile Points: A Challenge to the Virginia Archaeological Community. Archeological Society of Virginia Quarterly Bulletin 39(2):65-71.
(1973) The Cattail Creek Fluting Tradition and Its Complex-Determing Lithic Debris. Massachusetts Archaeological Society, Bulletin, Vol. 34, Nos. 1-2, pp. 6-12.
(1965) The Cattail Creek Fluting Tradition. Chesopiean, Vol. 3, No. 1.

Parry, W. J.
(1994) Prismatic Blade Technologies in North America. In: The Organization of North American Prehistoric Chipped Stone Technologies, edited by P.J. Carr, pp. 87-98. International Monographs in Prehistory, Ann Arbor, MI.

Patten, Bob
(1978a) The Denver Series – Point #13: Eden. Flintknapper's Exchange 1(1):18-20.
(1978b) The Denver Series – Point #3: Fluted Sandia. Flintknapper's Exchange 1(2):28-29.

(1978c) The Denver Series – Point #7: Hells Gap. Flintknapper's Exchange 1(3):29-30.
(1979a) The Denver Series – Point #34: Blackwater Draw Clovis, New Mexico. Flintknapper's Exchange 2(2):5-6.
(1979b) The Denver Series - #5, Folsom Point from Folsom, New Mexico. Flintknapper's Exchange 2(3):16.

Peck, Rodney M.
(2006) Data – North Carolina Fluted Point Survey.
(no date) Fluted Point Survey (List) From the author.
(2004) The Boney Site: A Paleo Indian Site in Greenville County, Virginia. Central States Archaeological Journal, Vol. 52, No. 1, pp. 20-23.
(2003) Paleo Indian Tool Kit of the Williamson Site. Central States Archaeological Journal, Vol. 50, No. 3, pp. 154-157.
(1988) Clovis Points of Early Man in North Carolina. Vol. 6, Piedmont Journal of Archaeology, Peidmont Archaeological Society.
(1985) The E. R. Callicut Clovis. Chesopiean, Vol. 23, No. 3, pp. 26-27.
(1969) Isle of Wight County Paleoindian Sites. Chesopiean, Vol. 7, No. 1.

Perkinson, Phil H.
(1971) North Carolina Fluted Projectile Points Survey Report Number One. Southern Indian Studies, Vol. XXII, Chapel Hill, NC.
(1973) North Carolina Fluted Projectile Point Survey Report Number Two. Southern Indian Studies 25:2-60. Chapel Hill.

Perino, Gregory
(1991) Selected Preforms, Points, and Knives of the North American Indians, Vol. 2, Points and Barbs Press, Idabel, OK.
(1985) Selected Preforms, Points, and Knives of the North American Indians, Vol. 1, Points and Barbs Press, Idabel, OK.

Phillips, Philip and Gordon Willey
(1953) Method and Theory in American Archaeology: an operational basis for cultural-historical investigation. American Anthropologist, Vol. 55, pp. 615-33.

Pickles, R. W.
(1946) Discovery of Folsom-like Arrowpoint and Artifacts of Mastodon Bone in Southwest Virginia. Tennessee Archeologist, Vol. 3, No. 1, pp. 3-7.

Piperno, Dolores R.
(2006_ Phytoliths. AltaMira Press, Blue Ridge Summit, PA.

Plew, Mark G., James C. Woods, and Max G. Pavesic
(1985) Stone Tool Analysis – Essays in Honor of Don. E. Crabtree. University of New Mexico Press, Albuquerque, NM.

Prufer, Olaf H.
(1964) Survey of Ohio Fluted Points, No. 10. Cleveland Museum of Natural History. Cleveland.
(1960) Early Man East of the Mississippi. Cleveland Museum of Natural History, Cleveland, OH.

Prufer, Olaf H. and Garretson W. Chinn
(1960) Survey of Ohio Fluted Points No. 2. Cleveland Museum of Natural History. Cleveland, OH.

Purdy, Barbara A.
(1996) How to Do Archaeology the Right Way. University Press of Florida, Gainsville, FL.

(1986) Florida's Prehistoric Stone Technology. University of Florida Press, Gainesville, FL.

Purdy, B. A. and H. K. Brooks
(1971) Thermal Alteration of Silica Minerals: An Archaeological Approach. Science, Vol. 173, pp. 322-25.

Ramsay, Pauline and David Thompson
(1990) Pens for Museum Documentation. Conservation News, No. 43, pp. 12-14.

Rapp, Jr., George and Christopher L. Hill
(1998) The Earth-Science Approach to Archaeological Interpretation. Yale University Press, New Haven, CT.

Renfrew, Colin
(2000) Loot, Legitimacy and Ownership. Duckworth Debates in Archaeology. Bookcraft (Bath) Ltd, Midsomer Norton, Avon, GB.

Reynier, Michael
(1994) A Stylistic Analysis of Ten Early Mesolithic Sites in South East England. In: Stories in Stone, eds. A. Ashton and A. David, Lithic Studies Society, Occasional Paper No. 4, Oxford, UK.

Robbins, Maurice
(1966-1981 version) The Amateur Archaeologist's Handbook. Harper & Row, New York, NY.

Roberts, Frank H. H. Jr.
(1938) The Folsom Problem in American Archeology. Annual Report, Smithsonian Institution, Washington, DC.

Roux, Valentine and Blandine Bril (eds.)
(2005) Stone Knapping – the Necessary Conditions for a Uniquely Hominin Behavior. McDonald Institute Monographs, Oxbow Books, Oxford, England.

Schuldenrein, Joseph
(1999) Charting a Middle Ground in the NAGPRA Controversy Secularism in Context. SAA Bulletin, Vol. 17, No. 4, pp. 22-333.

Seeman, M., and O. Prufer
(1982) An Updated Distribution of Ohio Fluted Points. Midcontinental Journal of Archaeology 7(2):155-169.

Semenov, S. A.
(1964) Prehistoric Technology. Cory, Adams, & MacKay, London, UK.

Shafer, Harry J. and Richard G. Holloway
(1979) Organic Residue Analysis in Determining Tool Function. In: Lithic Use-Wear Analysis, B. Hayden, ed., Academic Press, New York, NY.

Shennan, Stephen
(1997) Quantifying Archaeology. University of Iowa Press, Iowa City, IA.

Shetrone, H. C.
(1936) The Folsom Phenonmenia as Seen from Ohio. Ohio State Archaeological and Historical Quarterly, Vol. 45, No. 3, pp. 240-256.

Shott, Michael J.
(1989) On Tool Class Use Lives and the Formation of Anthropological Assembleges. American Antiquity, Vol 54, pp. 9-27.
(1986) Technological Organization and Settlement Mobility: An Ethnographic Examination. Journal of Anthropological Research, Vol. 42, pp. 15-51.

Sollberger, J. B.
(1994) Hinge Fracture Mechanics. Lithic Technology, Volume 19, Number 1, pp. 17-20.
(1988) On Replicating Fluted Projectile Points. Bulletin of the Texas Archeological Society 59:1-17.

Sollas, W. J.
(1924) Ancient Hunters and Their Modern Representatives. Macmillan Company, New York, NY.

Solso, Robert L.
(2005) The Psychology of Art and the Evolution of the Conscious Brain. MIT Press, Cambridge, MA.

Sorrell, Charles A.
(1973) Minerals of the World: A Field Guide and Introduction to the Geology and Chemistry of Minerals. Golden Press, New York, NY.

Speth, J.
(1972) Mechanical Basis of Percussion Flaking, American Antiquity, Vol. 37, pp. 34-60.

Spiess, Arthur E. and Deborah B. Wilson
(1987) Michaud – A Paleoindian Site in the New England-Maritimes Region. Occasional Publications in Maine Archaeology, Maine Historic Preservation Commission, Maine Archaeological Society, Inc., Augusta. ME.

Stanford, Dennis
(2004) Personal communication, Oregon Ridge Primitive Weekend, Baltimore County, Maryland.
(1991) Clovis Origins and Adaptations: An Introductory Perspective. In: Clovis: Origins and Adaptations, ed. R. Bonnichsen and K. Turnmier, pp. 1-14. Center for the Study of First Americans, Corvallis, OR.

Stillings, Neil A., Mark H. Feinstein, Jay L. Garfield, Edwina L. Rissland, David A. Rosenbaum, Stephen E. Weisler, and Lynne Barker-Ward
(1987) Cognitive Science. MIT Press, Cambridge, MA.

Stoltman, James B., and K. Workman
(1969) A Preliminary Study of Wisconsin Fluted Points. Wisconsin Archeologist, Vol. 50, No. 4, pp. 189-214.

Stronge, W. J.
(2004) Impact Mechanics. Cambridge University Press, Cambridge, England.

Sullivan, Lynne P. and S. Terry Childs
(2003) Curating Archaeological Collections: From the Field to the Repository. AltaMira Press, Walnut Creek, CA.

Thompson. S. K.
(1992) Sampling. John Wiley and Sons, New York, NY.

Tixier, Jacques
(1974) Glossary for Descrption of Stone Tools. Newsletter of Lithic Technology, Special Publication 1, Washington State University, Pullman, WA.

Van Buren, G. E.
(1974) Arrowheads and Projectile Points. Arrowhead Publishing Co., Garden Grove, CA.

Vaughn, P.
(1985) Use-Wear Analysis of Flake Stone Tools, University of Arizona Press, Tuscon.

Verrey, Robert A.
(1986) Paleoindian Stone Tool Manufacture at the Thunderbird Site (44WR11) Ph.D. Dissertation, Department of Anthropology, Catholic University of America, Washington, DC.
(1976) An Analysis of Paleo-Indian Projectile Points from the Middle Shenandoah Valley, Virginia. Master's Thesis, Catholic Univesity of America, Washington, D.C.

Vickery, K. D., and J. C. Liftin
(1994) A Proposed Revision of the Classification of Midwestern Paleoindian, Early Archaic, and Middle Archaic Projectile Points. In: The First Discovery of America: Archaeological Evidence of the Early Inhabitants of the Ohio Area, edited by W.S. Dancey, pp. 177-210. The Ohio Archaeological Council, Columbus, OH.

Vitelli, Karen D. and Chip Colwell-Chanthaponh (ed.)
(1996) Archaeological Ethics. AltaMira Press, Walnut Creek, CA.

Waldorf, D. C.
(1984) The Art of Flintknapping. Mound Builder Arts and Trading Company, Branson, MO.

Wall, Robert D.
(1966) The Lockhart Site: Functional Analysis in a Paleoindian Complex. M.A. Thesis, Department of Anthropology, Catholic University of America, Washington, DC.

Waters, Michael R. and Thomas Stafford
(2007) Clovis Dethroned. Mammoth Trumpet, Vol.22, No. 4, pp.1-3 and 13.

Wells, Spencer
(2003) The Journey of Man – A Genetic Odyssey. Random House, New York, NY.

Whittaker, John C.
(1998) Evaluating Consistency in Typology and Classification. Journal of Archaeological Method and Theory, Vol. 5, pp. 129-164.
(1994) Flintknapping - Making and Understanding Stone Tools. University of Texas Press, Austin, TX.
(1987) Making Arrowpoints in a Prehistoric Pueblo. Lithic Technology 16(1):1-12.
(1955) Texas Street Artifacts. New World Antiquity, Vol. 2, No. 9, pp. 132-133.
(1952) A Paleo-Indian Site in Eastern Pennsylvania: An Early Hunting Culture. Proceedings of the American Philosophical Society, Vol. 96, No. 4, pp. 464-495.

Wilkison, Elizabeth M.
(1986) A Complex of Paleo-Indian Quarry-Workshop and Habitation Sites in the Flint Run Area of the Shenandoah Valley of Virginia. Chespoiean, Vol. 24, No. 3, pp. 2-36.
(1966) Paleo-Indian Components of the Flint Run Jasper Quarry Site 44-WC-1. Chesopiean, Vol. 4, No. 4.
(1965) Discovery of an Indian Jasper Quarry in N.W. Virginia. Anthropological Journal of Canada, Vol. 3, No.1.

Witthoft, John
(1952) A Paleo-Indian Site in Eastern Pennsylvania: An Early Hunting Culture. Proceedings of the American Philosophical Society 96:464-495. (Reprinted by Persimmon Press, Buffalo).

Wittkofski, J. Mark and Theodore R. Reinhart
(1989) Paleoindian Research in Virginia – A Syntheis. Special Publication No. 19, Archeological Society of Virginia.

Wormington, Hannah Marie
(1966) The Spirit of Worthwhile Collecting. Chesopiean, Vol. 4, Nos. 4-5, pp. 134-36.
(1962) A Survey of Early American Prehistory. American Scientist, Vol. 50, No. 1, pp. 230-242.
(1957) Ancient Man in North America. Denver Museum of Natural History Popular Series, No. 4, 4th edition.
(1947) Prehistoric Indians of the Southwest. Denver Museum of Natural History, Popular Series No. 7.

Young, David E. and Robson Bonnichsen
(1984) Understanding Stone Tools: A Cognitive Approach. Peopling of the Americas Process Series: Vol. 1, Center for the Study of Early Man, University of Maine, Orono, ME.

Zimmerman, Larry, Karen D. Vitelli, and Julie Hollowell-Zimmer
(2003) Ethical Issues in Archaeology. AltaMira Press, Walnut Creek, CA.

CD Available ...

The following CD is available which contains:
- North American Projectile Points
- Experimental Archaeology –
  A Science for Studying Native American Prehistoric Technology
- McCary Fluted Point Survey of Virginia
- A Model for a Fluted Point Survey
- Prehistoric Projectile Points Found Along the Atlantic Coastal Plain
- Excel McCary Survey Database

Cost: **$19.95** plus **$7.50** priority U.S. mail

Order from:

Virginia Academic Press
Post Office Box 11256
Alexandria, Virginia 22312 USA

Printed in the United States
by Baker & Taylor Publisher Services

Printed in the United States
by Baker & Taylor Publisher Services